MARKETING AND HIGHER MANA

MARKETING AND HIGHER MANAGEMENT

PA MANAGEMENT CONSULTANTS LTD

ESMOND PEARCE

London
GEORGE ALLEN AND UNWIN LTD
RUSKIN HOUSE   MUSEUM STREET

FIRST PUBLISHED IN 1970

This book is copyright under the Berne Convention. All rights are reserved. Apart from any fair dealing for the purpose of private study, research, criticism or review, as permitted under the Copyright Act, 1956, no part of this publication may be reproduced, stored in a retrieval system, or transmitted, in any form or by any means, electronic, electrical, chemical, mechanical, optical, photocopying, recording or otherwise, without the prior permission of the copyright owner. Enquiries should be addressed to the publishers.

© *George Allen and Unwin Ltd. 1970*

SBN 04 658032 8

PRINTED IN GREAT BRITAIN
in 11 pt. Times type
BY WESTERN PRINTING SERVICES LTD
BRISTOL

Contents

Introduction	*page* 9
PART 1 THE MARKETING CONCEPT	
1 The Fundamentals of Needs and Wants	13
2 The Function of Marketing	22
3 Financial Aspects of Marketing	45
4 Product Policy	81
5 Marketing Planning	111
6 Marketing Management	142
7 Corporate Long Range Planning	150
PART 2 MARKETING TOOLS AND TECHNIQUES	
8 Market Research	155
9 Market Forecasting	171
10 Product Planning	181
11 Advertising Research	190
12 The Function of the Sales Force	201
Glossary	220
Index	249

Introduction

The purpose of the marketing function in industry is to aid the management of a company to continue to secure the most profitable use of its resources. Marketing is therefore, fundamentally, an instrument of management. However, the ability to *produce* a particular instrument and the ability to *use* that instrument effectively are two quite separate and distinct arts. For example, the performance obtained from a violin depends not only on the skill of the technician who has produced that instrument but also, and perhaps to a greater extent, on the skill of the performer who uses it.

The techniques of marketing provide management with a highly sensitive instrument. It is the responsibility of the practitioners and specialists in marketing to produce the instrument, but successful marketing depends, above all, on the skill with which that instrument is used by higher management. The market orientation of a business can never start in a marketing or sales department, it can only start in the board-room. The effectiveness of a company's marketing operations must always depend on day-to-day policy decisions made at top management level.

In recent years, many books have been written for the marketing practitioner on the tools and techniques of marketing. Many of these tools, such as market research, have been the object of separate study. However, very much less guidance has been given to higher management on the use of marketing and on the essential part that must be played by the managing director and the other members of the top management team.

This examination of the marketing function therefore has two principal objectives:

a. To provide higher management with a better understanding of the use of marketing and of the policy decisions that must be made at Board level;
b. to provide the marketing practitioner with a composite, overall view of marketing in relation to his own particular role.

The book is divided into two parts. Part 1 is concerned with the fundamental nature of marketing, the role of higher management and the policy decisions that have to be made at that level. Part 2 reviews the principal tools and techniques of marketing, to give an understanding of its capabilities and limitations and lead towards its more effective use. No attempt has been made to provide a detailed technical treatise for the staff who are actually concerned in the management and operation of the various procedures. For this they should refer to the appropriate textbooks.

Specialists in any field tend to develop their own technical terms and jargon. However, as directors and senior managers are not always familiar with these terms, their use has been avoided as far as possible in the text. The more commonly used terms are given in a Glossary at the end of the book.

The reader will find occasional instances of repetition between one part of the book and another. This has been done deliberately so that, when the book is used for reference purposes, a particular chapter or subject can be referred to individually, from the index, with the minimum amount of reference to previous chapters. A comprehensive alphabetical index is included for this purpose.

The book is based on a long experience gained in helping clients with their marketing problems in a very wide variety of industries. In addition, the author has taken account of the various discussions in which he has engaged over many years on the marketing courses for higher management at the Sundridge Park Management Centre. Many of the past members of these courses will recognise certain passages in the book. Thanks are due to all those who have contributed either directly or indirectly in providing the material on which the book is based. For professional reasons, the names of clients have not, of course, been revealed in any of the case examples that are quoted; and, where there was any possibility of recognition, the examples have been suitably disguised.

PART 1

The Marketing Concept

Chapter 1

The Fundamentals of Needs and Wants

'Our company is different.' There can be few directors and managers who have not, at some time, either used these words themselves or heard them used by others when discussing some industrial problem. This is hardly surprising since, in fact, almost every company *is* different and nowhere is this more apparent than in the field of marketing. A procedure that may be eminently suitable for one company may be quite unsuitable for another, even in the same industry.

Nevertheless, there are certain fundamentals which are universally applicable to any selling situation. An examination of these fundamentals provides a guide to the inherent nature of the marketing function.

Every activity stems from some basic need. In a community we satisfy some of our needs by our own activities, but for many of our needs we rely on the activities of others. In return, many of our own activities are concerned with satisfying the needs of others.

However, even for the most elementary needs of life itself, the existence of the need is not, on its own, sufficient to bring about the associated activity that will satisfy that need. Some particular arrangement has to be made for each activity to occur. In nature, two methods have evolved for producing these primary activities. The first and simpler method is to arrange for the need to be satisfied by some repetitive activity, or cycle of activities, that can continue without interruption. For example, the need to circulate blood round the body is satisfied by the repetitive action of the heart. Because this can be made a continuing repetitive activity, it is unnecessary for us to be made aware of the need, or to be provided with any stimulus to make us want to take any specific action to satisfy it.

There are, however, many of our elementary needs that cannot be satisfied in this way. Immediately a need arises that requires us to take some non-repetitive action, some stimulus is necessary to make us *want* to take the necessary action that will satisfy the need. For example, if we left a finger over a flame, the skin would be severely damaged. Therefore, we are provided with a mechanism that makes us feel pain so that we *want* to satisfy the need to remove the finger from the flame as quickly as possible. (The words 'need' and 'want' are sometimes given different meanings from those implied in the above context. However, it is this interpretation of their meanings that is used throughout this book.)

A number of ingenious mechanisms have evolved for the sole purpose of providing the stimulus that converts a need into a want. This is the essence of any selling operation. In nature, these selling mechanisms and processes are often very much more elaborate than the functional need which they are designed to satisfy.

For example, in order that any form of life can continue to exist, the essential primary need is for the reproduction of the species. This primary need gives rise to a number of resultant needs for a variety of activities. Some of these, such as ovulation, can be satisfied by a repetitive cycle of activities. But there are other activities that are needed in the reproductive process where it is necessary to create awareness of the need and to stimulate a want to satisfy that need. In many species, this requires a highly involved selling system that demonstrates the natural evolution of all the arts of salesmanship. Indeed, in birds, visual display and advertising are freely used for this purpose.

Two basic forms of motivation are used in nature for providing the stimulus that converts a latent need into an active want. These are fear and pleasure. Fear of pain is more commonly used when a quick and urgent response is required, for example in removing the finger from the flame. Pleasurable sensations are used when the need can be satisfied by a less urgent activity. For instance, the need for food is converted into a want through the pleasurable sensations of eating. But if this fails, and the need becomes more urgent, pain takes over as the pangs of hunger begin to develop. In every selling situation, it is some form of one or other of these two basic motives that converts a need into a want.

The necessity for instituting some procedure for converting a need into a want is not, therefore, as is sometimes supposed, an extraneous commercial requirement that has had to be tacked on to the processes of production and distribution in a competitive economy. It is a fundamental part of the evolutionary process and no activity can occur unless this requirement is fulfilled. Many of the procedures that are used in nature for this selling function have developed into highly complex systems. There is, however, no fundamental difference between these systems and their commercial counterparts.

The practical application of these principles is illustrated in the old selling axiom: 'You cannot make a sale merely by convincing a prospective customer of his need for your product. The need must be converted into an active want before he will be ready to place his order.' Essentially, the selling operation consists of demonstrating a need and converting the need into a want. The demonstration of a need is a straightforward matter of conveying information. Its conversion into a want requires the skilful selection and application of appropriate motivating factors in the design of the product and in its presentation to the prospective buyer.

FROM BASIC NEED TO PRODUCT SALE

A 'product' can be described as the outcome of any industrial or commercial activity. Therefore a company's product may be a physical article, a service, or a combination of both. It is the existence of some basic need that leads to the potential demand for a product to satisfy that need. The need to keep warm in winter and the need to occupy leisure hours are typical examples of basic needs. There are often a number of stages between a basic need and an active want to buy a particular product. The basic need gives use to a series of resultant intermediate needs, each of which must be converted into an active want before the next stage can occur. Taking toothpaste as an example, the various steps can be illustrated as follows:

1. The prospective purchaser has a need to prevent dental decay.
2. He is made aware of the need to prevent dental decay.
3. His need to prevent dental decay is converted into a want to prevent dental decay.
4. He is made aware of the need to clean his teeth in order to prevent dental decay.
5. His need to clean his teeth is converted into a want to clean his teeth. (Any parent knows the importance of this step.)

6. He is made aware of the need to use toothpaste to help him to clean his teeth effectively.
7. His need to use toothpaste is converted into a want to use toothpaste.
8. He is made aware of the need to buy toothpaste in a suitable and convenient form.
9. His need to buy toothpaste in a suitable and convenient form is converted into a want to buy a particular brand of toothpaste.

The need for the product stems from but should not be confused with the basic need. For example, the purpose of the toothpaste is to help in cleaning the teeth, any prophylactic properties that it may possess are incidental in this particular context.

In the everyday buying of consumer goods, the purchaser does not, of course, go through the various steps in this chain, even subconsciously, every time a repeat purchase is made of the same product. A primitive population would first have to be educated in dental hygiene before attempting to sell them toothpaste, but the ordinary housewife is thinking only of the need to buy a new tube of toothpaste when she is doing her shopping.

However, this does not mean that the various steps in the chain cease to play any part in repetitive purchasing. The conversion of a need into a want is not something that either has or has not happened. The more important aspect is the *extent* to which each of the needs in the chain has been converted into a sufficiently urgent and continuing want. It is this that governs the quantity and frequency of the customer's purchases. In the case of the housewife buying toothpaste, it is this alone that governs how often and how regularly the members of her household clean their teeth, hence how often she has to buy a new tube of toothpaste.

A chain is only as strong as its weakest links. The successful manufacturer does not make the mistake of concentrating the whole of his selling effort on the final link. He is looking for intermediate needs that have not yet been converted into sufficiently active and urgent wants.

In the toothpaste example, only a single comparatively simple chain of events was shown between the basic need and the sale of the product. In practice, the chains are often very much more elaborate than in this simple example and a complex network can sometimes emerge. For

THE FUNDAMENTALS OF NEEDS AND WANTS

instance, the basic need may give rise to different intermediate needs which lead to entirely different types of products. The need to keep warm in winter leads to the need for an overcoat as well as the need for an electric fire. Similarly, there are some products that may play a part in satisfying more than one basic need. The final need that is satisfied by buying golf clubs may stem from the need for physical exercise as well as the need to occupy leisure hours.

Therefore, at any one of the links in the chain, two or more chains may converge or two or more chains may lead from it. The occurrence of some incident that affects one part of the chain can often have repercussions throughout the whole network and can affect the sales of products that at first might seem to have little relationship to one another. The introduction of television affected not only the demand for the cinema but also the demand for a wide range of other products such as furniture for the home.

Superficially, there may appear to be certain products that are not satisfying any inherent need at all, and for which an artificial want has been created by advertising or other forms of sales promotion. However, if people continue to buy a product it must be satisfying some need – it may be an abstract need, like the need to occupy leisure hours, or it may be some deeper psychological need such as the need that is satisfied by smoking. Nevertheless, these needs are no less real than the need to keep warm in winter which has already been quoted as an example. The fact that neither the seller nor the buyer may be able to identify and define the particular need that is being satisfied by the purchase of the product is irrelevant, and does not affect these fundamental principles.

Therefore, for every product, there is some chain of events between a basic need and its sale to a customer. The basic need gives rise to a series of resultant needs. At each stage, a 'selling operation' is necessary to convert the need into a want before the next stage can occur. The quantity sold will be governed by the extent to which each of the needs in the chain has been converted into a sufficiently active and urgent want.

THE NATURE OF A POTENTIAL DEMAND

It has already been pointed out that it is the existence of a need that leads to the potential demand for a product or service to satisfy that need. The 'potential demand' should not be confused with the 'actual demand' which is quite simply a statement of the current total purchases of the product. A dentifrice manufacturer might be securing 40 per cent of the current demand for toothpaste in Nigeria, but this would probably be only a very small percentage of the potential demand. It is also important to distinguish between the potential demand for the company's own particular product and the total potential for that type of product. The potential demand for a particular car costing £3,000 is very different from the total potential for the car industry.

The size of the inherent potential demand for a particular product will depend on:

1. The number of people who have some need that could be satisfied at least as well by the purchase of the product as by any other available means.
2. The proportion of these people who have the financial ability to satisfy that need by the purchase of the product.
3. The quantity and frequency of their purchases that would be necessary in order to satisfy their need.

The nature, design and cost of a product will determine the kind of need that it will satisfy and its ability to satisfy that need at least as well and economically as any other available means. It therefore follows that, at any particular moment in time, the size of the potential demand for a product is governed *only* by its design and selling price.

In spite of loose statements that are sometimes made, a potential demand is not and cannot be 'created' by any selling or promotional activities. It is the design of the product itself that creates the potential demand *and fixes its size*. The greater the potential demand, the greater will be the scope for converting it into profitable sales.

However, the design of the product not only fixes the size of the potential demand but, in many cases, it also plays an important part in influencing the proportion of that demand that is converted into profitable sales. The buying decision of a prospective purchaser is usually influenced by very much more than the product's intrinsic fitness for his purpose. His personal opinion of its design, shape and appearance can be one of the most important factors in the 'selling operation' of converting his need into an active want to buy that particular product rather than some competitive product.

Similarly, such things as the company's reputation for the quality and reliability of its products, the reliability of its delivery date promises, credit facilities, and after-sales service all play their part in converting the potential demand into profitable sales.

Therefore, in a manufacturing company, the type of products that it produces will govern the nature of the basic needs that it will be satisfying. The process of converting those needs into active wants starts with the designer of each product and continues throughout the subsequent manufacturing and selling operations.

CORPORATE ACTIVITY AND OBJECTIVES

It was pointed out earlier that, in a community, we satisfy some of our needs by our own activities but that, for many of our needs, we rely on the activities of others. In return, many of our own activities are concerned with satisfying the needs of others.

In a primitive community, some of its members develop a greater aptitude than others for certain forms of activity. As a result, the exchange process is started. The various members of the community begin to concentrate their activities on satisfying those particular needs of the community which fit their own individual skills and abilities. As the community develops, some of the needs change and the individual members have to adapt or change their activities. But the form of activity which each member elects to undertake is still the one that fits his own particular experience and ability.

In an industrialized society, many of the activities are carried out by groups of people formed into companies. However, the same fundamental principles apply to the company as to the individual in a more primitive community. The successful existence of any company depends upon its ability to satisfy some particular need or needs of the community in a way that will provide the most profitable utilization of its resources. As a corporate body, the company consists of buildings, plant and people. Together, these resources constitute an aptitude to carry out certain kinds of activities. Fundamentally, it is this aptitude that represents the company's saleable commodity.

The needs of the community are today changing at a faster rate than ever before. If a company is to continue to be successful it must be constantly watching these changing needs – and selecting new ones if necessary – to ensure that it is continuing to satisfy those particular needs which require the activities for which it has the greatest aptitude. It is only in this way that it will be able to continue to secure the most profitable utilization of its resources.

In the past, there have been many companies that have failed to recognize these fundamental principles. A manufacturing company may have been set up to produce a certain type of product. In the course of time, it comes to believe that the purpose of its existence is to produce these products. It bases its operations on the assumption that, if it employs good salesmen and makes good products, it should have no difficulty in selling them. It assumes that its success depends upon its ability to make these products as efficiently and economically as possible. This becomes the objective of its activities and it institutes financial controls to ensure that it is achieved. Indeed, if there happens to be a large unsatisfied demand for the company's products, this may, for a time, be all that is necessary to make it a highly successful business.

However, under the frequently changing conditions of today, it is more than ever important that a manufacturing company should recognise that it is *not* in business to make a product. The only reason that it is in business is to satisfy certain needs of the community. This reason is not dictated by any altruistic considerations, it is a fundamental necessity if the company is to survive. (In fact, for the purpose of these considerations, it is irrelevant whether or not the satisfaction of a particular need happens to be socially or ethically desirable.) Therefore, the primary objective of any business is to satisfy a need to the mutual benefit of the company and its customers. Its ultimate success must always depend upon how efficiently it achieves this objective.

SUMMARY – THE NEED FOR CO-ORDINATION

The practical significance of many of the fundamental aspects that have been examined will have been apparent. The more important features can be summarized as follows:

1. Every activity stems from some basic need.
2. No activity will occur unless the need has been converted into a want.
3. Even for our most elementary needs, which we satisfy by our own

THE FUNDAMENTALS OF NEEDS AND WANTS

     activities, the conversion of the need into a want may require a highly elaborate process.
4. There may be many stages between a basic need and an active want to buy a particular product.
5. A need cannot be 'created' by advertising or salesmanship. The nature and size of the need for a product is governed only by the design and selling price of the product itself.
6. The continued existence of any industrial or commercial enterprise depends upon its ability to satisfy some particular need or needs of the community.
7. This requires the selection of a suitable need and the production of some article or service that will convert the need into a want to buy that article or use that service.
8. A company's financial success must always depend upon how effectively it uses its resources to convert a basic need into an active want to buy its products.

The fundamental purpose of every activity concerned with designing, producing and selling a product is, therefore, to convert a need into a want in such a way that it will provide the most efficient use of the company's resources. If a company is to continue to be successful, it is important that the individual activities should be planned and co-ordinated so that, collectively, they achieve this single objective. To be effective, this planning and co-ordination must be based on a thorough understanding of market needs and of the factors that influence the buying decisions of prospective purchasers.

The marketing function in industry stems from and is based on these fundamental considerations of needs and wants.

Chapter 2

The Function of Marketing

There is, of course, nothing new about the word 'marketing' when used in its literal meaning of 'buying and selling goods in the market-place'. However, it was not until several years after the Second World War that the word was adopted by industry and used to describe a specific activity. It is, therefore, a comparatively recent addition to our industrial vocabulary. The word itself has gained wide acceptance and is, today, freely and frequently used, although its precise meaning and purpose are often imperfectly understood.

BACKGROUND

It was in the early 1950s that certain industrial companies began to recognise the need for a re-appraisal of management functions. This was partly due to the increasing complexity of modern industry and, more particularly, to the conditions which had by then arisen as a result of the war. Between 1939 and 1950, the world demand for most manufactured goods had considerably exceeded the available supplies of labour and raw materials to produce them. The shortages tended to increase rather than diminish in the years that followed the war, as the demand began to expand. As all essential commodities were rationed and buyers rarely had any choice between alternative products, they were thankful to get anything they could obtain.

In order to be able to run a business successfully under these conditions of acute shortage, it was necessary for management to concentrate on obtaining the greatest possible output from the available labour and materials. Little or no consideration had to be given to selling the goods once they had been produced. An increase in output usually meant an automatic increase in sales.

After ten years of these conditions, it was not unnatural that management thinking, and the whole structure of management, had become centred on production. It was during this period that some of the biggest advances were made in management techniques for planning and controlling production operations. A new generation of managers was growing up under the assumption that a company was in business to make certain products and that its success depended almost entirely upon the ability of management to produce these products as efficiently and economically as possible.

These conditions applied not only in Britain but throughout most of the world. When, around 1950, the market conditions began to return to those of a normal peacetime economy, there were certain companies, particularly in the United States, that quickly recognised that their management thinking would have to be re-examined. They could no longer afford to go on paying scant regard to the customer in their top management decisions. Moreover, they realised that this reorientation would require a drastic change in the whole philosophy of management, and that it was not something that concerned only the sales manager and his department. The whole of the company's activities would have to be re-oriented towards its markets instead of its products. These considerations led to the development of the function that has come to be known as 'marketing'.

THE MEANING AND PURPOSE OF MARKETING

In the early days, when the word 'marketing' first started to be used in industry, there was often considerable misunderstanding about its meaning. It was sometimes assumed that marketing was merely some kind of comprehensive term for a company's promotional and selling activities. It was this assumption that occasionally led some companies to believe that the right approach was achieved by employing a so-called 'marketing manager' to be responsible for directing and controlling these external activities. In reality, such a company had not even begun to employ the principles of marketing, it had merely changed the title of its sales manager.

It is, perhaps, the literal meaning of the word 'marketing' that has led to these misunderstandings. From this meaning, it would be quite logical to assume that 'marketing' is almost the same as 'selling'. However, this is true only in the sense that, as shown in the previous chapter, the *whole* of a company's activities are fundamentally concerned with the processes of converting a need into a want. 'Marketing' relates to this overall activity whereas the word 'selling' is used to refer to that particular part of this activity that is carried out by the sales department.

In order to try to explain marketing, many attempts have been made to define its meaning in a few words. However, none of these abbreviated definitions has been completely successful and many of them have tended to add to the confusion rather than diminish it. Moreover, it is doubtful whether a brief definition of the *meaning* of marketing serves any useful purpose. What is very much more important is that the precise *purpose* of marketing should be clearly understood. This purpose can be defined as follows:

1. To determine and define the market or markets that will provide the most effective (or most profitable) utilization of the company's physical, technical and financial resources.
2. To ensure that these resources are being used to DESIGN, PRODUCE and SELL a product or range of products in such a way as to win favourable buying decisions from the prospective customers in the defined market at an economic cost.

The implications of this definition should be clearly understood. This is the inherent purpose of the marketing function. Its objective is to aid management in continuing to secure the most effective or most profitable use of the company's resources.

It will be seen that, based on a definition of the most suitable market, the marketing function is concerned with planning and co-ordinating all those activities throughout the company that will in any way, either directly or indirectly, influence the buying decisions of prospective customers in that market.

It has sometimes been said that marketing starts with an 'attitude of mind' on the part of management. It is certainly true that, if it is fully to achieve its purpose, the managing director and every executive in the company must not only understand this purpose but must also recognise that the success of the business depends upon the efficiency with which each one of them plays his own part in using the company's resources to convert a need into an active want to buy the company's

THE FUNCTION OF MARKETING

products. If this is consciously recognised and understood, it will lead to an overall approach to the management of the business in which every decision and every activity is planned and co-ordinated to achieve this objective. This specific approach to the management of a business is inherent in the fundamental concept of marketing, and is not something that is achieved by the independent activities of some particular individual or department.

The marketing function itself is essentially a fact-finding, planning and co-ordinating function. It does not in any way replace the administrative functions of the design, production and sales managers and it should not be confused with these functions.

SELECTING AND DEFINING THE MARKET

Marketing starts with a consideration of the company's existing or potential resources and with the determination of the particular sectors of the community whose needs will provide the most profitable utilization of those resources. It is only too easy for a company to be dissipating its effectiveness because some of the needs which it is trying to satisfy are not relevant, while others for which it may be very much better equipped are overlooked.

In the definition of the purpose of marketing, this process is referred to as 'selecting and defining the market'. In its original sense, 'a market' is a place where buying and selling is carried out. To the seller, it represents a particular group of buyers who are congregated together. The term thus comes to mean, in its industrial context, a particular group of people who have SOME COMMON CHARACTERISTIC. It is the nature of this common characteristic that defines a particular market. This basis for defining a specific market is important although it is sometimes overlooked.

If the subsequent marketing operations are to be successful, it is essential that the common characteristic which makes certain people suitable potential customers for the company should be clearly and precisely defined. Loose definitions are dangerous. To define the market for a particular machine tool as 'firms in the engineering industry' is much too broad and imprecise, because this assumes that every engineering firm has an existing need for the tool and overlooks the fact that it is people and not corporate bodies that make buying decisions. Since marketing is concerned with the buying decisions of certain particular people, it is essential to know who these people are.

Moreover, as has already been pointed out, this determination is not something that can be instituted at some particular time and then left on the assumption that the same people will continue indefinitely to provide the most effective use of the company's resources. In a market, nothing is ever static. In some markets the changes may be of greater magnitude and may occur more frequently than in others. However, in a market where there are frequent changes, this will be known and recognised. The greater danger lies in those markets where small changes may be unsuspected although, over a period of time, they can build up and reach substantial proportions. The determination of the most suitable sector or sectors of a market in relation to a company's resources is, therefore, a vital part of successful marketing. The techniques and procedures that are used for this purpose are described in Chapters 8 and 9.

THE FACTORS THAT INFLUENCE A BUYING DECISION

A company's success also depends upon its ability to win favourable buying decisions from its customers. Therefore, when the potential customers have been defined, marketing is concerned with determining the factors that will influence the buying decisions of those customers so that the company's products and the whole of its activities can be designed and planned accordingly.

It is this knowledge and understanding of the factors that are influencing the buying decisions of the company's customers that is at the root of successful marketing. The whole of the company's marketing operations should be based on these factors.

There are many things that can influence a purchaser's buying decision. What these influences are will depend upon the buyer and upon the particular product he is buying. Moreover, it is usually not a single factor but a combination of various factors that will consciously or subconsciously influence his decision.

There are ten basic factors which, to varying degrees, can influence a purchaser's buying decision. These ten factors can be defined as follows:

1. The fitness of the product for the buyer's purpose.
2. The buyer's personal opinion of the design and appearance

THE FUNCTION OF MARKETING

of the product (as distinct from its intrinsic fitness for his purpose).
3. The selling price of the product in relation to the buyer's opinion of its design and fitness for his purpose – and, where applicable, in relation to the intensity of his need.
4. The availability of the product to the buyer or, where applicable, the time required for its delivery to him.
5. What the buyer knows from his own experience or has heard from others about the supplier's reputation for the consistency in quality of its products and for their reliability in use.
6. Where applicable – what the buyer knows from his own experience or has heard from others about the reliability of the supplier's delivery date promises.
7. Where applicable – what the buyer knows from his own experience or has heard from others about the speed and effectiveness of the after-sales service provided by the supplier.
8. Where applicable – the credit facilities provided by the supplier that are available to the buyer.
9. The predisposition to buy the product that has been created in the buyer's mind by advertising or other promotional activities.
10. The persuasion exercised by a salesman.

The relative importance of each of these factors will, of course, vary widely from one type of product to another.

Therefore, the first step in planning the marketing of a particular product is to examine it in relation to each one of these ten basic factors and to determine whether and to what extent each factor will play a part in influencing a prospective purchaser's decision to buy that product.

This appraisal will show which are the primary factors that must be taken into account in planning the way in which the product is to be designed, produced and sold. It will ensure that attention is being specifically directed to those particular factors which will govern the volume of sales and the share of the market that is obtained.

Through failing to make this appraisal, many companies have devoted a great deal of time, money and attention to some factor that may be playing only a small part in influencing a customer's buying decision while, at the same time, they have been giving scant attention or even completely overlooking some more important factor. For example, with certain products it is easy to waste money on advertising when a fraction of that money spent on some other influencing factor would have a far greater effect on the share of the market obtained.

There are certain important considerations that must be borne in mind in making this appraisal. One of the first things that is evident from an examination of the ten basic influencing factors is how many of them are entirely dependent upon the personal opinions and beliefs of customers rather than on concrete facts. Therefore, the appraisal must be based on a thorough knowledge and understanding of the customer. It is only too easy for a producer to assume that he knows what influences his customers' decisions whereas, in fact, even the customers themselves may not be consciously aware of all the reasons why they are buying one product rather than another.

If the customer is making a choice between competing products, it must be remembered that he will be considering each of the relevant influencing factors in relation to the same factor in competitors' products. Therefore, there are many situations in which the factors must be viewed in a relative rather than an absolute sense. It will be necessary to know not only what customers think about the company's own products but also what they think about competitors' products.

It is also necessary to consider whether some customers are being influenced by quite different factors from those that are influencing others. For instance, the factors that influence a man when he is buying the product may be different from those that influence a woman, or that influence people in one age-group may be different from those that influence people in another. With industrial products, there may be a difference between the buyers in large organisations when compared with those in the smaller companies. In all these cases, the appraisal must be sub-divided and carried out separately for each sector of the market.

Also, if there are intermediaries between the company and the ultimate users or consumers of its products, it must be remembered that the factors that influence a distributor are likely to be very different from those that influence the ultimate buyer. Therefore a separate appraisal must be made for each.

The appraisal essentially consists of analysing the product in relation to each one of the ten basic influencing factors. Therefore, it is necessary to consider the implications of each factor.

THE FUNCTION OF MARKETING

Factor 1 – Fitness for Purpose
It might at first sight appear that the fitness of the product for the customer's purpose should be self-evident or easily determined – either it will fit his purpose or it will not. In some situations it may be as simple as this; but, more often than is sometimes realised, it can be far from simple even to determine the precise purpose for which the customer buys the product although, unless this is known, it is clearly impossible to know whether the product fits that purpose. For example, the purpose for which a customer buys a car costing over £2,000 can hardly be to enable him to travel comfortably, quickly and efficiently, because he could achieve this purpose at much lower cost. The customer himself would probably find it extremely difficult to define his purposes in buying the car. Consciously or subconsciously these purposes may include such things as acquiring a 'status symbol' and 'keeping up with the neighbouring Joneses'.

As another example, it would be quite wrong to assume that the only purpose for which people buy expensive fountain pens is to use them as writing tools. Some of the pens are bought for this purpose, but a substantial proportion are bought for the purpose of presenting them as gifts – particularly as the kind of prestige gift that the recipient will know to be rather more expensive. Knowing this purpose, the manufacturer markets the pen accordingly. For example, it is supplied in an attractive and expensive box which may serve no useful purpose to the user who is quite likely to throw it away. There are many other products such as cigarette lighters and electric razors that come into this category.

These are fairly simple and obvious examples. Nevertheless, there have been many products which have not secured as large a share of the market as they could have done merely because the manufacturer failed to recognize some of the underlying purposes for which the product was being purchased and had not, therefore, taken these into account in designing the product or in planning the way in which it was to be presented and sold. This does not only apply to domestic goods; it can often apply to products or services that are sold to industry. Therefore, in order to ensure a product's fitness for the buyer's purpose, it is obviously essential that this purpose should be carefully analysed and thoroughly understood.

In terms of the fundamentals of 'needs' and 'wants' (Chapter 1), the manufacturer must recognize all the conscious and subconscious needs that are being or could be satisfied by the purchase of the product.

Factor 2 – Design and Appearance
The buyer's personal opinion of the design and appearance of the product can often be of much greater importance than its intrinsic fitness for his purpose, particularly when he is likely to be making a choice between various competing products all of which may be more or less equally suitable for his purpose.

Good technical design is, of course, important in relation to such considerations as economy in production and performance and reliability in use. However, this second influencing factor does not relate to design as viewed from some technical standard. It relates only to the buyer's own opinion of the product's design and appearance, and it depends entirely upon his personal beliefs, whims, fancies and prejudices. Moreover, the buyer himself is not always conscious of some of the aspects of the product's design and appearance that may be influencing his buying decision. For instance, such things as the shape of a bottle, or the colour of the paint used on a machine tool and the shape of its control levers, can often be playing a larger part than is realized by the buyer himself when he makes his choice.

When considering this factor it is sometimes difficult not to be influenced by one's own opinion of the product's design. This influence is particularly strong for the expert in the product. He knows the things which the customer *ought* to be taking into account when making his decision; he knows what is important and what is trivial or irrelevant. However, it is essential that he should forget his technical knowledge when considering the effect of this factor on the buyer. He must find out the customer's opinion, because this is the only opinion that matters, regardless of whether it is right or wrong.

Factor 3 – Selling Price
With any product, there will be some relationship between the selling price and the quantity sold; there are few situations where an increase in price would not cause some reduction in quantity. It is, perhaps, because of this that there is sometimes a tendency to over-estimate the importance of the part played by the selling price in relation to the other

THE FUNCTION OF MARKETING

factors that are influencing the buyer's decision. This varies considerably from one type of product to another. A buyer will almost certainly take the price into account when he is choosing between competing products, but whereas some products are bought largely on price, there are others where other factors will play a very much larger part in influencing the decision.

However, it is the selling price of the product that governs the profit earned by the company in relation to the costs of its production and sale. Therefore, regardless of the relative importance of the part that it is playing in influencing a buying decision, the selling price is always one of the most important considerations in the marketing of any product. The theory of selling prices and the selection of the most suitable price is discussed in Chapter 3.

Factor 4 – Availability
The availability of the product to the buyer must inevitably play some part in almost any purchasing decision. For example, in the case of consumer goods, the housewife is unlikely to be prepared to spend her time going from shop to shop looking for some particular brand or make. Sooner or later (and often at the first attempt) she will accept some alternative that is available in the absence of her preferred brand. So the sales of such products must always be affected by the proportion of the appropriate retail outlets at which the product can be obtained.

If it is the type of product that the buyer does not expect to obtain from stock, the time required for its delivery can sometimes be an important factor in influencing the buying decision. In some cases this can be the factor that determines which company receives the order. Therefore, in making a marketing appraisal the possible effect of the availability factor should always be examined even in those situations where it may not be immediately apparent.

Factor 5 – Reputation for Quality and Reliability
The preceding factors have been directly concerned with the product itself and its delivery to the prospective customer. They relate specifically to the particular product, or batch of products, that he is about to buy. However, there are other factors that the buyer will consciously or subconsciously take into account in reaching his decision. Although the

buyer himself may not recognize the distinction, these factors relate to the company that supplies the product rather than to the actual product he is buying. Such factors depend entirely upon the personal belief and opinion of the prospective customer. He will form this opinion either from his own previous experience in buying the company's products, or from what he has heard from others about them. (In the case of branded goods, this refers to the brand name and not the maker's name.)

The first of the factors in this category is what the buyer knows from his own experience or has heard from others about the company's reputation for the consistent quality of its products and for their reliability in use. When he is buying the product the customer normally has no means of knowing (apart perhaps from a superficial inspection) whether there may not be some fault in the product when it is delivered to him. Similarly, he has no means of knowing directly whether the particular product he is buying will be reliable when it is in use later.

Therefore, consciously or subconsciously, the prospective purchaser will judge this factor by what he knows or believes about the supplier's reputation for consistent quality and reliability. From the marketing point of view it is extremely important to recognize this distinction. It is the company's *reputation* and not the actual quality or reliability of a particular batch of products that influences the buying decisions of prospective customers. For example, a temporary fault in some production process can affect the company's sales long after the fault has been corrected and forgotten about in the works. (There is a case of a well-known company in which a batch of faulty raw material slipped through inspection and caused a fault to develop in its products when they were in use. The trouble was quickly corrected but the company's sales were affected by a loss of confidence in the market for at least three years.) For the same reason a fault that is confined to only one of the products that the company produces can affect the sales of all its other products.

As with the other factors that influence a buyer's decision, the importance placed on the company's reputation for quality and reliability will vary from one type of product to another. There are few products in which this factor can be ignored and there are many in which it is extremely important. Even minor faults which escape inspection and get through to the customer can very quickly build up an adverse company image. A company can easily lose sales from this cause without being fully aware of its extent or even of its existence. Many dissatisfied customers merely stop buying or buy elsewhere rather than take the trouble to write in and make a complaint. Even if complaints are received, their number is likely to be only a small proportion of the real number of dissatisfied customers.

In this context, it is quite irrelevant whether or not the customer's complaint is justified. The customer's personal opinion of the company's products may be wrong; his complaint may appear to be trivial or unimportant; it may even be argued that he did not read the instructions correctly. Nevertheless this is what the customer thinks, and as *his* opinion it is the only opinion influencing his buying decisions. If the customer is wrong, the fault lies not with the customer but with the company and the way in which it has marketed the product.

Factor 6 – Reliability of Delivery Date Promises
There are a number of industries in which far more repeat business has been lost through broken delivery promises than through poor salesmanship in the field. The delivery date quoted for a particular order may appear to be satisfactory, but the buyer will be considering what reliance he can place on that promise. This is another factor in which his opinion will be based largely on his own previous experience in buying from the company. In some situations, a weakness in this factor may be merely a source of intense irritation and annoyance which can, nevertheless, do severe damage to the company's image in the mind of the buyer. There are other situations, particularly when supplying materials and components that another company uses in its products, where an outstanding reputation for a quick, reliable and efficient delivery service can be an extremely valuable asset which a company can offer to its customers as one of the most important factors in influencing their buying decisions.

Therefore, whether he realises it or not, the manager who is responsible for production planning and control may be playing one of the most important parts in marketing his company's products. He may sometimes have a far greater effect than the salesmen in influencing the buying decisions of the company's prospective customers.

Factor 7 – Reputation for After-Sales Service
Where an after-sales service is relevant to the product, this factor is often underestimated as a contributory effect on sales. As with quality

and reliability, a poor reputation for after-sales service may be losing far more business than would be suspected from the actual number of complaints received from customers. Conversely, a reputation for a speedy and efficient after-sales service can be a deciding factor with many buyers. Therefore, in all cases where after-sales service is relevant the company's reputation in this respect should be investigated to determine its effect on buying decisions.

Factor 8 – Credit Facilities
It is generally recognized today that credit facilities, in one form or another, can often play an important part in winning sales. Nevertheless, there is still a substantial minority of companies who have not fully recognized the implications of this factor and have what might be called a split personality over the way in which they regard their customers. Until the moment when the goods are delivered, these companies treat their customers as important individuals who are to be wooed and cosseted. But immediately these same customers receive the goods and owe the company money, they are regarded with suspicion and treated as if every customer was a potential rogue. A regular indicator of this attitude is the letter from the accounts department which is often phrased in very different terms from that leaving the sales department. In the case of cash transactions, there are still some companies who refuse to accept cheques in situations where the financial risk associated with their acceptance would be only a minute fraction of the money spent on other ways of promoting and selling the company's products.

Similarly, the cost of providing credit is sometimes regarded in the wrong perspective and without relation to the other costs of selling and distribution. For instance, the cost of providing an additional month in which to pay is a tangible cost which can be determined precisely. It will usually be a very small percentage of the value of the order and its effect on sales can, in certain situations, be considerably greater than a very much larger percentage spent on some other form of selling or promotion. In some industries, extended time in which to pay can be more attractive to a distributor than the small difference which its cost might make to the amount of discount which he receives for handling the goods.

There are, therefore, a number of different aspects to be considered when examining the relevance of this factor in a particular marketing situation. There is the more obvious situation in which the facilities or terms offered by one supplier may be different from those offered by another and this can have a direct bearing on the buyer's decision. Other aspects are more likely to affect the general image of the company that is created in the minds of its customers, but this image itself can play an important (although perhaps subconscious) part in influencing buying decisions.

When considering this factor, the risk of incurring bad debts must, of course, be taken into account. Although a company should be careful not to create the impression that it doubts the credit-worthiness of every one of its customers, it would be equally unwise to assume that there are no customers who will be unable to pay. Some form of discreet credit rating should always be used if immediate payment is not being made. It is a matter of balancing the loss that would be incurred in bad debts against the loss that would be incurred from reduced sales if an over-cautious policy is pursued. The essential point to consider is the way in which the policy that is adopted will affect the company's image with its customers.

Factors 9 and 10 – Advertising and Selling
It would, of course, be impossible for any company to sell its products if the prospective users or distributors of those products were quite unaware of their existence. Therefore, every company must use some form of visual or verbal communication to inform prospective customers of the existence of its products.

Having fulfilled its role of creating awareness of the product's existence, this communication with the prospective customer can also be used to influence his buying decision. However, it is extremely important to remember that the effect of a company's advertising and the persuasion of its salesmen are only two of the many factors that influence a prospective customer to buy the company's product rather than some competitive product.

For example, an efficient and well organized sales force can play a very important role in providing information to customers. Nevertheless it is easy for a company to over-estimate the extent to which its salesmen can influence the actual buying decision. This error sometimes arises

MARKETING AND HIGHER MANAGEMENT

from a subconscious tendency to believe that 'a good salesman ought to be able to sell anything to anyone' and, therefore, that the share of the market the company obtains depends almost entirely on the skill of its salesmen. In practice, there are many situations where the salesman plays only a small part in relation to other factors far more influential on the buyer's decision. Moreover, in any situation and no matter how brilliant the salesman, the effectiveness of the part that he can play must always depend upon the extent to which each of the other relevant factors has been satisfied.

Therefore, in making an appraisal of a particular marketing situation, it is important to distinguish between:

(a) informing the prospective customer of the existence and purpose of the product, and

(b) influencing his decision to buy that product.

The extent to which either advertising or salesmanship can be effective in the second aspect always requires very careful examination; it will depend entirely upon the nature of the product and the channels that are used for its distribution. For example, with certain mass consumer goods sold through retail outlets, advertising can be one of the most important factors in influencing a buying decision. But with other products, even a massive advertising campaign can have only a very small effect on sales once the prospective buyers are aware of the product's existence.

When planning marketing operations, it is always important that the precise purpose for which advertising is to be used, and the precise role of the salesman, should be specifically defined (see Chapter 5).

SUMMARISING THE BASIC INFLUENCING FACTORS

In making an appraisal of a particular product, the objective should be, first, to determine which of the ten basic factors play important parts in influencing a decision to buy that product. These factors should then be placed in their approximate relative order of importance. (It would be impracticable and unnecessary to attempt to place the factors in a precise order of importance since the most important factor in the opinion of one customer may be different from that of another.) This analysis will reveal which aspects in the design, production, distribution and sale of the product will govern the share of the market that it obtains.

Next, the attitude of prospective buyers should be examined in relation to each of the relevant factors. This procedure will show *what action should be taken* in regard to that factor in order to win favourable buying decisions consistent with the economic use of the company's resources.

For example, the initial appraisal might show that the appearance of the product is one of the most important factors in influencing a buying decision. It would then be necessary to determine which particular features in the product's appearance are consciously or subconsciously influencing the buyer and what are the preferences of the majority of buyers in regard to these features. In the light of this knowledge, the product can then be designed accordingly – or if it is an existing product, its design can be appropriately adapted. Similar action in relation to each of the other relevant factors will ensure that the product is being designed, produced and sold in the way that will be most certain to win good sales.

Although this analytical appraisal must always be based on a thorough knowledge of the attitudes and opinions of the customer, it should not be assumed that this will necessarily involve the company in highly elaborate and expensive market research. In most situations, the cost of finding out about prospective buyers is usually small in comparison with the other costs of producing and selling the product. This research is often carried out with considerable success by quite small companies with only limited financial resources.

This basic approach ensures that the whole of a company's activities are directed to the fundamental task of converting a need into an active want to buy its products. If this approach is not adopted, a company may spend much time, money and attention on matters that have only a marginal effect on influencing the buying decision to the partial or complete exclusion of much more effective measures.

THE NATURE OF MARKETING – DIFFERENCES
BETWEEN ONE INDUSTRY AND ANOTHER

Because the relative importance of each of the basic influencing factors varies so widely, the nature of the marketing activities in one industry may need to be very different from those in another.

For example, a consideration of the ten factors in relation to two competing brands of cigarettes might show the following:

> Both brands are equally suitable for the buyer's purpose and both are sold at the same price.
> The only difference in design and appearance that can be detected by the buyer is the design of the pack.
> There are no significant differences in consistency of quality and the aspect of reliability in use does not arise.
> The ultimate buyer is not concerned with such things as delivery dates or credit facilities. (This point may, however, affect the distributor.)
> The buyer will have made up his mind which brand he is going to ask for before he goes inside the tobacconist's shop and his choice will very rarely be influenced by the persuasion of a salesman.
> Therefore, with this product, the principal factors that influence a buying decision are likely to be:
> Factor 9. The predisposition to buy the product that has been created through advertising.
> Factor 4. The availability of the product through effective retail distribution.
> Factor 2. The design and appearance of the pack.

This does not, of course, mean that none of the other factors play any part at all or that they can be ignored completely. However, based on these three major factors, the company's marketing activities are likely to be primarily concerned with:

> Determining the range of brands that should be produced (price, type, size, etc.).
> Considering diversification into other products using tobacco.
> Reviewing selling price policy, including distributors' discounts.
> Re-thinking pack design in relation to its effect on the buyer.
> Securing effective and adequate retail distribution.
> Considering the design of point-of-sale promotional material and arrangements for its display, including the amount that should be spent on this activity.
> Determining advertising policy and budget. Copy-testing to determine the most suitable form of advertising. Media Selection.

THE FUNCTION OF MARKETING

Obviously in this kind of situation, advertising and promotional activities play an extremely important part in influencing a buying decision. For this reason marketing is closely associated with advertising in many mass consumer products.

However, the situation is very different if the ten basic influencing factors are examined in relation to a domestic durable product such as an electric cooker. The investigation might show the following:

Factor 1. Fitness for Purpose. The cooker has a number of different purposes to fulfil: boiling, roasting, grilling, etc. One cooker may fulfil some of these purposes more effectively than another. It must also compete with gas and other cookers that fulfil these same purposes in a different way. Therefore, the effect of this factor in influencing a buyer's choice must be taken into account.

Factor 2. Design and Appearance. When the customer has reached the point of deciding which of a number of similarly performing cookers should be purchased, it is the design and appearance of the various models that is likely to be one of the most important factors in influencing that decision.

Factor 3. Selling Price. Although the price is almost certain to be given some consideration, there will be many buyers whose choice will not be influenced by small differences in price between competing cookers.

Factor 4. Availability. A favourable buying decision is much less likely to be obtained if the cooker is not on display in the showroom where the buying decision is being made. Similarly, delivery from stock on one model and a delay of several weeks on another may influence the buying decision.

Factor 5. Quality and Reliability. Many buyers will give little thought to the reliability of the cooker when making their choice, but will assume that whichever cooker they purchase will work properly when it is installed. This factor is only likely to be important if a manufacturer has had trouble and, as a result, has acquired a poor reputation for quality or reliability.

Factor 6. Reliability of Delivery Promises. This may influence a distributor's decision about continuing to stock the cooker. It will not directly affect the ultimate buyer, except through the availability factor.

Factor 7. After-sales Service. This service will probably be carried out by the distributor and not by the manufacturer. It will not, therefore, affect the buyer's choice between alternative cookers.

Factor 8. Credit Facilities. A large proportion of cookers are bought on hire purchase terms. However, in many markets, these are not arranged or financed by the manufacturer and the terms will be the same for competing cookers. The effect of this factor must therefore be considered in relation to the distributor rather than the ultimate buyer.

Factor 9. Advertising. It is possible to create in a buyer's mind a certain predisposition to buy a particular cooker before he or she enters the showroom. However, it has to be remembered that this may be completely obliterated during the subsequent conversation with the showroom assistant. Nevertheless, familiarity with the name on the cooker may play some part in influencing the choice as there is often some reluctance to buy a product if a buyer has never previously heard its name.

Factor 10. Persuasion by the Salesman. The remarks that are made by the showroom assistant will often have an important bearing on the customer's choice. With some buyers, this factor and the appearance of the cooker may be the two most important factors in influencing the decision.

It will be seen that, in this situation, there are very many more factors that may be influencing the buyer's choice than in the previous example of cigarettes. Moreover, certain factors that are of considerable importance in one example are of negligible importance in the other. For example, advertising plays only a minor role for the cooker sale as compared with the extremely important role for the cigarette sale, because in the latter case the customer has usually made up his mind which brand he is going to buy before he goes inside the shop. In the case of the cooker, it is such things as design and appearance that have most influence over the decision.

The marketing activities required for successfully selling cookers have therefore, a very different emphasis from the requirements for the sale of cigarettes. A typical example of these activities might be as follows:

A continuing study of the nature and size of the present demand for cookers and of the demand that is likely to exist in five and ten years' time.

The determination of the most suitable sector of the market; for

THE FUNCTION OF MARKETING

example, whether to cater for all buyers or whether to concentrate on some particular sector, such as those who are prepared to pay a higher price for a better quality product or, alternatively, those who want a reliable cooker at a low price.

An investigation into opportunities for expansion in overseas markets that the company has not yet fully exploited.

Research into the effect on the sale of cookers of other products in the company's range and the inter-relationship between cookers and those products.

An appraisal of the scope for diversification, with particular reference to other domestic electrical products.

Determination of the range and selling prices of the cookers that the company should be producing to cater for the selected markets.

A continuing and comprehensive study of the particular features in the design of a cooker that influence a purchaser's choice.

Close co-operation with the company's research and development activities to ensure that effective influencing features are incorporated in the design of the cookers.

Regular forecasts of the demand for each of the cookers in the company's range.

A review of distribution policy. The selection of suitable distributors, distributors' discounts, alternative channels of distribution.

Decisions regarding promotional and selling strategy and relating to the size and deployment of the sales force required for the selected channels of distribution; the nature of promotional and advertising activities and the amount that should be spent on them.

Initiation of procedures for briefing and training distributors' sales staff, including demonstrators and showroom assistants.

This list is not intended to be complete and is given only to illustrate the kind of marketing activities that are likely to be involved in the production and sale of this kind of product.

These two examples demonstrate that, after the market has been defined, the subsequent marketing operations stem from and are governed by the relative importance of each of the ten basic factors that influence the buying decision.

It will have been seen that there are few facets of a company's activities that are not related in some way to one or other of these influencing factors. Factors 1 to 3 are related to the nature and design of the product itself. Factor 4 depends upon the organization for production and distribution. Factors 5 to 7 depend upon the company's image and the buyer's personal opinion of the company and its products and every manager in the company plays some part in creating this image. Factor 8 is concerned with financial considerations and the activities of the accounts department. Factors 9 and 10 are related to the company's advertising, promotional and selling activities.

The marketing function is concerned with planning and co-ordinating all these activities in such a way that the company is making the most effective use of its resources to convert a need into an active want to buy its products.

THE PROCEDURES AND TOOLS OF MARKETING

There are various activities that must be carried out to enable the marketing function to be performed effectively. These activities can be divided into five categories as follows:

1. Finding out who and where are the potential purchasers, when and how they buy, and what are the conscious and subconscious motives that influence their buying decisions (Market Research).
2. Examining market trends and estimating future demands (Market Forecasting).
3. Determining from 1 and 2:
   What products should be made.
   How they should be designed in regard to those features that will influence a buying decision.
   At what price they should be sold.
   What quantities should be produced (Product Planning).
4. Planning the most suitable channels between the producer and the user for the distribution and sale of the product (Distribution Planning).
5. Planning the most suitable means and methods of communication between the company and the distributors and users of its products (Promotion and Sales Planning).

The techniques and procedures that are used for carrying out these activities constitute the tools of marketing and are described in the various chapters in Part II. This physical separation is made because it is extremely important to avoid confusing the tools of marketing with the marketing function itself.

THE DISTINCTION BETWEEN MARKETING AND THE TOOLS OF MARKETING

Reference has already been made to the misunderstandings that often exist about the exact nature and purpose of marketing. A not uncommon misconception arises from the fact that it is often assumed, perhaps only subconsciously, that marketing comprises a collection of tools and procedures such as market research, market forecasting, and so on. However, just as when thinking about a cocktail cabinet, one is not concerned with a bag of cabinet-makers' tools, so when discussing marketing, one should not dwell solely on the available range of marketing tools. Nevertheless, one could not make a cocktail cabinet or market a product without knowing about the relevant tools and how to use them.

It should also be remembered that efficient tools do not necessarily mean an efficient product. Many masterpieces in cabinet work were produced with what would today be regarded as very primitive tools. Similarly, many very successful marketing operations have been carried out at little cost and without the use of any highly elaborate procedures. However, good tools used in the right way, *for the right purpose*, must always facilitate any operation. The cost of acquiring and using a particular tool must be balanced against the benefits that will be obtained from its use.

The distinction between the product and the tools is particularly important in relation to the use of marketing in the management of a business. Marketing is an instrument of management. It is the instrument itself that has to be used by management, not the tools with which the instrument is produced. It is a sensitive instrument and as such its performance depends upon the aptitude and skill of the user. From the same instrument, the virtuoso will produce very different results from the novice. The expert user has a complete understanding and mastery of the instrument, knowing its capabilities and limitations. Such expertise has a very tangible worth in the business environment.

The effectiveness of the marketing function depends on an understanding of its implications and skill in application by every member of the management team. For this reason it is so often emphasized that marketing is largely an attitude of mind on the part of management. The purpose of techniques and procedures is to assist management in making decisions. The techniques and procedures do not, themselves, run the business. The application of the principles of marketing depends upon decisions that are made and actions that are taken in every department of the business. The adoption of the marketing concept requires the recognition by every member of the management team of the paramount importance of the customer and the realization that every activity that is carried out anywhere in the business constitutes a part of the total operation of converting the customer's need into an active want to buy a company's products or to employ its services. It is the adoption of this overall approach to the management of a business that constitutes marketing, not the employment of a variety of techniques and procedures.

However, the staff who must implement the marketing procedures must know what techniques and procedures are available for their particular purpose and how to use them to the best effect.

THE MARKETING FUNCTION – SUMMARY

Marketing is an instrument of management. Its purpose is to provide management with the means of designing, producing and selling a product or range of products in such a way as to secure the most effective use of the company's resources.

Marketing is based on the needs and requirements of the market. The activities in a market-oriented company are governed by the conscious and subsconscious factors that influence the buying decisions of prospective customers. These factors vary widely from one type of product to another and a detailed analysis is necessary in relation to each product. This analysis provides the guide to the company's marketing operations.

Successful marketing depends upon the adoption of the right attitude by management. It does not necessarily require the use of any highly elaborate or costly procedures, and is just as applicable to the small business as to the large industrial organization.

Chapter 3

Financial Aspects of Marketing

The purpose of marketing is to secure the most effective use of the company's resources. It is concerned with the customer, but its purpose is to maximize profit rather than sales volume. A company with a turnover of £500,000 can, of course, sometimes be far more profitable than one with a turnover of £1,000,000.

In the past, there has often been a tendency for marketing and sales managers to devote far too much attention to sales volume as an end in itself. But volume for volume's sake is of no value whatever; if the company as a whole pursued volume as its objective this could quickly lead to disaster. Of course, marketing and sales managers are not completely unaware of this; they recognize that the cost of securing the sales is a factor that has to be taken into account. Even so, many of them still regard these costs as being something that should always be considered *in relation to sales volume*. For instance, costs are often expressed as a percentage of sales and it is assumed that, if the percentage increases, something is wrong and that a reduction must inevitably represent some improvement. The measurement of costs as a percentage of sales volume can be a useful guide for controlling a company's day-to-day activities once its marketing strategy has been decided, but it can be extremely misleading in deciding what that strategy should be. For example, an alteration which reduces the cost of the sales force from 5 per cent to 4 per cent of sales will not necessarily increase the profitability of the company and it could easily reduce it.

The financial objective in running any business is to continue to secure the optimum return on the capital employed in the production and sale of its goods or services. The sole purpose of the marketing function is to aid in the achievement of this objective by determining the ways and means by which the company's resources can continue to be most profitably employed. This is fundamental to the marketing concept.

Moreover, if the company is pursuing a policy of expansion, it is the function of marketing to show which resources and which markets can be most profitably expanded in relation to the additional capital employed.

EVERY MARKETING DECISION IS A FINANCIAL DECISION

It is not always sufficiently recognized that every marketing decision is, in fact, a financial decision and that the only result that matters is the effect of that decision on the continued optimization of the return on the capital employed in the business. This applies to every decision whether it is concerned, for example, with the way in which a product should be designed or with the number of salesmen that should be employed.

It is therefore important that any manager who is making a marketing decision should have a sufficient knowledge of financial matters to be able to understand the full implications of that decision. This is often a serious weakness in marketing and sales management that the return on capital is assumed to be concerned with the mysteries of the balance sheet and therefore within the sole province of the accountant. As a result, many decisions are made without full regard to their financial effect and without knowing the true facts on which those decisions should have been based. This is seldom because the information was not available but because the marketing man did not know the right questions to ask the accountant in the first place.

The first part of this chapter therefore reviews the basic nature of capital, profit and costs. This has been reduced to the bare essentials since it is not necessary to be an expert in accountancy to be able to make a marketing decision. Many of the complexities that occur in practice, and as much financial 'jargon' as possible, have been deliberately excluded in order to provide a clearer picture of the fundamental principles. The purpose is merely to enable marketing and sales managers to understand the implications of their decisions and to enable them to ask the right questions. Many readers will therefore already have a very much more advanced knowledge of financial matters than is given in these elementary considerations and, as explained in the Introduction on the use of the book, they should omit the first two sections in this chapter.

FINANCIAL ASPECTS OF MARKETING

THE NATURE OF CAPITAL

In order to start any industrial or commercial enterprise, certain expenditure is necessary on such things as buildings, plant and equipment. Expenditure will also be necessary to provide sufficient stocks of materials and finished goods to enable the company to carry on until it receives payment for the goods from its customers. All expenditure of this nature represents the capital that is being used in running the business. As the business expands, more equipment may be needed and larger stocks will be required, and the capital employed will therefore be increased.

It should be noted that money spent in this way remains in the business and is distinct from the ordinary trading expenditure. For instance, if a company buys a machine costing £1,000, it has merely transferred a thousand pounds' worth of money in the bank to a thousand pounds' worth of machinery in the factory. It still owns a thousand pounds but in a different form. However, if the machine has a life of, say, ten years, it will not still be worth a thousand pounds after it has been in use for a year, whilst at the end of ten years it will be valueless. Therefore an allowance must be made each year for the depreciation in the value of the machine and this must be recovered from the company's trading revenue.

Although the money remains in the business in one form or another, someone has had to provide this money in the first instance. In a private company, the money will either have come out of the owner's pocket or he will have borrowed it. If he has spent £100,000 in this way, he will measure his success in terms of his annual profit in relation to this outlay. So, for instance, if the annual profit from his trading was £3,000, the return on his investment would be 3 per cent per annum. In this case he would have been completely wasting his efforts in trying to run the business, and would have done much better to stay at home and invest the money in some other way. If, on the other hand, he had spent only £10,000 on equipping and running the business, a trading profit of £3,000 per annum would represent a 30 per cent return on his investment and he would have every reason to be satisfied with his efforts. In other words, it is the percentage return that indicates the efficiency with which the affairs of the business have been managed.

It will be seen that the volume of sales, as such, has not entered anywhere into this measurement of efficiency. Moreover, the amount of profit earned is not, by itself, of any significance since, in both examples, the profit was the same. The profit only becomes meaningful when expressed in relation to the amount of capital employed in equipping and running the business.

Exactly the same principles apply, of course, in a public company in which it is members of the public who have provided the money for the buildings, equipment and stocks. By doing so, they have acquired a share in the ownership of the company. The principal purpose of the annual balance sheet is to show the owners that their money still exists, either in cash at the bank or in the form of buildings, machinery, stocks of goods and other similar assets. It 'balances' the amount of money invested by the owners on the one hand, against the value of the assets on the other.

The function of management is to use the money invested in the company in the most efficient way. This must be the controlling factor in every policy-making decision. An increase in sales may necessitate an increase in stocks and, therefore, an increase in the amount of money that is tied up in this way. It may also increase the amount of money that is tied up in goods delivered but not yet paid for by customers. Hence, an increase in sales can result either in an increase in the overall amount of capital that is being used or in tying up some part of that capital and preventing it from being used in a more profitable way. Any action that will increase sales or increase profits is of no benefit to the company if it ultimately results in a reduction in the return on the capital employed. It is the relationship between the capital and the profit that shows how well or how badly the company has been managed.

In practice, a company's capital is usually divided into various categories for the purpose of more detailed financial consideration. For instance, a company's 'working capital' is not necessarily the same as the value of its assets shown in the balance sheet, which may include other items. However, this does not affect the basic principles described above.

THE NATURE OF COSTS AND PROFIT

It has already been shown that capital expenditure on such things as buildings and equipment is of a different nature from the operating costs incurred in the production and sale of the company's products.

These costs include such items as the purchase of materials and supplies, salaries, wages, power, depreciation, rates, insurance and all other services. For example, the purchase of a car for a salesman is a capital expenditure since the company still owns the car and the cost of the car therefore does not form part of the selling costs; it is only the amount by which the car has depreciated in value each year that is included in these costs.

These operating costs, when deducted from the revenue, govern the amount of profit that is earned from that revenue. The profit that is earned in a given period of time will therefore be the revenue received from the goods sold during that period less the *cost of those goods*. It is important to note that this cost will not necessarily be the same as the costs actually incurred during that period – some of the goods may have been produced in an earlier period and some of the costs during the period may have been incurred in the production of goods that have not yet been sold. For example, a company has received an income from its sales of £1 million during the last twelve months. Its total operating expenditure during that period was £900,000. It could not be assumed from this that the company has made a profit of £100,000. The actual position might have been as follows:

Cost of materials and goods in stock at beginning of year	£300,000
Costs incurred during year	900,000
	1,200,000
Cost of materials and goods in stock at end of year	150,000
Cost of goods sold during year	1,050,000
Revenue from sale of goods	1,000,000
Loss	£50,000

Therefore, instead of making a profit of £100,000, the company had, in fact, made a loss of £50,000. It is for this reason that the profit earned by a company over a particular period cannot be determined without knowing the value of the stocks of raw materials, work-in-progress and finished goods, both at the beginning and end of the period.

The situation is even more complex when it comes to relating the costs to the products themselves and determining the profit that is made from the sale of an individual product. Some of the costs, such as the cost of materials, can be related to a particular product and the expenditure will depend directly upon the quantity of those products that is produced. But many of the costs, such as staff salaries, are not directly related to a particular product. Nor are they directly related to the quantity produced, because many of them would remain the same if there was a change in the volume of production or sales. Therefore, the cost per article is never some precise constant figure that can be calculated by dividing the total costs by the quantity produced.

In order to determine the effect of a change in volume, it is necessary to differentiate between those costs which vary according to the quantity produced and those which do not. These are the 'variable costs' and the 'fixed costs', defined as follows:

VARIABLE COSTS – Those elements of the total costs which vary in *direct proportion* to a change in volume

FIXED COSTS – Those elements of the total costs which are not affected by a change in volume that is within the limits of the situation under consideration

It is important to note the qualification that applies to the fixed costs. Few costs, if any, would remain constant under all conditions. For instance, the clerical costs in the sales office may be a fixed cost for a small change in sales volume as there would be no alteration in the size of the staff, whereas part or all of these costs would be variable if a large change in sales volume were considered, such as doubling the number of orders to be handled. Therefore, before attempting to analyse the costs into their fixed and variable elements, it is important to be clear about the range of sales volume within which the analysis is to be carried out.

There will be certain individual items of cost, such as the cost of electricity, which may contain a fixed element as well as a variable element. Electricity used for lighting the premises is likely to be fixed, whereas electricity used to drive a machine may vary with the output of the machine. However, in most cases there is little difficulty in making a reasonably reliable estimate of the division which is sufficiently accurate for the purpose. The following is an extract from a typical cost analysis, it is not complete and shows only some of the more significant items in order to illustrate the division into the fixed and variable elements for a variation in sales volume within the range of plus or minus 20 per cent.

	Total Cost	Fixed Elements	Variable Elements
Materials	£414,326	£9,000	£405,326
Wages	606,824	401,413	205,411
Salaries and bonuses	58,715	52,702	6,013
Lighting and heating	12,482	11,234	1,248
Power	13,920	2,000	11,920
Postage	1,806	903	903
Legal expenses	750	750	—
Repairs to buildings	5,037	5,037	—
Depreciation	8,213	8,213	—
Carriage	24,511	7,408	17,103
Commissions	32,805	—	32,805

By analysing the whole of the costs into their fixed and variable elements, the effect on profits of a change in sales volume can be determined. This is shown in the following simplified examples where the total costs are £900,000 and the current profit is £100,000:

Variable costs	£500,000
Fixed costs	400,000
	900,000
Sales	1,000,000
Profit	£100,000

If the sales were increased by 10 per cent, the variable cost would, by definition, also be increased by 10 per cent. The fixed costs would remain unaltered:

Variable costs	£550,000
Fixed costs	400,000
Total costs	950,000
Sales	1,100,000
Profit	£150,000

Therefore, in this example, a 10 per cent increase in sales would result in a 50 per cent increase in the company's profits. If the figures are plotted on a graph, the profit at various levels of sales volume can be determined as shown in Figure 3.1. This graph is known as a Break-even Chart. It shows that, in this example, the company breaks even at a sales volume of about £800,000 per annum. Below this volume, the company would be running at a loss.

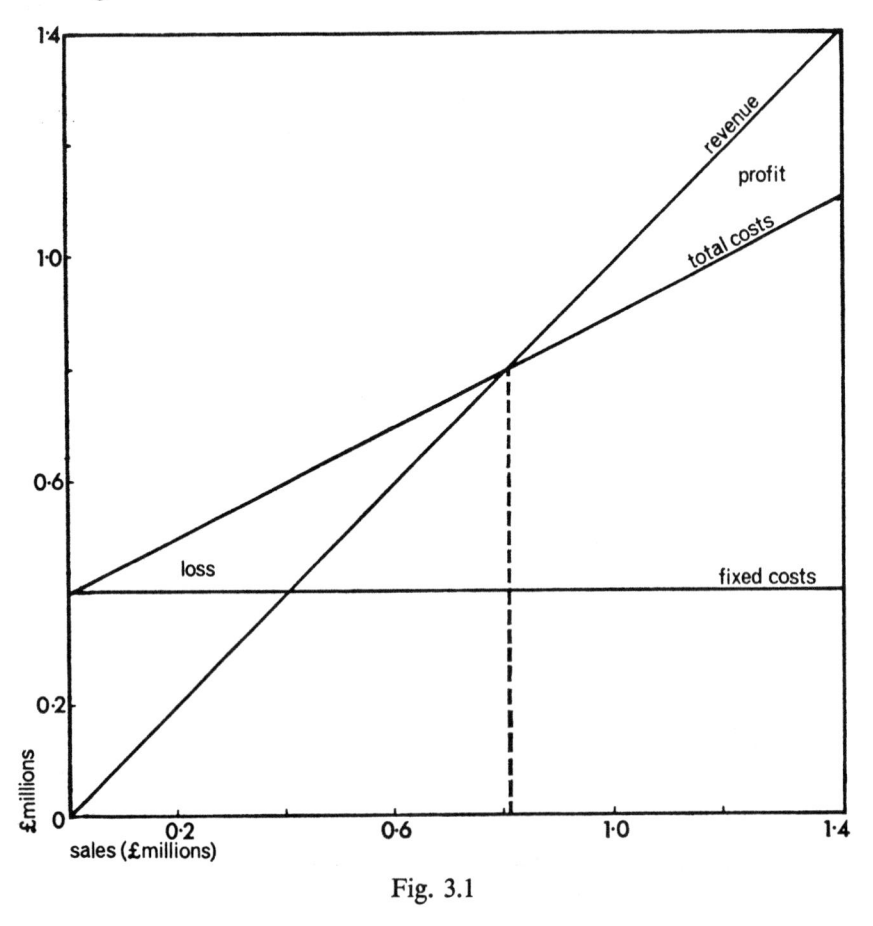

Fig. 3.1

The Break-even Chart provides a useful guide to the financial position of a company. This is shown in the following case example in which all the figures have been rounded off in order to clarify the illustration.

A certain company manufactured a range of products in powder form. These products were produced almost entirely on fully automatic mixing and packaging machines with very few manual operations. The raw materials were not particularly expensive but their purity and the formulation of the mixes had to be under continuous laboratory inspection and control. The capital employed was £1,312,000 and, during the previous twelve months, the trading figures had been as follows:

Revenue from sales	£2,610,000
Total cost of goods sold	2,270,000
Profit	£340,000

The company had a 24 per cent share of its market and, although the sales were slightly lower than in the previous year, it might seem from its trading figures to have been in a reasonably satisfactory financial position. The profit of £340,000 represents a return of about 26 per cent on the capital employed and is 13 per cent of its sales revenue. However, a cost analysis showed that, because of the nature of the business, the fixed costs represented a high proportion of the total. The principal variable cost was the cost of the raw materials. The summarized analysis of the fixed and variable costs for a plus or minus 20 per cent change in sales volume showed the following:

Fixed costs	£1,520,000
Variable costs	750,000
Total costs	£2,270,000

Under these conditions, the Break-even Chart is as shown in Figure 3.2. It will be seen from this chart that the company was, in fact, in a potentially dangerous situation. A small drop in sales would make a very big difference to the profits. Competition was becoming more intense and it only required the market share to fall from 24 per cent to 20 per cent to bring the company to its break-even point. The Board recognized that immediate action was necessary to safeguard the return on its capital and to put the company into a less dangerous position. This required a major reorganization with severe pruning of the fixed overhead costs together with product modifications to increase the sales volume. It was only because the company was aware of this position at a time when its profits still appeared to be satisfactory that it was able to avoid running into serious financial difficulties.

Fig. 3.2

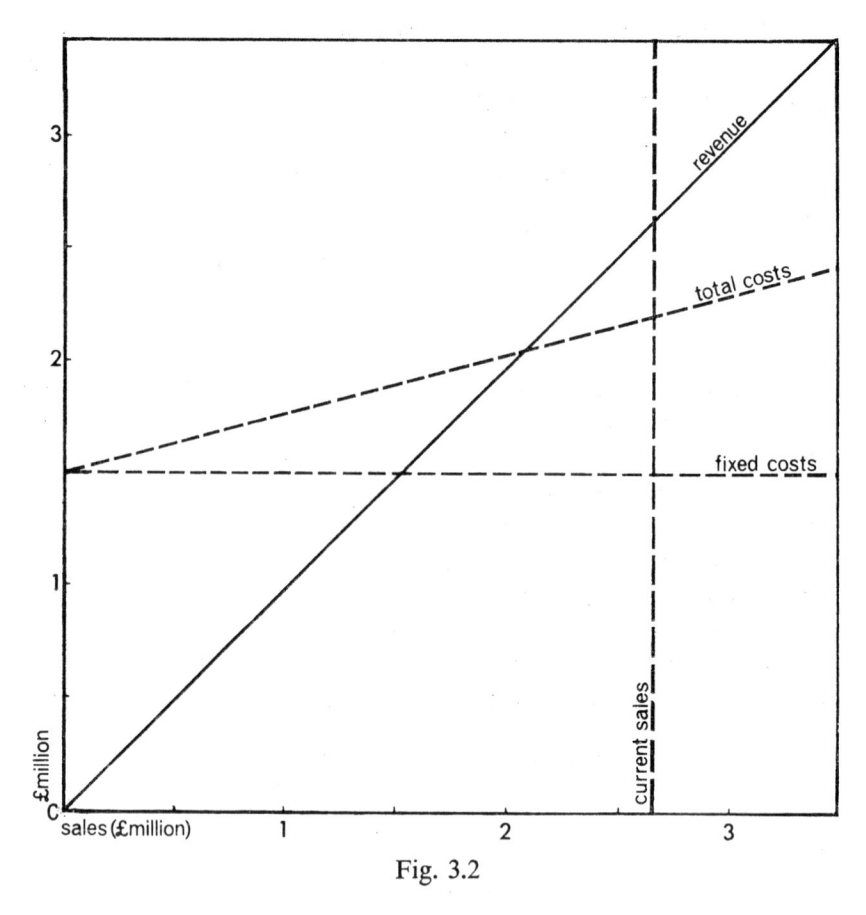

This case example illustrates the value of a Break-even Chart in examining a company's financial position. It is particularly important to know the shape of the chart and the company's current position on that chart before planning any change in its marketing strategy. For instance, if the cost and revenue lines are nearly parallel, a substantial increase in sales volume would have only a small effect on the company's profits. Under these conditions it would probably be most unwise to increase the costs by spending additional money on promotional activities in order to increase sales. A reduction in selling costs or an increase in selling prices, even if these meant a reduction in sales volume, might be a simple way of securing a substantial increase in the company's profits.

FINANCIAL ASPECTS OF MARKETING

THE THEORY OF SELLING PRICES

One of the areas in which finance and marketing are most closely related is in determining the price at which a product should be sold. This cannot be done correctly without an understanding of the simple principles which govern the relationship between selling price and profit. It is perhaps not unnatural that many practical managers are apt to adopt a somewhat reluctant approach to theoretical considerations which seem to be far removed from the realities of everyday situations. Nevertheless, in the case of selling prices, an understanding of the basic principles is essential if mistakes are to be avoided. At the same time, the principles themselves will not fix the selling price. It is the practical application of these principles that enables the most suitable price to be determined.

The selling price which will produce the maximum profit from the sale of a particular product in a given period depends upon the relationship between the selling price and the quantity that would be sold. The nature of this relationship is shown in Figure 3.3. In general, as the price increases, the quantity that would be sold diminishes. With many products, the curve tends to flatten at both ends as shown in the illustration. In a few cases, when the selling price is reduced below a certain level, the quantity sold may begin to diminish. The steepness of the

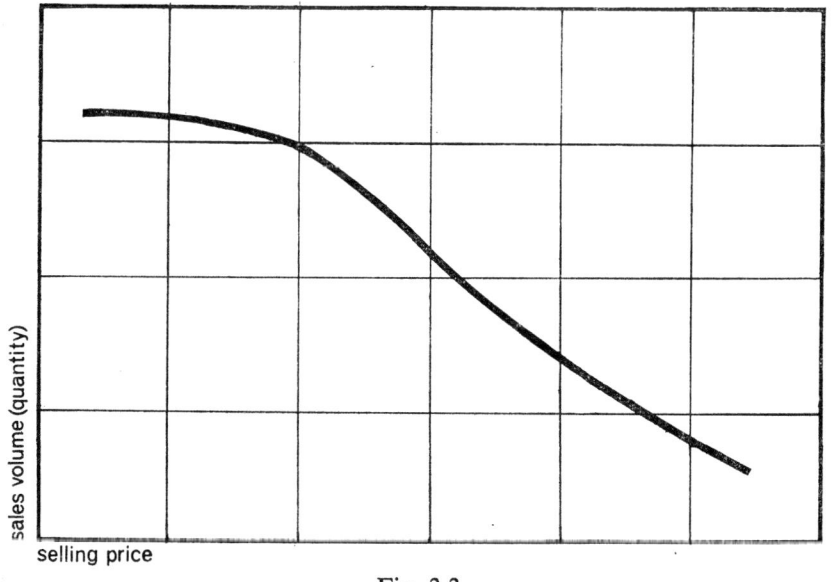

Fig. 3.3

curve will, of course, vary widely for different products depending upon the relative importance of the part that is being played by the selling price in influencing the purchaser's decision (see Chapter 2). For instance, the curve for a brand of tobacco would be very much steeper than the curve for the pipe in which it is smoked.

In practice, the curve would not be continuously smooth as shown in the illustration. It is more likely to follow an irregular sawtooth pattern owing to the incidence of such things as psychological selling prices. For example, an increase from £4 18s. to £4 19s. is likely to have a much smaller effect than an increase from £4 19s. to £5. However, for the purpose of these considerations, such irregularities have been smoothed out as they do not affect the principles involved.

This relationship between a change in selling price and the resultant change in demand is sometimes referred to as 'the elasticity of the demand'. If a 1 per cent reduction in price would increase the demand by more than 1 per cent, the demand is said to be elastic; if it would increase the demand by less than 1 per cent, the demand is said to be inelastic.

In a given period, the revenue that would be obtained from the sale of a product is, of course, the selling price multiplied by the quantity that would be sold at that price. If, for instance, each vertical division in Figure 3.3 is a unit of volume and each horizontal division is a unit of selling price, the revenue that would be obtained at each selling price becomes as follows:

Selling Price	Quantity	Revenue
1	3·25	3·25
2	3·0	6·0
3	2·25	6·75
4	1·5	6·0
5	0·7	3·5

The typical curve of the relationship between selling price and revenue is shown in Figure 3.4.

The variable costs incurred in the production and sale of the article (direct labour, material, etc.) are, by definition, directly proportional to the quantity. The relationship between the selling price and the variable costs is, therefore, exactly the same as the relationship between selling price and the quantity as shown in Figure 3.3. Therefore, by combining

FINANCIAL ASPECTS OF MARKETING

Figures 3.3 and 3.4, we get the relationship shown in Figure 3.5 between the variable costs and the revenue at various selling prices.

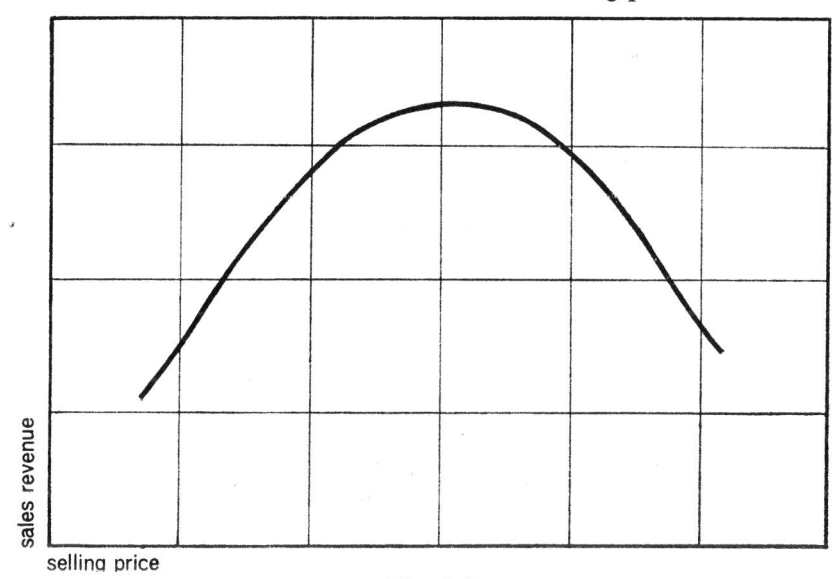

Fig. 3.4

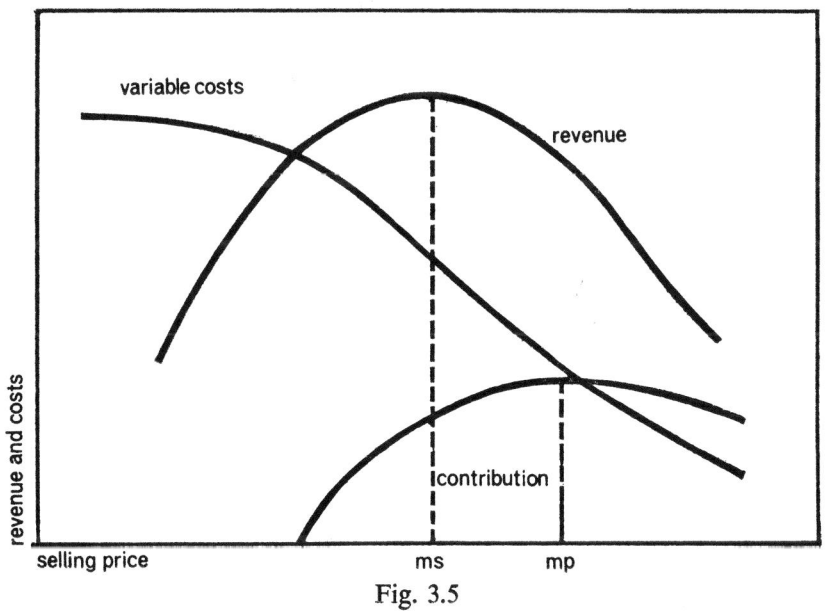

Fig. 3.5

The difference between the variable costs and the revenue at each selling price is, of course, the contribution to the fixed overheads and profit at that price. Since the fixed overheads remain constant within the limits of the situation being considered (see Fixed Costs), the selling price which will produce the maximum profit is the price at which the difference between the variable costs and the revenue reaches a maximum. This difference is shown by the third curve in Figure 3.5.

It will be seen that the selling price which produces maximum profit is quite different from the selling price which produces maximum revenue. In practice, the price of maximum profit (m.p.) is always considerably higher than the price of maximum revenue or maximum sales (m.s.), since the two prices could only be identical if the whole of the costs were fixed and there were no varialbe costs at all.

This theoretical consideration demonstrates that there are only two factors that govern the selling price which will produce the maximum profit. These are:

(a) The variable cost of the product.
(b) The relationship between selling price and sales volume for that particular product.

IT WILL BE SEEN THAT THE FIXED OVERHEAD COSTS HAVE NO BEARING WHATEVER ON THE SELLING PRICE WHICH WILL PRODUCE THE MAXIMUM PROFIT.

In practice, it would be extremely difficult if not impossible to reproduce the theoretical curve in Figure 3.3 of the precise relationship between selling price and sales volume over a wide range of actual selling prices. Nevertheless, this relationship *and the effect of this relationship* must always exist for any product. This essential factor must be taken into account in practical methods of determining the most suitable selling price for a particular product.

Although, in most cases, the objective in fixing a selling price is to secure the maximum profit, there are some circumstances in which the most suitable selling price may be below this price. However, even in these cases, the most suitable selling price cannot be determined without first determining the price for maximum profit. These basic theoretical principles are therefore fundamental to any effective procedure for fixing selling prices.

FIXING SELLING PRICES

Because of the difficulty in determining the precise relationship between selling price and sales volume, there is no simple arithmetical method of determining the most suitable selling price for a product. Various methods are commonly found in practice.

One method is to estimate the cost per article and to add a certain percentage to this cost to provide the profit. In order to estimate the cost per article, it is necessary to have some device for allocating the fixed overhead costs to each product, this is usually in the form of percentages added to the variable costs. This allocation can never be made with complete accuracy. Moreover, the estimated cost per article is not a factual cost because the true cost will depend upon the quantity produced and sold, so that the cost can easily vary from month to month by more than the percentage that has been added to provide the profit. This method of fixing the selling price therefore introduces a quite unnecessary source of error since, as shown in the review of basic principles, the amount and allocation of the fixed overheads does not affect the most profitable selling price. In addition, this method has the much more serious disadvantage that it takes no account whatever of the effect of the selling price on the quantity that would be sold. The method has, therefore, little to recommend it unless the company is quoting for a single specific job or contract where there will be no variation in the quantity sold, and for which the order will be either obtained or lost.

Another not uncommon method is that which is sometimes referred to as basing the selling price 'on what the market will stand'. However, those who use this expression never seem to be quite clear what they mean by it. It seems to imply that there is some maximum price that purchasers would pay for a product and that, above this mystic price, few if any would be sold. It is true that there are a few products that do have a recognizable price plateau and that, beyond this plateau, sales begin to fall off fairly sharply. But, even in these special cases, the most profitable price is not necessarily at the edge of the pleateau.

In practice, this method usually means that account is being taken of the effect of price on quantity in order to determine some optimum selling price. This would be satisfactory were it not for misunderstandings about 'the optimum price'. The optimum price is clearly not the price at which the greatest quantity would be sold, this would be absurd. Therefore the individual who is fixing the price is often basing his estimate on his knowledge of the effect of price, not on quantity, but on sales turnover. As a result, although perhaps only subconsciously, he tends to arrive at the price which will produce the maximum revenue. He has found that, above this price, the revenue will start to fall.

However, as was pointed out in the previous section, the price that will produce the maximum profit is a very different price from that which produces the maximum revenue (see Figure 3.5). The difference in the profit that would be earned at each of these two prices can amount to substantial proportions over twelve months. Moreover, as will be seen from Figures 3.3 and 3.5, at the point of maximum contribution there is nothing unusual about the shape of the curves of either quantity or revenue. Neither of the curves reaches a peak or undergoes any unusual change at this point. Therefore, no matter how much experience a price-fixer may have of a particular market, there is nothing about the quantity or the revenue that will, by itself, provide any kind of intuitive guide to the most profitable selling price. As a result, a company that fixes its prices in some such way can be quite unknowingly obtaining a much smaller profit from its products than that which it is capable of obtaining.

A simple method of assessing the price that will produce the maximum profit is to use a trial and error process in which the effect of various trial prices is examined. The existing selling price can be used as a starting point or, alternatively, a tentative price can be obtained from conventional costing procedures. In either case, the essential requirement is to determine the variable cost of the article. In most cases this can be done with reasonable accuracy and, since this cost will be directly proportional to quantity, the variable cost per article remains the same and is unaffected by the quantity sold. The difference between the variable cost and the trial selling price will show the contribution to the fixed costs and profit that would be obtained by selling the product at that price.

The following is a typical example where a tentative selling price has been obtained by additions to the variable costs to cover overheads and profit:

Variable cost	£5
Fixed costs	4
Profit	2
Tentative selling price	£11

At this tentative selling price, the contribution to the fixed costs and profit would be as follows:

Selling price	£11
Variable cost	5
Contribution	£6

For convenience, the contribution per article is multiplied by 100 so that it can be expressed in terms of contribution per 100 articles sold:

Contribution per 100:   £600

The next step is to examine the possible effect of reducing the price to, say, £10. This would reduce the contribution per article to £5 but would probably increase the quantity that would be sold. For example, if the reduction in price increased the quantity by 10 per cent, then 110 articles would be sold at £10 for every 100 articles sold at £11. Based on a knowledge of the market and the prices of competitors' products, various possible effects are examined. If it is considered that the reduction in price from £11 to £10 would *at most* increase the quantity sold by as much as 15 per cent, the effect of a change in volume within this range can be tabulated as follows:

Increase	Quantity	Unit Contribution	Total Contribution
5%	105	£5	£525
10%	110	£5	£550
15%	115	£5	£575

However, since the total contribution at a selling price of £11 was £600, it would clearly be unprofitable in this case to reduce the selling price to £10. In fact, even if the reduction in price from £11 to £10 increased the sales by as much as 20 per cent (120), the resulting contribution of £600 would be no better than the contribution at £11 although 20 per cent more work would have had to be done in the production and sales departments to produce that same contribution.

It is evident from this that unless the product was being sold in some exceptionally competitive market, a selling price of less than £11 should not be considered. The effect of various tentative selling prices above

£11 is next examined. It is normally impossible to make a precise estimate of the percentage effect on quantity of a change in selling price. Therefore, at each selling price, the likely maximum and minimum percentage change should be examined. For instance, in this example, after examining the market, it might be considered that an increase in price from £11 to £12 might reduce the quantity by anything from 5 per cent to 15 per cent. The effect at various selling prices can be tabulated as follows:

Selling Price	Unit Contribution	Assessed Quantity Min.	Max.	Total Contribution Min.	Max.
£11	£6	100		£600	
12	7	85	95	595	665
13	8	75	85	600	680
14	9	60	75	540	675

On this assessment, the selling price that is most likely to provide the maximum profit is evidently around £13, but it might be dangerous to exceed this price. A suitable selling price for the product would therefore probably be about £12 18s.

It will be seen that, in this procedure, it is unnecessary to make a forecast of the actual monthly or yearly sales at each of the tentative selling prices. The assessment is limited to an estimate of the likely *percentage effect* of a *change* in selling price. The accuracy with which the most profitable selling price can be determined will depend only on the accuracy with which this assessment can be made. It should rarely, if ever, be assumed that this could be made with such complete accuracy that only a single estimate of the relative quantity need be made at each selling price. However, it will be found that in most cases, as in the foregoing example, the selling price that is most likely to produce the maximum profit becomes apparent even if there is a considerable range between the maximum and minimum estimates at each of the tentative prices.

It is, of course, quite impossible to determine the most profitable selling price without having some knowledge of the relationship between price and volume for the particular product. Therefore, even a rough approximation must inevitably be better than an arbitrary price based only on the costs.

As pointed out in the examination of the theory of selling prices, the objective in fixing the price is, in most cases, to secure the maximum profit. There are, however, certain situations in which the most profitable selling price may not be the most suitable selling price in that particular situation. For example, if a company has the sole monopoly in a product for which there is a large demand, it may be found that the most profitable selling price would yield an abnormally high return on the capital invested in that product. Therefore, before selling the product at this price, two possible effects must be considered:

a. The high return may encourage other companies to invest money in developing a similar product.
b. Selling at the higher price may limit the volume of sales and leave a large unsatisfied demand.

Therefore, although the most profitable price will yield the maximum profit in the short term, this success may encourage competition to enter the field and result in a lower profit in the long term. Similarly, the high selling price may restrict the development and expansion of the product and of the market for that product. Although, initially, the maximum profit might be obtained by meeting only 10 per cent of the potential demand, this may not be a wise long-term policy. There are few industries today in which a company can afford to stand still no matter how profitable its present activities. Growth and expansion are essential if it is to continue to be successful.

In these and similar situations, after the most profitable selling price has been determined, a policy decision must be made as to whether it might be more suitable to sell the product at some lower price. However, a sound decision cannot be made unless the most profitable price has first been determined. Without this knowledge the company would have no means of knowing the financial effects of its decision.

A RELIABLE ASSESSMENT OF THE MOST PROFITABLE SELLING PRICE IS THEREFORE AN ESSENTIAL FEATURE IN THE SUCCESSFUL MARKETING OF ANY PRODUCT.

CHECKING EXISTING SELLING PRICES

An adaption of the procedure for determining the most profitable selling price can be used to provide a quick and simple check on the profitability of existing selling prices. This consists of calculating the volume of sales that would be necessary to provide the same contribution if the existing price was raised or lowered.

The procedure can best be illustrated by the actual case example of an electric heater that was being sold to distributors for £24. The normal price to the user was £36. Rounded off, the manufacturer's cost analysis was as follows:

Selling price	£24
Variable costs	13
Unit contribution	£11
Contribution per 100 heaters	£1,100

In order to check the suitability of the existing selling price, a simple calculation is made of the additional quantities that would have to be sold to provide a contribution of £1,100 if a reduction was made in the selling price. For convenience, the calculation is usually made for a reduction of 10 per cent in the selling price, but this is not important. A similar calculation is then made of the quantities that would have to be sold if the price was increased by the same amount:

Retail Price	Manufacturer's Price	Variable Cost	Unit Contribution	Quantity to Produce £1,100
£ s. d.	£ s. d.	£ s. d.	£ s. d.	£
36 0 0	24 0 0	13 0 0	11 0 0	100
32 8 0	21 12 0	13 0 0	8 12 0	128
39 12 0	26 8 0	13 0 0	13 8 0	82

It should be noted that all the figures in this table are actual calculations, not estimates. It follows from these figures that:

a. If a 10 per cent reduction in the price of the heater would increase the quantity sold by *more* than 28 per cent, then a reduction in price would increase the profit and the existing price is too high.
b. If a 10 per cent increase in the price would reduce the sales by *less* than 18 per cent (100–82), then an increase in price would increase the profit and the existing price is too low.

A simple examination of the market and of the prices of competitors' products showed that a reduction of £3 12s. in the retail price would not result in an increase in sales of anything like as much as 28 per cent. Therefore, the existing price could certainly not be reduced. On the other hand, it seemed unlikely that a similar *increase* in the price would reduce the sales by as much as 18 per cent. Therefore the existing price was probably too low.

If it had appeared that a 10 per cent increase in the price would have been likely to reduce the sales by as much as or more than 18 per cent, then the check would have shown that the existing price was satisfactory. However, as there was preliminary evidence that the price was probably too low, a more detailed investigation of this heater was carried out using the procedure previously described for estimating the most profitable selling price. This confirmed the check and at a subsequent general revision of prices the retail price of this model was increased from £36 to £39 18s. with a substantial increase in profit.

It will be seen from this example that the steps in the checking procedure are as follows:

1. Determine the variable cost of the article and, hence, the current contribution per 100 articles sold (a)
2. Calculate the contribution per article if the selling price were reduced by 10 per cent (b).
3. Divide the current contribution (a) by the new unit contribution (b) to determine the percentage increase (c) in the quantity that would have to be sold to maintain the same total contribution.
4. Calculate the contribution per article if the selling price were increased by 10 per cent (d).
5. Divide the current contribution (a) by the unit contribution (d) to determine the percentage reduction (e) in the quantity to maintain the same total contribution.
6. Examine the market and competitors' prices.
7. If a 10 per cent reduction in the price would be likely to increase the quantity sold by *more* than (d), then the existing price is too high.
8. If a 10 per cent increase in the price would be likely to reduce the quantity sold by *less* than (e), then the existing price is too low.
9. If the variation in quantity would be less than (d) and more than (e), then the existing selling price is probably providing the maximum profit from the sale of the article.

In making the check it is of course important to take account of the possible incidence of any abnormal steps that may occur in the price/volume relationship – for example the effect of an increase in price from 9s. 11d. to 10s. The check is comparatively simple to carry out. Of course it will only show whether the existing selling price is either approximately correct, too high, or too low to provide the maximum profit. If it is too high or too low, it will not show what the price should be. The procedure previously described must be used to determine the selling price that will provide the maximum profit.

SELLING PRICES AND THE BREAK-EVEN CHART

The Break-even Chart can be used to provide a useful check on the effect of an overall change in the selling prices of a company's products. Such a change will, of course, alter the company's break-even point. The chart in Figure 3.6 is a typical example and shows the effect of an overall increase or reduction of 10 per cent in the selling prices of a company's products. The company's current cost and profit situation is as follows:

Fixed costs	£75,000
Variable costs	100,000
Total costs	175,000
Sales	200,000
Profit	£25,000

In drawing a Break-even Chart for this purpose, a convenient method is to draw the horizontal scale of quantity in such a way that 100 represents the existing volume of sales. This shows that, with the current selling prices, the company would break even at 75 per cent of the present level of sales (Point A on Figure 3·6).

If the selling prices were reduced on average by 10 per cent, an increase of 25 per cent in the quantity sold would be necessary to enable the company to maintain its present trading profit. However, such an increase would probably increase the working capital in stocks and outstanding accounts. Therefore, an overall reduction of 10 per cent in selling prices would result in a reduction in the return on the capital employed unless it produced an increase in the quantity sold of considerably more than 25 per cent. Moreover, the break-even point would

FINANCIAL ASPECTS OF MARKETING

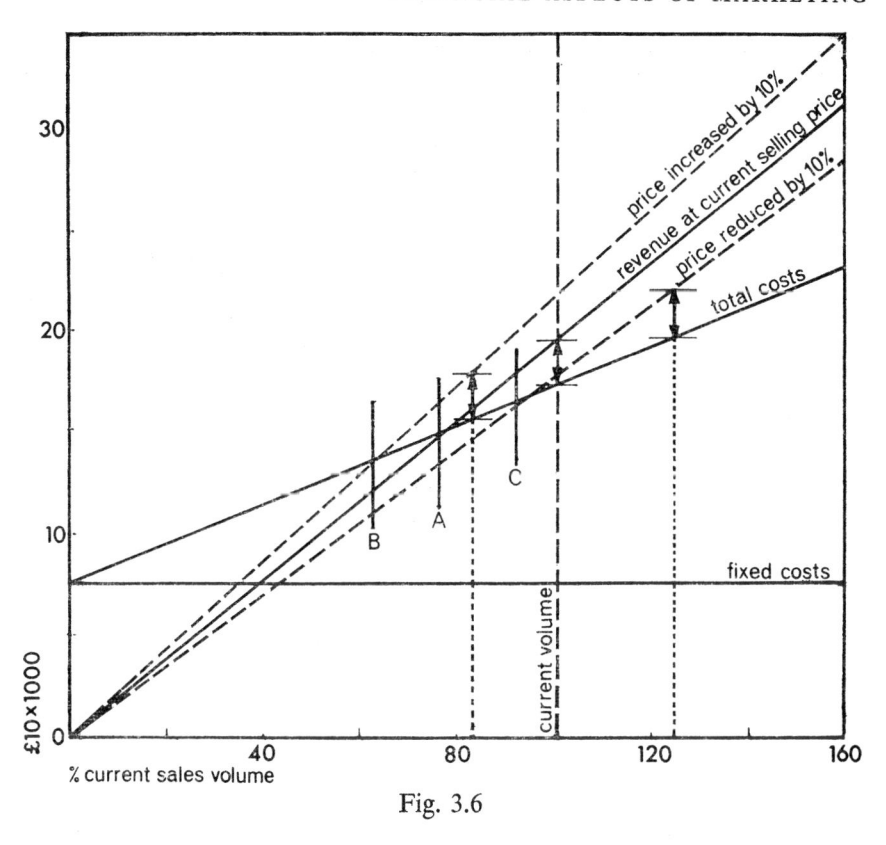

Fig. 3.6

be raised to 92 per cent of the current sales volume (Point C), so that a decline in the overall demand would put the company in an extremely dangerous position.

A 10 per cent *increase* in selling prices would also reduce the company's trading profit if it resulted in a reduction of more than 17 per cent in the quantity sold. If the reduction was less than 17 per cent, the profits would be increased, because the break-even point would be lowered from 75 per cent to 62 per cent of the current sales volume (Point B).

It will be seen from this example that, if a company is contemplating an overall revision of its selling prices, the Break-even Chart can be used to examine the situation and to show the effects of various changes in selling price. This enables the change which is likely to have the most beneficial effect to be selected.

67

MARKETING AND HIGHER MANAGEMENT

RELATIVE PROFITABILITY OF INDIVIDUAL PRODUCTS

The factors that govern the range of products most suitable to be marketed in relation to the company's resources are discussed under Product Planning in Chapter 4. The potential profitability of a product is, of course, a decisive factor in deciding whether or not it should be included in the range. Even so, if a company is selling a range of products, it is unlikely that every one of those products will be equally profitable. Therefore the company's overall profit will be influenced by the 'Product Mix' – i.e. the proportion of each product in its total sales. The relative profitability of individual products is therefore an important consideration during the planning of a company's marketing strategy.

It has already been pointed out earlier in this chapter that it is not possible to establish a precise constant cost per article. Even if the fixed costs could be accurately allocated to each product, the cost and profit *per article* must always depend upon the quantity sold. However, if the variable cost of an article is deducted from its selling price, the difference will show the contribution to the fixed overheads and profit obtained on every one of those articles that is sold. Therefore a precise figure can be given to the 'contribution per article' that is independent of the quantity sold.

This contribution per article, or 'unit contribution', is used to determine the relative profitability of two or more different articles produced from the same plant and employing the same overhead resources. Let us assume that two articles 'X' and 'Y' are being produced and that the selling price and variable cost of each article are as follows:

	Article 'X'	Article 'Y'
Selling price	£10	£20
Variable costs	4	12
Unit contribution	£6	£8

Two deductions could be made from these figures about the relative profitability of the two articles:

a. Every order for Article 'X' provides a contribution of £6 to the fixed costs and profit as compared with an £8 contribution for Article 'Y'.

b. The revenue from the sales of Article 'X' provides a contribution of 60 per cent to the fixed costs and profit as compared with a 40 per cent contribution for Article 'Y'.

It might appear from (a) that article 'Y' is the more profitable whereas, from (b), article 'X' might seem to be the more profitable. In fact, contrary to common assumption, it is quite impossible to tell solely from the costs which article in a range of products will provide the most profitable utilization of the company's resources. Under some circumstances, a company might be able to increase its profits by putting greater selling emphasis on article 'X', whilst under other circumstances the greater emphasis should be on article 'Y'. This is illustrated in the following examples.

If the two articles were produced by the same type of labour, the situation might be as follows:

	Article 'X'	Article 'Y'
Labour cost	£2	£4
Material and other variables	2	8
Total variable costs	4	12
Selling price	10	20
Unit contribution	£6	£8

In this case, two of articles 'X' would be produced in the same time and at the same labour cost as one of article 'Y'. Therefore, in this time, the contribution to the fixed costs and profit from the sales of article 'X' would be £12 as compared with £8 from article 'Y'. Hence, if the total output of the two articles was governed by the availability of labour, article 'X' would provide the more profitable utilization of the company's resources.

If machines were used in the production of the articles and if both articles were made on the same machines, the situation might be as follows:

	Article 'X'	Article 'Y'
Output per machine—hour	12	10
Unit contribution	£6	£8
Contribution per machine—hour	£72	£80

Under these conditions, if the output is governed by the capacity of the machines, article 'Y' would provide the more profitable utilization of the company's resources.

However, this measure of the relative profitability of the two articles would not apply if the machines were sometimes idle and were not being used to their maximum capacity throughout the week. A similar situation arises in the first example if the output is not restricted by the availability of labour. Under those conditions, the output would be governed by the quantity sold. The position might be as follows:

	Article 'X'	Article 'Y'
Annual sales (revenue)	100,000	£300,000
Annual sales (quantity)	10,000	15,000
Unit contribution	6	£8
Total annual contribution	£60,000	£120,000

Therefore, although the percentage contribution on article 'X' is 60 per cent compared with only 40 per cent for article 'Y', it is article 'Y' that has produced the greater total contribution to the company's fixed costs and profit during the year. Article 'Y' has been 'more profitable' than article 'X'. A 10 per cent increase in the sales of article 'Y' would produce a much greater increase in profit than a 10 per cent increase in the sales of article 'X' (providing that sufficient labour was available or could be obtained to produce the additional output). This suggests that the profitability of the product mix could be most effectively improved by increasing the proportion of the selling effort on article 'Y' and, similarly, that any additional promotion would be more profitable if it was directed at article 'Y' rather than article 'X'.

However, this assumes that both products have an equal sales potential and that it would be just as easy to obtain an increase in sales with one product as with the other. In practice, this is unlikely to be the case. For instance, the selling expenditure that produces sales of 100 article 'Y' might produce sales of 200 article 'X'. Under these conditions, the relative contribution potential of the two products would be as follows:

	Article 'X'	Article 'Y'
Ratio of sales potential	200	100
Unit contribution	£6	£8
Ratio of contribution potential	1,200 = 150	800 100

Therefore, every pound spent on selling article 'X' is capable of producing 50 per cent more contribution to fixed costs and profit than the same amount spent on selling article 'Y'. It follows from this, and only from this, that it is considerably more profitable to promote additional sales of article 'X', rather than article 'Y', up to the limit of the plant capacity.

In summary, the relative profitability position of these two products is as follows:

1. Article 'X' is capable of providing more profit than article 'Y' unless the demand for the two articles is exceeding the maximum production capacity.
2. If the output is being limited by machine capacity, article 'Y' is capable of providing more profit than article 'X'.
3. If the output is being limited by the availability of labour, article 'X' is capable of providing more profit than article 'Y'.

These examples serve to demonstrate that the determination of the 'most profitable' products in a product range is far from a simple matter of product costing, as is sometimes supposed, but is rather another area in which finance and the marketing function are intimately related. Costing methods are required to determine the unit contribution of each product and the contribution in relation to the use of labour and equipment. A thorough knowledge of the market is necessary to determine the relative sales potential of each product. Based on this information, the relative profitability of the products in the range under varying conditions can be ascertained by means of the calculations used in the examples.

It has, of course, been assumed in these examples that the products are produced in the same plant and use the same overhead resources. The product that provides the greatest contribution to fixed costs and profit is therefore making the greatest contribution to the profitable use of those resources. However, if the amount invested in the production and sale of one product, or group of products, is greater than another, the profitability must be considered in relation to the return on the investment for each product. In the example given above, the company that is producing articles 'X' and 'Y' may be spending considerable sums on development and research. Article 'X' may be capable of producing a 50 per cent greater annual contribution than article 'Y'. But, if twice as much has been spent on the development of article 'X', the return on the investment would be greater with article 'Y'.

However, this does not mean that the products which are showing the highest return should receive the greatest attention when planning the sales of the product range. Such a bias would be likely to reduce the sales of those products which have the lowest return, resulting in an even lower return on the investment which has been made in them. If there are differences in the amount invested in different products or product groups, it is necessary to know the relative potential return from each in order to plan investment expenditure and decide upon the product range. But, once a range of products has been decided, the objective must be to secure the maximum total contribution to fixed costs and profit from the range as a whole. It is only in this way that it will be possible to maximize the return on the overall investment.

RELATION BETWEEN SELLING COSTS AND PROFIT

If the level of efficiency remains unchanged, the value received from an item of expenditure will normally be directly proportional to the cost. Doubling the expenditure on materials would double the quantity received; doubling the production costs would double the output from the factory; doubling the clerical costs would double the amount of work done in the offices, and so on. The selling costs are, however, an exception to which this general rule does not apply. The sales volume is not directly proportional to the amount of money spent on advertising and promotion, nor is it directly proportional to the number of salesmen employed and, hence, to the cost of the sales force. In this respect, the selling operations differ fundamentally from the other operations carried out in the business, where the value obtained from the expenditure depends only on the internal efficiency.

There are certain basic factors that govern the amount that must be spent on selling in order to provide the maximum profit. The general nature of the relationship between the number of salesmen employed and the volume of sales obtained is shown in Figure 3.7. There is some maximum volume of sales that would be reached when there were sufficient salesmen to call on every potential customer at sufficiently frequent intervals. Beyond this, any further increase in the number of salesmen cannot produce any further increase in sales. If every potential customer was of the same type, had a need of exactly the same size and had the same purchasing ability, the volume of sales would, theoreti-

FINANCIAL ASPECTS OF MARKETING

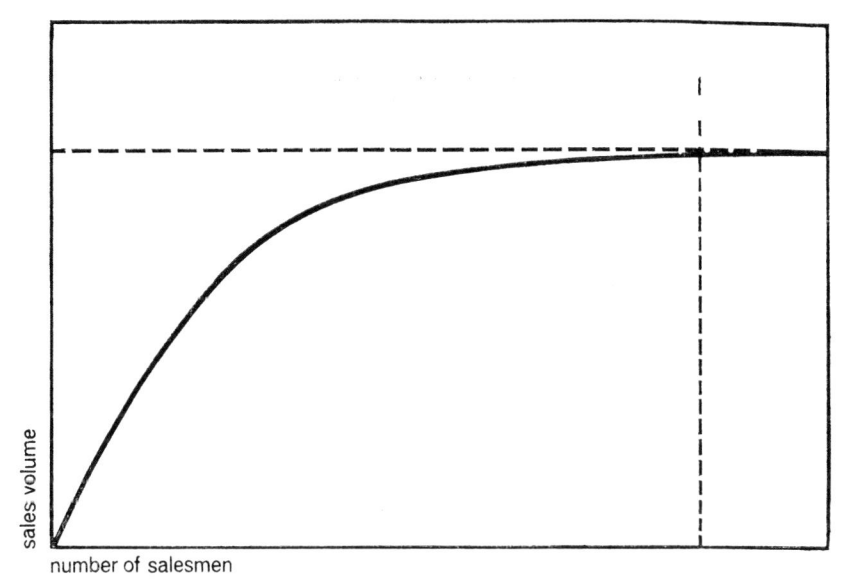

Graph showing sales volume (y-axis) vs number of salesmen (x-axis), curve rising and leveling off at saturation volume (dashed horizontal line).

Fig. 3.7

cally, be directly proportional to the number of salesmen employed up to the saturation volume. In practice this never occurs, and it is by no means uncommon for less than one quarter of the total number of potential customers to be responsible for three quarters of the total demand. Hence, the ratio of sales volume to salesmen diminishes at an increasing rate until it levels out at the saturation volume as shown in the illustration.

If the salesmen were being paid only on commission, with no other remuneration, and if they had to pay their own expenses, the cost of the salesmen would, of course, be directly proportional to sales volume. The whole cost would therefore be a 'variable cost'. However, in most situations, a substantial part of or even the entire cost of the sales force is in the form of salaries and expenses. This cost will be approximately proportional to the number of salesmen employed.

The gross contribution to fixed costs and profit is directly proportional to the volume of sales obtained. Therefore the relationship between the number of salesmen and the gross contribution will be exactly the same as the relationship between the number of salesmen and the volume of sales in Figure 3.7. The fixed cost of the sales force has to come out of the total contribution. Therefore, for any given number of salesmen, the difference between the gross contribution and the cost of the sales force will be the remaining net contribution to fixed costs and profit, as shown in Figure 3.8. The maximum profit will be obtained with the number of

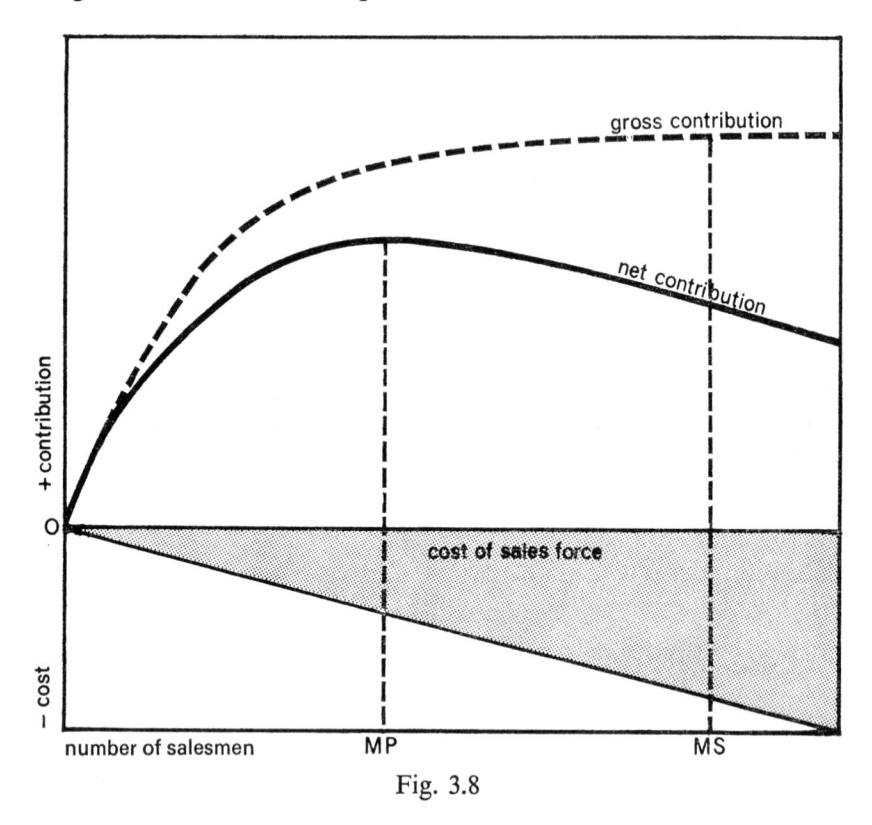

Fig. 3.8

salesmen that produces the maximum net contribution. This is shown at 'MP' in Figure 3.8 where 'MS' is the number of salesmen that would be required to obtain maximum sales volume. (Note that any part of the selling cost which is in the form of bonus or commission on sales is a variable cost and does not affect these considerations.) In planning and controlling a selling operation, it is therefore necessary to know the number of salesmen required to obtain maximum profit. Procedures for determining the optimum size of the sales force are described in Marketing Planning in Chapter 5.

A similar situation arises when determining advertising expenditure. The effect of advertising on sales volume will, of course, depend not only

FINANCIAL ASPECTS OF MARKETING

on the amount that is spent but also on such things as the design of the advertisements and the media in which they are displayed. However, assuming a constant level of advertising efficiency, a typical relationship between expenditure and sales volume is shown in Figure 3.9. There is a

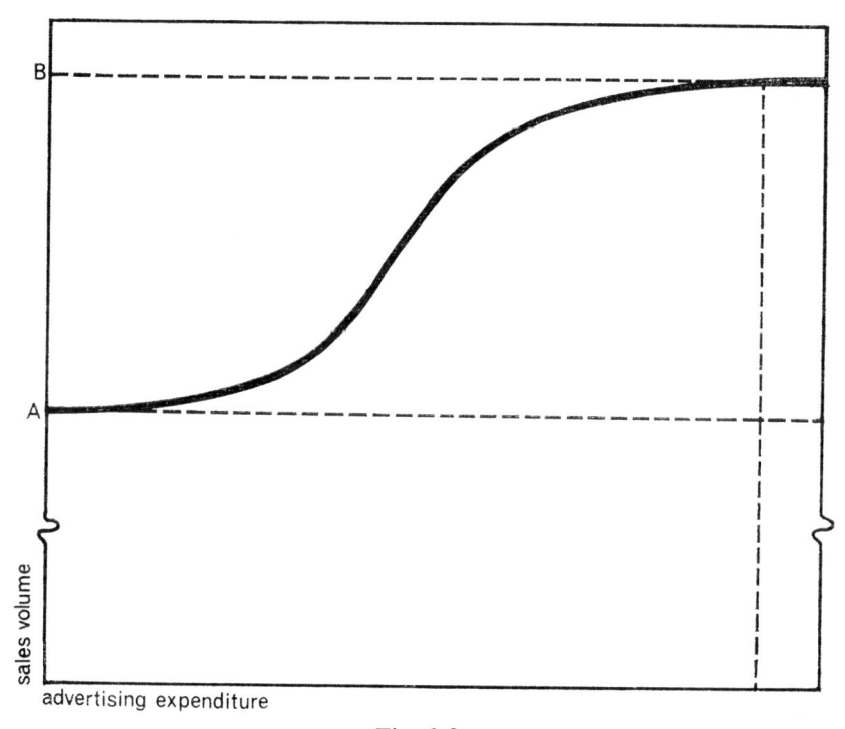

Fig. 3.9

certain volume of sales, 'A', which would be obtained without any advertising. Depending on the size of the potential demand, there must also always be some maximum volume 'B' that could be obtained as a result of advertising, beyond which an increase in advertising expenditure could not produce a further increase in sales. The shape of the curve between 'A' and 'B' will depend upon such things as the amount that is being spent on advertising by competitors. It will not always be the same shape as that shown in Figure 3.9 but this is typical of many situations. Advertising has a cumulative effect and a small expenditure may make little difference to sales. But, as the expenditure is increased, its impact and effect on sales increases by a greater proportion. This will again decline as the maximum potential sales volume is approached, as shown in the illustration.

Employing the same considerations as those used for the sales force, it follows from Figure 3.9 that the relationship between advertising expenditure and gross contribution is as shown in Figure 3.10, where 'C'

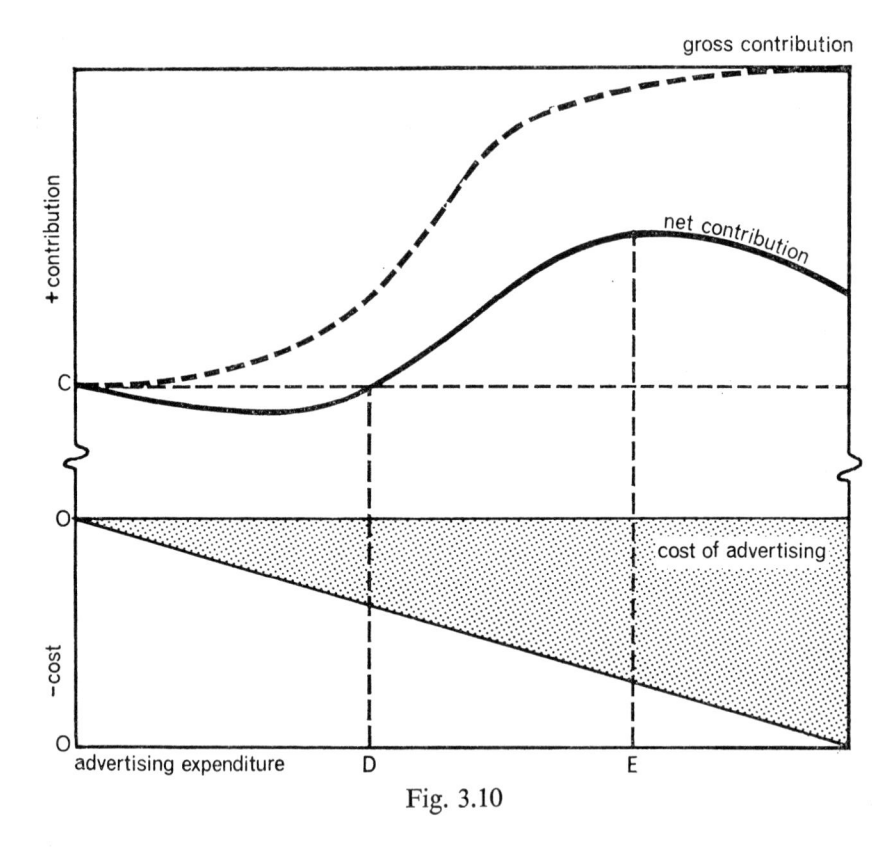

Fig. 3.10

is the contribution that would be obtained without any advertising. It will be seen that a small expenditure on advertising may, in fact, reduce the net contribution and profit. No benefit is obtained until the expenditure exceeds the amount 'D'. The maximum profit is obtained at the amount 'E'.

It will be seen from these examples that, in order to obtain the maximum profit, a company's selling costs, unlike its other costs, are governed not only by its internal activities but also by sensitive external factors in the market. An important part of the marketing function is the study of these external factors in order to determine the optimum situation. (See Marketing Strategy, Chapter 5.)

RELATION BETWEEN SALES VOLUME AND CAPITAL EMPLOYED

If the amount of capital remained constant, irrespective of the volume of sales, then the return on the investment would be directly proportional to the profit earned. Doubling the profit would result in doubling the percentage return on the investment. However, even if an increase in sales does not necessitate additional capital expenditure on plant or equipment, it must almost inevitably result in an increase in the amount of money owed by customers for goods already delivered and not yet paid for. It is also likely to result in an increase in the amount of capital invested in stocks and work-in-progress. Since the fundamental purpose of marketing is to secure the optimum return on capital, it is obviously important that, when planning any change in the marketing strategy, the effect of the change on the capital investment is taken into account.

Executives outside the financial department do not always realize how much cash is required to fill the monetary pipe-line between payments and receipts. Expenditure on wages and materials may be incurred in the production of goods weeks or months before payment for those goods is received from the customer. Even after goods have been delivered, a delay of four weeks until payment is received alone represents a capital investment that is equivalent to more than 8 per cent of the annual sales revenue. In the total pipe-line, this amount is often somewhere between 10 per cent and 25 per cent of the annual sales and, in some cases, can be very much higher. For instance, on an annual turnover of £1,000,000, the amount invested in this pipe-line alone might be £200,000. This is in addition to the capital that has been invested in buildings, machines, and other assets. It would absorb £20,000 out of the company's annual profits to provide even a 10 per cent return on this pipe-line investment.

Some part of the total investment will therefore fluctuate with the volume of sales. In order to determine the effect of a change in sales volume, the capital employed in the business can be divided into its fixed and variable elements. The procedure is exactly the same as that used in analysing the operating costs to determine the relationship between volume and profit.

During a period of rapid sales expansion, there may be a temporary need for a considerable amount of additional cash to finance the increased production. Because of the time lag between expenditure and income, additional expenditure may be incurred on wages and materials many weeks before the corresponding additional revenue is received from customers' payments. More than a few companies have run into financial difficulties through this cause, and over-trading through a too rapid sales expansion is always a potential danger. Therefore, when planning any appreciable expansion of sales, it is extremely important to determine the amount of additional cash that will be required during the period of expansion. A suitable procedure is to prepare a plan showing the anticipated income and expenditure in each month throughout the period. If additional cash is difficult to obtain, it may be necessary to time the expansion so that the worst periods do not coincide with the times of the year when large occasional payments have to be made, such as the payment of dividends.

In addition to the effect of a change in sales volume, there are other ways in which the capital employed is influenced by the marketing strategy. This is particularly important in relation to distribution policy. For instance, if an intermediate distributor is by-passed, it may be possible to increase profits; the cost of the larger sales force that would be required may be considerably less than the discount that has to be paid to the distributor. However, if the distributor takes bulk deliveries and holds local stocks, it may be necessary, when selling direct, for the company itself to hold very much larger stocks of finished goods in order to provide the same service to customers. The capital required would be still further increased if it was necessary for separate local stocks to be held throughout the country in warehouses owned by the company. Therefore, in all such cases, it is the return on the investment that must be considered and not merely the relative profit that would be obtained from one channel of distribution as compared with another.

PROFIT PLANS AND BUDGETS

The preparation of profit plans and budgets is not, of course, part of the marketing function, but a matter for the financial department.

FINANCIAL ASPECTS OF MARKETING

Nevertheless, the full benefits of marketing cannot be obtained unless the company is working to a specific profit plan. It was pointed out at the beginning of the chapter that marketing is concerned with profits rather than sales volume. Therefore, a forecast of sales is not an end in itself, nor is it complete until it has been converted into a profit plan. From this, short and long-term budgets can be prepared by which to control the financial stability and growth of the company.

However, plans prepared by the financial department are of little value if they are based entirely on its records of what has happened in the past. The marketing function has a vital part to play in supplying the information on which realistic and attainable plans can be based. This again demonstrates the need for a complete and continuing association between the marketing and financial functions in the business. This amounts to more than mere co-operation, because the extent of the company's success depends upon the two functions working jointly to achieve their common objective of ensuring the continued profitability of the business.

FINANCIAL ASPECTS OF THE CUSTOMER'S BUSINESS

Securing a satisfactory return on the investment is just as important for the customer as it is for the supplier. However, its value and importance as a 'selling benefit' is sometimes overlooked.

Selling to retailers can be taken as an example. The major part of a retail organization's investment is in the form of stocks and in the space required to accommodate those stocks. Therefore, the profitability of a product to the retailer depends, not so much on the mark-up and the quantity he will sell, as on the profit that it will provide per square foot of his floor area – or, in the case of shelved products, the profit per cubic foot of shelving.

Nevertheless, in selling a product to retailers, the appeal is often consciously or subconsciously based on persuading the retailer that there will be a demand for the product and that he will be able to sell it in substantial quantities. In fact, the retailer is being besieged by manufacturers who are trying to sell him their products. He is quite prepared to assume that there will be a demand for those products, otherwise the manufacturers would not have wasted their time producing them, and he is little concerned with the relative merits of one product as compared with another. The products in which he will be interested are those from which it can be demonstrated that he will obtain the greatest profit per cubic foot of his space. This is the real 'selling benefit' as far as the retailer is concerned.

A manufacturer should know as much about the basic financial aspects of his customer's business as the customer knows himself – preferably more. This knowledge plays an important part in successful marketing. It should be taken into account both in the way in which the product is designed and packaged as well as in the way in which it is sold. Salesmen should be trained, not only in salesmanship and a knowledge of the products they are selling, but also in the part which those products play in influencing the profitability of the customer's business.

Without this knowledge and understanding of the customer's business, there cannot be complete customer-orientation in the marketing and selling operations. Matters of this kind distinguish the company that is marketing its products from the one that is merely trying to sell them.

Chapter 4

Product Policy

It was shown in the first chapter that, fundamentally, the successful existence of any company depends upon its ability to continue to satisfy some particular need or needs of the community in a way that will provide the most profitable utilization of its resources.

The variety of a community's conscious and subconscious needs is almost beyond number. Each of these needs represents a potential demand for some product or service to satisfy that need. A company, on the other hand, has certain specific resources consisting of buildings, equipment, people and money. The first step in marketing is to match the one with the other in order to ensure that, out of the vast number of products for which there is a potential demand, the company is producing the particular types or varieties of products that will make the most profitable use of its resources.

This is a very important fundamental aspect in the overall management of any business. Nevertheless, it is easy to take this matching process for granted and to assume that the company is continuing to produce products of the right type, variety and design to achieve this objective. No matter how highly efficient a company may be in other aspects of its business, its ultimate success must *always* depend on its products. Yet there are still many companies that give far less time and attention to ensuring that their products are right for the market than they give to almost any other sphere of the company's activities.

Product policy is concerned first with the type of product – for example a car or a refrigerator – and then, within that type, the range and particular versions that should be produced. Having determined the most suitable types and varieties of products it is, of course, equally important that they should be designed and presented in the most suitable way to win favourable buying decisions. However, this chapter is concerned only with top management decisions on product policy, for these affect every member of the management team. The design of the company's products is part of the routine marketing activities that are covered in the second part of the book – see Chapter 10.

The product which a company is marketing is not necessarily a physical article: it may be anything from a breakfast cereal to the professional services of a banker or chartered accountant. This does not in any way affect the principles that are involved. In some industries, however, it is important to be clear about the nature of the product that the company is, in fact, marketing. For example, a jobbing iron foundry is producing castings to the design and specification of its customers, but it is not marketing castings, it is marketing a foundry service. Its product policy will be concerned with the nature of the service and not with the design of the castings that it is producing. It is important that this distinction should be borne in mind in all considerations of product policy and planning.

The objective of the product policy is to ensure that, in the light of the ever-changing conditions in the market, the company's resources continue to be used in the most profitable way. The achievement of this objective requires not only a knowledge of what is happening outside the company in the market, but also a complete understanding of the precise nature and extent of the company's internal resources. Contrary to what is sometimes assumed, the starting point for successful marketing is inside the company, and not outside in the market.

ANALYSIS OF RESOURCES

A modern company is a complex organism. It consists partly of its physical assets, in the form of buildings and machines, and partly in the corporate knowledge, experience and expertise of its management, staff and employees. It also possesses an 'image' which, to a greater or lesser extent, has earned it the goodwill of a particular group of purchasers with whom it has established connections.

If the most effective use is to be made of this complex organism, it must be taken apart and analysed in detail. This provides the only basis for a sound product policy. The most suitable way of carrying out this examination will obviously depend on individual circumstances. One of its most important purposes is to pinpoint the company's particular strengths and weaknesses. No company is so strong that it does not possess some weaknesses and no company is so weak that it does not possess some strengths. The objective is to market those products that will most fully exploit the company's strengths and minimize its weaknesses. The principal features to be considered are as follows:

a. *Land, Buildings and Machines*
If the company has a considerable capital investment in highly specialized buildings and equipment – for example, a chemical works or steel rolling mills – this will obviously dictate the general *type* of product to be produced so long as there continues to be a profitable demand. In these cases, the consideration is limited to the kind and range of products within that type.

In other cases, such as a general engineering works, it may be possible to produce many different types of products in the same buildings and with perhaps the same or only mildly modified machines and equipment.

The examination will be concerned with the general suitability of the plant for producing different varieties of products. It will search for any particular advantages over competitors that might be more fully exploited.

b. *Location of Plant*
The location of the plant can occasionally have a bearing on the type of products that can be most profitably produced. This may be in relation to supplies of certain raw materials or in relation to the outlets for the products.

c. *Design and Technical Expertise*
This is often one of the most important factors in determining the most suitable type and range of products. It is especially important when diversification is being considered (see Product Diversification). Given the money, any company can acquire efficient machines and equipment. Design skills and technical expertise may take years to build up. The search here is for the *fundamentals* of the things that the company is really good at doing, for example, not that the company is good at making certain products but *why* it is good at making those products. It is this that will often suggest the scope for alternative applications.

Here, more than anywhere else, careful consideration must be given to strengths and weaknesses. For instance, one furniture manufacturer might be weak in designing for appearance but extremely good at designing for efficient and economic production. In another manufacturer, the situation might be reversed. The most suitable articles and styles that each company should produce will be those that exploit their strengths and avoid their weaknesses. (This may seem to be obvious but it is surprising how often an examination shows that it is being overlooked in practice.)

d. *Production Skills*
The degree of skill required in the production of different products varies widely. Some products can be produced almost entirely by unskilled labour with very little training; others require the employment of skilled craftsmen with long experience.

Here again, the objective is to examine the particular skills that can be most usefully exploited and the weaknesses to be avoided.

e. *Distribution Network*
A company's existing distribution network and the goodwill of its customers can sometimes be one of its most valuable assets. For instance, in some cases it would be comparatively easy for a company to sell any product that passed through its existing network to its existing customers. Typical examples can be seen in certain companies that market a number of quite different consumer products that pass through the same network.

However, with all these factors, it is the deeper rather than the more superficial application that may be more significant. The case history of a particular engineering company provides a good example. The company started by producing a single piece of equipment that was used by civil engineering contractors. This was a unique product that proved to be very successful and a considerable amount of goodwill was built up.

The company then made a careful study of the needs of its customers. By designing specialised machines and equipment to meet these needs, the company rapidly expanded and is today a large and prosperous organization.

PRODUCT POLICY

f. *Promotional and Selling Facilities*
The nature of a company's promotional and selling experience will depend upon the type of product it produces and the markets in which it sells them. This experience can be successfully used in selling other products that require the same expertise even though the products may have to pass through new channels to new customers.

For example, a company that is selling machines and equipment to one industry will not have any selling problems in selling other machines or equipment to another industry. The company would, however, need to use different selling methods – and perhaps even a different sales force – if it wished to start selling consumable materials to industrial customers.

g. *Finance*
A company's financial resources obviously form an important part of its assets and may influence its product policy in regard to such things as the rate at which it can expand. However, unlike the other assets, money is universally applicable to any type or variety of product. Nevertheless some products may require more money to develop than others.

Procedures for determining the relative profitability of different products were described in Chapter 3. The potential profitability of a product is obviously one of the most important factors in determining its suitability.

It is on considerations of this kind that a company's product policy should be based. The steps that follow in the determination of the most suitable types, varieties, and range of product all stem from this detailed analysis of the company's own particular resources. As has been said, the objective is to make the fullest possible uses of those resources which constitute the company's greatest strengths. These may be within its physical resources or they may be within the specialized knowledge, experience and skills of management and employees.

Like the market, a company's strengths and weaknesses are not static. New strengths can be developed and weaknesses can be eliminated. However, the foundations for any development will always be stronger if they are built on strengths rather than on weaknesses.

THE PRODUCT RANGE

Variety in a range of products can occur in different forms. These forms can be broadly grouped into three classes:

1. Variety in type of product.
2. Variety in style or design of products of the same type.
3. Variety in size within the same style or design.

For example, a company may be producing men's shirts and pyjamas – a Class 1 form of variety. The shirts may be produced in different styles or designs – a Class 2 form of variety. Each style is produced in a range of sizes – a Class 3 form of variety. Some varieties, such as the different degrees of hardness in a pencil (H, HB, etc.) are of the same nature as a variety in size and come within Class 3.

Confusion sometimes arises in discussing problems of variety through failure to distinguish between these three different forms. Each requires different consideration. However, precise border line distinctions as to whether some particular form of variety is in one class or another are not important.

Class 1. Variety in Type of Product

The principal factors that govern the type of product can be summarized as follows:

a. Its suitability in relation to the company's design and production facilities. Does it exploit the strengths and avoid the weaknesses? If applicable, to what extent does it affect the balance of the load in relation to machine capacities?
b. Its relative profitability in relation to the investment – as described in Chapter 3.
c. The nature of the market for the product and the channels of distribution.
d. The availability of materials or components required in its production.
e. Its suitability in relation to the company's selling and promotional facilities.
f. Its suitability in relation to the company's image. Does it enhance or impair that image?

PRODUCT POLICY

g. Its effect, if any, on the sales of other types of products in the company's range.
h. The nature and intensity of competition.
i. The size and trend of the demand for that type of product.

The above factors are not placed in any order of importance as this varies in different situations. The last factor (i) is particularly important when considering the abandonment of an existing product or the introduction of a new one. In this context, a 'new' product means a type of product that is new to the company, although other companies may be already marketing that type of product. The size of the total demand for a particular type of product varies with time, and has the characteristic trend shown in Figure 4.1. When an entirely new product is first placed

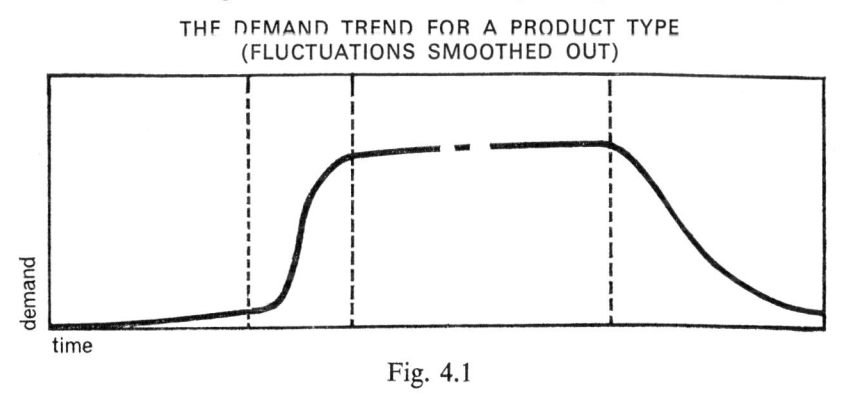

THE DEMAND TREND FOR A PRODUCT TYPE
(FLUCTUATIONS SMOOTHED OUT)

Fig. 4.1

on the market, the demand may be quite small for a considerable period of time. In some cases, many years have elapsed before the curve begins to turn upwards to approach the saturation potential for that type of product. For example, the first motor-cars were produced at the end of the last century, but it was some twenty years before there were any signs of the rapid expansion in the demand that subsequently occurred. Similarly, efficient dish-washers were on sale in Britain before 1940, but sales were negligible until the upturn in the demand started to occur around 1963. The upturn, as in these examples, often occurs quite suddenly and dramatically. This is due to a variety of causes working in combination and has been a common characteristic with many new products. The upward incline in the plateau itself is due to the natural rate of growth in an expanding economy.

Pioneers often do not reap the full benefits from their innovations. Financially, the ideal time to enter the market is at the point where the upturn begins to occur. It was at this stage that men like Ford in America and Morris and Austin in Britain entered the market and made considerable fortunes out of the sales of cars. (The acceleration in the upturn was largely due to the activities of these men themselves, which is one of the typical contributory causes to which reference has already been made. However, from many similar instances, there is no evidence to suggest that they would have fared any better than the original pioneers had they entered the market twenty years earlier.)

Therefore, before a company embarks on a new product, it is important that a careful study should be made of the trend in the demand for that type of product. After the plateau has been reached, competition is likely to be intense and profit margins low. However, instead of the single plateau shown in the diagram, there may be two or more plateaux at different periods of time. For example, the sales of gramophone records had sunk to a fraction of their original plateau before the new teenage demand sent them soaring to a new and much higher plateau.

Similarly, there should be no hesitation in abandoning an existing product if it has ceased to be profitable and if the demand is unlikely to increase. In the overseas markets, British industry has tended to earn the reputation of hanging on to existing products long after they should have been abandoned and replaced by new ones. Although there are many notable exceptions, there are still many products being made in Britain that were originated at a time when our most valuable asset was an abundant supply of cheap coal to provide fuel and power for industry. It is not surprising that such products, based on an obsolete asset, have ceased to be competitive in the world's markets unless they are now exploiting some other specialized resources.

Class 2. Variety in Form, Style or Design
Although a particular type of product may be eminently suitable for a company, it does not necessarily follow that all varieties of that product will be equally suitable or that the company should attempt to produce them.

However, within certain limits, an increase in the number of varieties will, in itself, increase the company's potential share of the market. This can best be illustrated by taking a simple hypothetical example. Let us assume that there were only two companies making marmalade and that each company was producing a single brand. Let us also assume that both brands were of the same quality, were sold at the same price and received the same weight of promotion. Under such conditions, the housewife going into the grocer's shop would have only two brands to choose from and each would have an equal chance of being selected. In other words, if all other things were equal, each company would secure 50 per cent of the total demand. However, if one of the two companies introduced a second brand under another name, the housewife would now have three brands to select from. Again, if all other things were equal, each brand would have an equal chance of being selected. The company that had the two brands would secure two-thirds of the market and the other company one-third. (The practical application of this principle can be seen in the case of a cigarette manufacturer who produces a variety of different brands.)

It is sometimes assumed that a particular variety is unnecessary if it is meeting the same demand as one of the company's other products. It will be seen from the example that this is not so. Nevertheless, there are severe practical limitations to the application of this principle. For instance, there is a limit to the number of different varieties which a distributor is prepared to stock and sell. However, the most important limitation is one of cost. The introduction of an additional variety always increases costs even if, as in the example, it merely means stopping a labelling machine to change the labels in the magazine. It may also necessitate holding larger stocks and increasing the amount of capital that has to be invested in this way.

Moreover, in the example, both varieties used exactly the same resources of the company. They required the same equipment, exploited the same skills and avoided the same weaknesses. Under these conditions, the Class 2 form of variety is primarily a matter of costs. The elimination of a particular variety is likely to reduce sales. But this will be no disadvantage if the loss in contribution from that variety is more than offset by the resultant savings in costs. Conversely, the introduction of a new variety will increase the costs; it will also increase the profit if the additional contribution is greater than the increased costs. Therefore, in these cases, the determination of the most suitable range depends primarily on a knowledge of market potentials and on accurate costing of setting-up times, stocks, etc.

There are, however, many forms of variety in Class 2 where the different varieties do not use exactly the same resources. This is, perhaps, the more common situation in many companies. Different varieties of the same type of product may require different equipment or different skills. They may even require different promotional and selling expertise although the channels of distribution are likely to be the same. An obvious but somewhat extreme example is the difference between a Rolls Royce and a low-priced, mass-produced car. The differences between Axminster, Wilton and tufted carpets is another example of this form of variety.

Because of this, many of the factors that govern the suitability of a particular variety in Class 2 are the same as in Class 1. They can again be summarized as follows:

a. The suitability of the variety in relation to the company's expertise in design. Is it well within the limits of this expertise? Does it exploit the strengths?
b. Its suitability in relation to production skills. Is it well within the limits of these skills? If not, can the necessary skilled labour be readily obtained?
c. Its suitability in relation to existing machines and equipment. What are the capacities of the machines and are there any bottlenecks? What special equipment, if any, is required for this variety?
d. Does the inclusion of the variety necessitate an increase in the overall ratio of value of stocks to sales revenue?
e. The suitability of the variety in relation to the company's selling and promotional activities. If there are intermediaries between the producer and user, does it pass through the same channels and is it stocked and sold by the same customers as other varieties?
f. The nature of the market. Is it an *alternative* variety that is purchased by exactly the same users as the other varieties? (For example, two brands of marmalade sold at the same price.) Or is it purchased by a different type or category of user (for example, a Rolls-Royce and a low-priced car?) In many cases, different sectors of the market may overlap but even small differences can be important in planning the most suitable policy – see 'Market Segmentation', Chapter 5.
g. The relative size of the potential demand for the variety in relation to the other varieties being produced. The trend in the demand.

h. The relative profitability of the variety based on the factors and procedures described in Chapter 3.
i. Its suitability in relation to the company's image. Does it enhance or impair that image?
j. Its effect, if any, on the sales of other varieties and other products in the company's range.
k. The nature and intensity of competition.

Once again, the objective is not merely to use the above factors as a check list but to formulate an imaginative policy that will fully exploit the company's own particular strengths and minimize its weaknesses (see the case example at the end of this section).

Class 3. Variety in Size
Variety in size, weight, degree or grade is almost invariably something that has first been introduced to meet the varying requirements of the market. However market requirements often change and some varieties continue to be produced and sold even though there is no longer a basic need for that variation – the purchaser might now be quite happy to accept an alternative if the existing variety was not available to him. This applies particularly where economies through variety reduction would enable a smaller standardized range to be offered at a lower price. For example, the additional cost of variety in this class is usually small if only small quantities are produced and the articles are largely handmade; it can be very considerable in large quantity mass production. Over the years many products pass from the former to the latter. In the earlier stages, variety can be introduced at little or no additional cost and users become accustomed to expecting these varieties. It may subsequently require considerable price advantages to wean them away from this expectation.

A company that has a large share of its market is likely to be in a better position to introduce a reduction in a range that has become recognized and established. The smaller company might be unable to do this without considerable loss in sales if its competitors continued to offer the greater variety.

On the other hand, the introduction of a *greater* variety in size or other similar characteristic can sometimes be a strong selling benefit that will increase sales. The resultant additional contribution to fixed costs and profit may be considerably greater than the additional cost of setting up, change-over times, stocks and so on.

The essential requirements in determining the most suitable policy in relation to this aspect of variety are reliable information about market potential and an accurate knowledge of the true costs involved. Without care, it is often easy to demonstrate on paper that savings should result from a reduction, but to find that these savings fail to materialize in practice.

PRODUCT DESIGN IN RELATION TO VARIETY

The cost of variety in Classes 2 and 3 can sometimes be considerably reduced if greater attention is paid to the need for variety in the basic design of the product. For example, if a car manufacturer started out by designing a car solely for the British market with a right-hand drive, it would be a very costly operation to produce an alternative model with a left-hand drive. Part of the car would have to be redesigned and many of the component parts would have to be different from those used on the British model. However, in practice, the need for this variety is taken into account in the basic design of the car and its component parts. As a result, a quite minor change on the final assembly operation will produce a model with either a left or right-hand drive. The cost of this variety is an almost negligible proportion of the total cost of the car.

In summary, the objective should be to plan a range of products that will make the fullest use of the company's strengths with the greatest possible degree of standardization in the materials and components used. Whenever practicable, the design of the products should be such that comparatively small variations in the use of the standardized materials and components will provide the variety necessary to cater for the varied and sometimes conflicting requirements of different customers.

CASE EXAMPLE

The following case history is a typical example of the way in which a company's product policy can be effectively changed in order to exploit its strengths and minimize its weaknesses:

PRODUCT POLICY

The company reviewed was producing a wide variety of men's and women's footwear. The range extended from women's 'fashion shoes' at one extreme to heavy industrial and agricultural boots at the other. Both the market share and profitability varied considerably for different varieties of footwear.

The company was one of the larger producers in its home market and had modest export sales. The overall return on capital was low and a reorganization was carried out in order to improve the company's financial position.

The first step in examining a market is to divide it into its various sectors. In this case, the first and most important division was between male and female purchasers. Each buys entirely different varieties from the other and there is no overlapping. Each of these divisions was then further sub-divided into types of purchaser and types of purchases. (The market examination must embrace *all* purchasers and *all* varieties of the product, and should not be confined to the range currently produced by the company.)

The particular factors that were influencing the purchasers' buying decisions were then determined and defined. It was found that many of these were subconscious factors of which the purchasers themselves were quite unaware and that there were considerable differences between one sector and another. For example, the kind of things which influence a woman when she is buying an evening shoe are different from those that influence her when she is buying the shoes in which she goes to work; or, much more obviously, the things that influence a teenager are very different from those that influence a middle-aged housewife buying the same type of shoe.

This market investigation is necessary, not only to determine the most suitable range, but also to plan the marketing strategy for the selected products – see Chapter 5 where the procedure is more fully described.

The company's resources were then examined in relation to the many different needs of the market. It was found that the company's principal weaknesses were in the field of women's 'fashion shoes'. In these shoes, frequent changes in design and style are necessary and sales depend largely upon the extent to which the designers have been able to predict the trend in fashions and colours for the ensuing season. The company's design expertise was particularly weak in this respect. Production skills were also weak on some of the finer work required for this kind of footwear. In other respects, however, the company's production efficiency was exceptionally good. High machine utilization and labour productivity was resulting in unusually low production costs. This was undoubtedly one of the company's most important strengths in relation to its competitors.

The examination of the market showed that, at that time, there was a rapidly expanding demand for women's 'casual' footwear both at home and overseas. The company had previously had little experience with this type of shoe but, nevertheless, such a trend would admirably suit its design and production resources. It would fully exploit the company's strengths and minimize its weaknesses. The decision was therefore made to abandon many of the fashion shoes and to concentrate on the production of this type of footwear. Two new ranges were developed with a variety of styles and designs in each. A new and well-chosen brand name was given to each range and promotional campaigns were launched. This proved to be a highly successful operation. Sales were particularly good in the company's export markets, and the export sales eventually exceeded those in the home market.

Attention was also being given to men's footwear. The market investigation showed that there were two previously unsuspected factors that were influencing a man's decision when he was buying leather shoes for town wear. A new range of men's shoes was therefore designed embodying these features. This type of shoe was well within the limits of the company's design and production facilities. This range also proved to be very successful with the result that the new ranges of men's and women's shoes were alone sufficient to provide a substantial part of the total load required to keep the plant fully utilized.

The company is today producing less than one-quarter of the number of varieties it had previously been producing. All the less profitable varieties have been eliminated and the company is making a more than adequate return on its capital investment.

The situation in this company was by no means unusual. It is one that can easily arise, particularly where there has been development and growth. Over the years, a range of products gradually emerges. Sufficient sales are being obtained to keep the plant employed at or near its full capacity and there is the normal reluctance to abandon any product that can still be sold. In many respects the company is operating efficiently,

PRODUCT POLICY

all that is lacking is a co-ordinated product policy to ensure, not merely that the plant is adequately loaded, but that the company's resources are being used in the most profitable way.

THE LIFE OF AN INDIVIDUAL PRODUCT

Consideration has so far been given only to the type and variety of products that a company produces. As already mentioned, the design of the individual products in relation to their markets is part of the company's routine marketing operations covered in a later chapter.

The company's product policy must, however, take account of the fact that each individual product has a finite marketable life. A company cannot go on selling the same version of a product indefinitely, because sooner or later the demand for that product in its existing form will begin to decline. The four principal phases in the life cycle of a product are:

1. Development
2. Launching
3. Maturity
4. Decline

These four phases are illustrated by the typical life cycle of a product in Figure 4.2.[1] This curve should not be confused with that shown in Figure 4.1 which related to the overall demand for products of a particular type. Figure 4.2 relates to the share of that demand which is secured by one particular model or version at some period of time during the total life of that type of product. Thus Figure 4.1 might relate to the overall demand for cars since their inception. Figure 4.2 would relate to the four phases in the life of one particular model of one manufacturer. The relative duration of each phase and the total length of the time cycle varies widely for different products. The overall time may range from many years to not much more than a few months, as is the case with certain 'fashion goods'.

[1] Some authors include a profit curve on this diagram which shows that, in the earlier stages, the product is running at a loss and that the profit reaches a maximum at some point in Stage 3. However, there are other factors that also affect the profit and, in practice, there are some products that have provided the greater profit in the earlier stages just after they have been launched.

95

MARKETING AND HIGHER MANAGEMENT

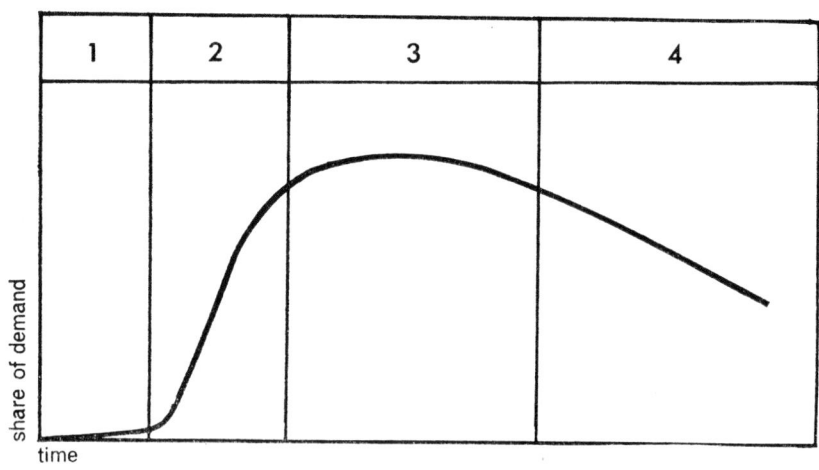

Fig. 4.2

It is not always sufficiently realized that the increasing tempo of change has meant that the marketable life of most products is being steadily and continuously reduced. For instance, less than a generation ago, if a manufacturer of industrial equipment put a new model on the market he might reasonably have expected to be able to go on selling that same model for about twenty years. Today he would be fortunate if he could sell it for five years without having to change it in some way. With some of the more advanced products the design has started to become obsolete almost as soon as it has come off the drawing-board.

Therefore, sooner or later, each one of a company's products has to be changed in some way if the company is to stay in business. It may require a major change in design or, as in the case of some consumer goods, it may require no more than a minor change in its packaging. However, whether the changes are large or small, it is important to plan ahead and be ready for these changes when they become necessary.

In the past, there have been many companies that have waited until the sales of one of their products have started to fall before taking any action to change that product or even to consider what that action should be. The effect of this is shown in Figure 4.3. At some point 'X', after the sales have been falling, a decision is eventually made to make some alteration to the product. Some time must inevitably elapse while the change is being made and before the revised product is ready to take over from its predecessor. By this time, sales of the existing product are

PRODUCT POLICY

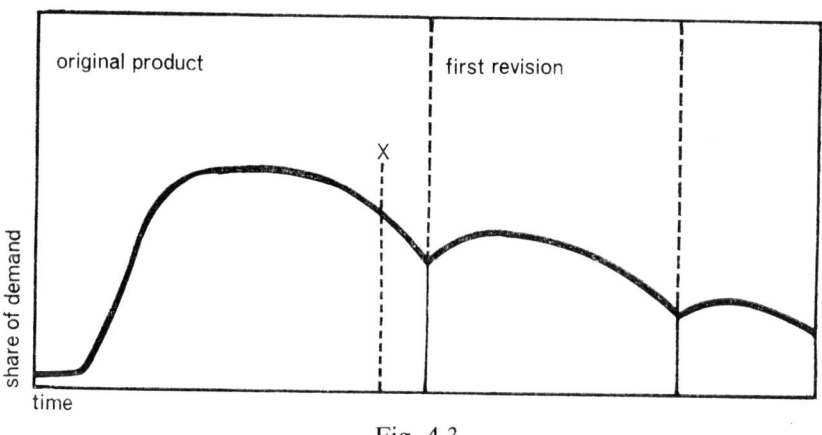

figure: graph with y-axis "share of demand" and x-axis "time", showing three successive peaks labelled "original product", "first revision", and an unlabelled third, with point X marked on the declining portion of the original product curve.

Fig. 4.3

likely to have dropped still further. Assuming that a suitable change has been made, the new version will improve the situation and stop the decline. However, the decline was caused through losing sales to competitors and, as every sales manager knows, it is extremely difficult to win back customers once they have changed over to buying the newer or improved products of other suppliers. For this reason, the revised product rarely succeeds in obtaining as large a share of the market as its predecessor. After a time, the revised product will itself pass into the decline phase and the same cycle is repeated, perhaps many times, with a diminishing share of the market on each occasion. The success of a business eventually depends on its products and in recent years this trend of events has been the cause and pattern of decline in the fortunes of many companies.

The risk of this occurrence is greatest in those companies whose products have a long life cycle and can be marketed without change for many years. In these situations it is only too easy for a company to become complacent about its products and to be taken unawares. Companies in those industries which regularly bring out new models at frequent intervals are at least aware that such dangers exist. The risk is also greater in those companies that are selling physical articles but whose real product is a service (for example, the jobbing iron foundry or the supplier of basic raw materials). Such companies may assume they do not have to bother about these changes, but in these cases it is, of course, the service that has to be adapted and improved.

MARKETING AND HIGHER MANAGEMENT

A sound product policy must therefore make provision for change. This is always important, regardless of whether the marketable life of the product may be a few months or many years.

A CHANGE THAT IS MADE ONLY WHEN IT IS EVENTUALLY FORCED ON MANAGEMENT BY DECLINING SALES IS ALWAYS A CHANGE THAT IS MADE TOO LATE.

In every company, there should be some organized procedure for the regular examination of each product's continuing suitability in relation to its market. The effect of such a procedure is shown in Figure 4.4.

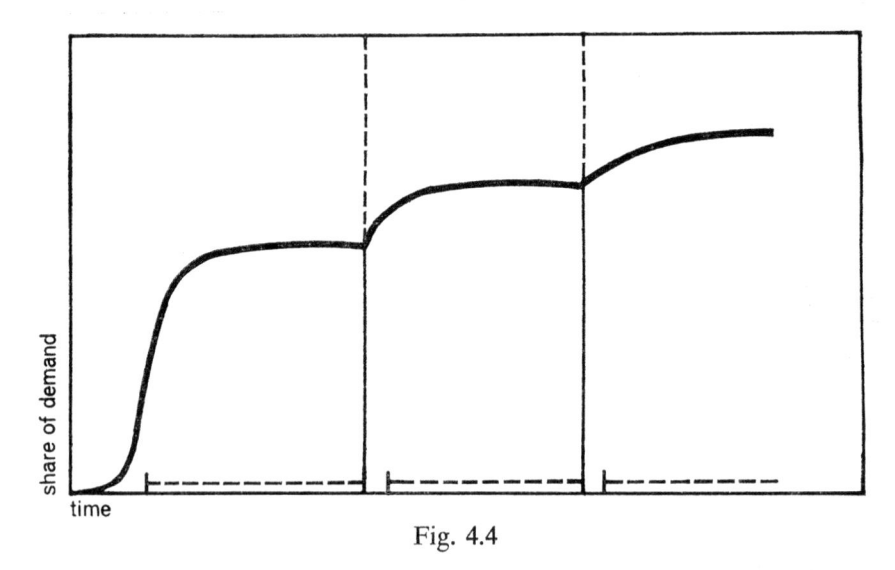

Fig. 4.4

A start is made in studying the purchaser's attitude to the product as soon as it is launched on the market – see Chapter 8. Technological and production improvements are examined and further marked information about the product is accumulated throughout the early stages of the product's life cycle. These activities are represented by the dotted line in the diagram. As a result, a new or improved version of the product is developed and ready well before it is needed. It is then only a question of judging the right time to put the revised product on the market. Because it is an improvement, based on a study of the market requirements, it will obtain a larger share of the market than its predecessor.

PRODUCT POLICY

The timing is important, particularly if expensive tools for making the existing product will have to be scrapped long before they are worn out. However it is much better to be too early than too late and there must be boldness in making the decision.

The introduction of the revised product does not always mean that the existing product has to be withdrawn. This depends on the product and the nature of the change. It may be possible to continue to sell both models so that the earlier model can be left on the market until such time as it ceases to make an effective contribution to the fixed costs and profits.

It should be emphasized that these considerations do not mean that change, as such, is in itself desirable and that the more often a company changes its products the better. On the contrary, the frequency of change often depends upon how well the company has been able to predict the needs of the market and has taken its predictions into account in the design of its products. The better the design of the product, the longer is likely to be its life and the less often will the company have to change its products in order to improve or maintain its position in the market.

Various factors dictate the need for change and the frequency at which it must occur. These factors can be broadly grouped into the following categories:

a. Changes in the needs of the market or changes in the particular factors that are influencing the buying decision of prospective customers.
b. Improvements that are originated within the company itself.
c. The introduction by other companies of new products that affect the demand for the company's products.

Changes in category (a) are rarely sudden and dramatic. They are often quite small changes that are continually occurring and of which even the customers themselves may be quite unaware. It is because of this that these changes can so easily escape detection until they have gradually built up beyond the point where the fatal decline in sales has already commenced. Constant vigilance is necessary if this is to be avoided.

The most suitable procedures must obviously depend upon the nature of the product and the size of the company. However, in every company, some individual should be given the authority and responsibility for ensuring that each one of the company's products is examined *at least* once a year, even if only to make sure that a change is not yet necessary. In the smaller companies, the managing director may have to undertake this responsibility himself.

DESIGNING FOR OBSOLESCENCE

In the preceding section it was suggested that there is no merit in changing a product merely for the sake of making a change. There is, however, an exception to this among durable products in those situations where, by making periodic alterations to the product, the customer can be induced to retain the product for a shorter period and to purchase a new model at more frequent intervals.

This policy was at one time much more common with such products as cars and radio receivers than it is today. For instance, it was considered necessary in these industries to bring out a new model each year in order to maintain the demand. The new models generally incorporated some improvement, but the essential requirement was considered to be that they should have some difference in their external appearance which would distinguish them from the designs of the previous year. In this way, each year's models could be given the appearance of obsolescence after a few years. This policy undoubtedly has some effect on inducing the customer to buy a new model more frequently than he might otherwise have done, particularly with those products and purchases where 'keeping up with the Joneses' is an important factor in influencing a buying decision. However, more recent experience suggests that its effect was perhaps over-estimated or that, with changing market conditions, today's customers have become less susceptible to it.

There is another and quite different aspect of designed obsolescence that sometimes has to be considered in relation to the company's product policy. This is the expectancy of useful life that should be built into the design of a durable product that is used either in the home or in industry. The shorter the life, the more often will the user have to buy a replacement. For instance, the demand for an electric light bulb that had a life of 10,000 hours would be only one-tenth of the size of the demand for a conventional bulb lasting 1,000 hours. On the other hand, the fact that one company's product has a longer life than another's may be an important factor in influencing the buying decision of a prospective customer. But, if building longer life into the product increases its cost, this may offset the benefit to the customer.

Therefore, as with so much else in marketing, the most effective policy is the one that stems from the basic analysis of the buying motives for the product – see Chapter 2. For example, the anticipated life of a refrigerator plays little of no part in influencing a purchaser's decision in choosing between one make of refrigerator and another. The majority of purchasers will give no thought to this at all. There would therefore be nothing to be gained by designing a refrigerator that had an appreciably longer life than that of competitors' models, particularly if this increased the price at which it would have to be sold. In products of this type, reliability is a very much more important factor than the life of the product in influencing the buyer's decision; the product that has a completely trouble-free short life will be more successful than the one that has a longer life, but in which even minor faults soon start occurring.

The situation is, of course, very different for those products where length of service is or could be made to become an important factor in influencing the buyer's decision. Under these conditions, if the life of the product can be extended without raising the price, this will initially increase the demand. However, because the product will last longer, the eventual demand will be reduced. For instance, doubling the life of the product might increase the company's share of the market by, say, 50 per cent. But, as the product would last for twice as long, it would eventually halve the replacement sales in that share of the market. Therefore, under these conditions, there might be no ultimate benefit from the change. Moreover, the initial increase in the demand would last only if and as long as similar action was not taken by competitors.

If the extension in the product's life is accompanied by an increase in price, its effect on sales will depend upon the relative importance of the parts played by the selling price and the life of the product in influencing the purchaser's decision. However, the financial effect of the eventual decrease in demand will be diminished. For instance if doubling the life of the product also doubled its unit contribution (Chapter 3), any increase in the company's share of the market would increase its profits even though the unit sales in that increased share of the market were eventually halved. (In practice, of course, the proportions are likely to be much less than those used to simplify this example.)

The determination of the most suitable policy in these circumstances is no easy task. It requires an intimate knowledge of the extent to which both the selling price and the product's life are influencing the purchaser's decision. Moreover, much will depend on the action taken by competitors. If a major competitor has already extended the life of its product, the company may have no option but to follow suit. If the company originates the change, it will be necessary to consider whether it will be able to retain this advantage or how long it will be before the same action is taken by competitors. The extent to which purchasers' decisions are influenced by brand loyalty and habit will also have to be considered, and this element varies considerably with different types of products. For example, if the initial advantage is strong enough to win over customers from a competitor, will these customers be retained or will many of them revert to their original buying behaviour if the competitor follows suit? The razor blade industry has provided a typical example of the problems that arise and have to be solved in this kind of situation.

PRODUCT DIVERSIFICATION

Product Diversification can be defined as the introduction of products that are of a different *type* from those previously produced by the company. In this respect it differs from the normal research and development of different varieties of the company's existing types of product. Its purpose is to enable the company to develop and expand the profitable use of its existing resources or of other additional resources that it can acquire. It may or may not embrace Market Diversification – that is to say, entry into different markets from those in which the company has previously been engaged.

Product diversification becomes essential for a company's survival as soon as its existing products reach that stage in their life when the demand for them begins to decline. At this stage, the introduction of new or improved versions of the product will, at best, merely enable the company to obtain a larger share of a steadily diminishing demand. Such action may delay a company's decline but it cannot prevent it. This stage may appear to be remote and there are, of course, many types of products for which there has been a constant demand for over a hundred years. However, with the introduction of new techniques, new materials and new habits, more and more of these long-established products are succumbing every year.

PRODUCT POLICY

Linoleum is a typical example and illustrates the trend in the demand already shown in Figure 4.1. It was first produced and sold in 1804, and during the early years of the last century there was a small but steadily increasing demand. However, it was not until 1860 that the upswing in demand occurred and linoleum became a standard item in almost every household. From then on, for nearly a hundred years, the demand for linoleum ran into millions of square yards per year. It became a large and prosperous industry in which many companies were engaged. Even in 1940, it may well have been difficult for these companies to imagine that any substantial change could occur in the demand. The decline, once started, very quickly gathered momentum with the advent of alternative floor coverings and with the rising standards of living of those householders who had previously been the largest users. Linoleum is, of course, still produced today but the output is only a fraction of its former size. Many factories had to be closed down completely or diverted to other products.

This is only one of many examples of the decline in the demand for an apparently well-established product. The last decade has seen the expansion in the demand for a vast range of entirely new products. There can be no doubt that these changes will go on occurring at an increasing rate in the future. No company in an established industry can consider itself entirely safe in this respect.

The companies that have survived these changes are those that have carried out a successful diversification operation. Some of these companies, by early adopting a policy of diversification that has been well planned and executed, are larger and more prosperous today than they were with their original products.

Successful diversification is built on a company's strengths. It starts, therefore, with the detailed analysis of the company's resources as already described at the beginning of this chapter. The act of carrying out this analysis will suggest possible products that might be used to exploit the company's own particular strengths, skills and resources. Each of these products is examined in detail in relation to its suitability, the size of the potential demand and the financial prospects.

The procedure for revealing possible products can be illustrated by taking as an example a company producing motor-cycles. As standards of living rise, more and more people can afford to buy cars. Therefore, although a limited demand for motor-cycles is likely to continue for racing and sporting purposes, the company is faced with an overall decline in the demand for its products. The examination of the company's resources will show the nature of its corporate skills and technical expertise. It will search for those particular strengths and resources that are not commonly possessed or available to industry in general. For example, the possession of power presses and lathes provides no particular strength. Nor does the ability to weld steel tubes together to form the frame of a motor-cycle, since this is a skill that any company can easily acquire. In this particular example, the company's most important diversifying asset is probably its ability to design and produce small internal combustion engines. The recognition of one or more assets such as this leads to the search for possible diversifying products. In this case, the products that immediately suggest themselves are such things as outboard engines, motor lawn-mowers, portable power tools, small motor-generator sets, and so on. An imaginative approach is essential in preparing this preliminary list of possible products; ideas and suggestions should be sought from as many sources as possible. The technique of 'brain-storming' is sometimes successfully used for this purpose.

The suggested products that result from this initial examination are then subjected to a series of screening processes during which many of them are likely to be rejected. The various stages are as follows:

1. *Preliminary Market Appraisal*
The purpose, at this stage, is merely to examine the likely scope for the product. This examination starts with a very rough approximation of the size of the demand that might be available, for example, is it likely to be thousands, tens of thousands, or hundreds of thousands? What is the *trend* in the demand for this type of product, is it rising or falling? What is its present position in relation to the life of the product shown in Figure 4.1 (remembering that the ideal time to enter the market is usually during the upswing)? What is the strength of competition – is it weak, moderate or intense? This preliminary examination does not require any elaborate and costly market research, which would be quite uneconomic at this stage since many of the tentative products on the list are likely to be rejected in the further screening processes.

PRODUCT POLICY

2. *Suitability in Relation to Company's Resources*
Although the product has been suggested by one of the company's existing resources, it may be quite unsuitable in relation to one or more of the others. This stage is therefore exactly the same as the detailed examination described more fully in the first section of this chapter for determining the suitability of a particular type of product. The tentative product is examined in relation to:

- a. Existing buildings, machines and equipment.
- b. Availability of materials.
- c. The company's design and technical expertise.
- d. Existing production skills.
- e. Existing distribution network.
- f. The company's promotional and selling expertise.

It has to be remembered that a potential product will not necessarily be suited ideally to each one of the above; the objective is to exploit one or more of the company's strengths. Some alteration to the company's other resources may be inevitable in order to achieve this.

3. *Preliminary Product Design*
What version or variety of that type of product would be produced? What would be the approximate cost of labour and materials? No attempt is made to design the product in detail at this stage, but these are rough approximations to enable a preliminary financial appraisal to be made.

4. *Preliminary Financial Appraisal*
What additional capital expenditure, if any, would be incurred in the production and sales of the product? What would be the degree of 'risk' associated with this capital expenditure? What would be the tentative selling price for the product and what is its potential profitability at this price? – See Chapter 3.

5. *Market Research*
A more detailed market investigation must now be carried out for those products that have survived Stages 1 to 4. What are the most suitable

sectors of the market? – See Chapter 5. What are the factors that influence the buying decisions of prospective purchasers in each of those sectors? – See Chapter 2. What is the trend in the demand and what is the nature and extent of competition? (This is a more detailed investigation than that carried out at Stage 1.) What would be the probable size of the demand at the tentative selling price?

6. *Development for Production*

This stage covers all operations in the design and development of the product to the point where either a prototype or the product itself can be put into production. Certain additional market information is often required after development has commenced and it may be necessary for Stages 5 and 6 to overlap.

7. *Detailed Financial Appraisal*

A more accurate financial appraisal is carried out at the earliest opportunity during Stage 6. This revises the preliminary appraisal of Stage 4 in the light of the more accurate information that is now available on markets and costs.

8. *Pre-launch Testing*

Every new product must, of course, be thoroughly tested before it is finally launched on the market. If there are any doubts about the product, deferment or rejection at this stage is always better than risking a failure after launching. Whenever practicable, the product should not only be tested internally but also by a selected sample of users. This may be part of a test marketing operation.

9. *Launching*

The launch of a new product requires careful planning if it is to be successful. Timing can sometimes be extremely important and some products have failed solely because they were launched either too early or too late.

Many products will be rejected at one stage or another during this

PRODUCT POLICY

screening process if it has been properly carried out. This high mortality rate is not always realized by companies that are embarking on a diversification operation for the first time. It is sometimes assumed that a preliminary examination should reveal one or two successful new products and that it should be unnecessary to spend money on researching and developing others. This can sometimes be true but, in general, is very unlikely to be the case. For example, a survey was carried out, by Booz, Allen and Hamilton Inc., of a large number of companies in the United States that had introduced new products. The findings in this survey, although in a different form, can be transposed to the various screening stages described above. This shows that, on average, fifty-eight new product ideas had to enter the screening process in order to obtain one successful new product. The mortality rate through the various stages was approximately as follows:

Products surviving the preliminary screening in Stages 1 and 2:	13 out of 58
Products surviving after Stages 3, 4 and 5:	6 out of 13
Products surviving through development, Stage 6:	3 out of 6
Products surviving after testing, Stage 7:	2 out of 3
Successful products eventually surviving after launching:	1 out of 2

The number of casualties shown in this survey as occurring in Stages 1 and 2 is probably not very meaningful. Some product ideas can be quite sensibly rejected from a simple consideration that could hardly be classified as a 'product examination', and it is obviously a matter of opinion as to where this line is drawn. The more significant figures are those in the subsequent stages. Somewhat surprisingly, these figures seem to show remarkably little variation over a wide range of products from electric motors to consumer goods. The obvious conclusion can be drawn that the proportion of products that failed after launching would not have been as high as 50 per cent if the screening had been carried out more effectively with a higher proportion of rejections at each stage.

There is often a reluctance on the part of management to make a decision to abandon something on which money has already been spent. Nevertheless, if subsequent failure is to be avoided, there must be no hesitation in abandoning doubtful products during the screening stages of a diversification operation. Any costs incurred on the abandoned products should be regarded as part of the total development costs of introducing the products eventually selected. The whole operation should be planned on the basis that there will and should be rejections if successful products are to be found.

There is an alternative form of diversification in which the company does not have to undertake the whole of the development work on the new product itself. Under some kind of licensing or other agreement, the company arranges to produce a product that has already been developed by someone else. However, the procedure for selecting suitable products for such an arrangement is exactly the same as that already described. Even if the product has been successfully marketed elsewhere (perhaps in another country), it should go through exactly the same screening stages in order to determine its suitability in relation to the company's own particular situation and resources. The proportion of rejections during the screening process is, of course, likely to be considerably lower and very much less expenditure will have been incurred on the development of abandoned products. This may partly offset the cost of acquiring the rights to produce and sell the products eventually selected. This is often the most suitable procedure for the smaller companies and those that have few facilities for carrying out research and development themselves.

PRODUCT ADAPTION

It is sometimes possible to adapt an existing product in order to make it suit some other purpose. This is an alternative form of diversification which may provide opportunities that might otherwise be overlooked. The development and growth of the rubber industry provides an outstanding example of this form of diversification.

In the latter part of the eighteenth century, it was found that the resinous gum exuded by certain trees growing in South America provided a substance that would rub out pencil marks. One or two companies were formed to import the material and convert it into a suitable form for this purpose. The raw material was at that time being obtained from South American Indians and the product was called an Indian 'rubber' in order to describe its purpose. It was not long before these companies began to examine the possibilities of using this new material for other purposes. Considerable research was carried out and the vulcanization process was invented in 1839. This considerably increased the scope of applications and, from then on, the process of developing and adapting the material for new uses has continued for nearly 150 years. A major world-wide industry has grown out of, and taken its name from, the pencil 'rubber' which was its single original product.

A great deal of imagination is often necessary to originate new products in this way although, once produced, they may seem obvious. Taking a specific example from the rubber industry: the rubber bands sold in a stationer's shop are cut from a tube of rubber that is virtually the same product and produced in exactly the same way as the inner tube of a bicycle tyre. The scope for this form of diversification is, of course, severely limited; nevertheless the possibility should always be considered. The development of a new use for an existing product in some suitably adapted form may be much simpler than changing to a different product.

However, the principles of successful diversification are exactly the same whether we consider the introduction of a new use or a new product. The difference is only a matter of degree as, for instance, in changing from a motor-cycle to an outboard engine. The basic requirement is not to find a new product, but to find a new use for the company's resources.

PRODUCT POLICY – SUMMARY

As modern industry developed, it was assumed that a company had two alternative courses of action: either to sell the products that the works could make, or to make the products that the sales department could sell. The relative merits of these two alternatives were argued in deciding the most suitable product policy that a company should adopt.

Such an approach stems from the concept that there are two sides to a business, one side being responsible for designing and producing the products and the other for selling them. It overlooks the fact that the process of satisfying a customer's need and influencing his buying decision does not start in the sales department, but with the design of the product and should be the sole objective of all the company's activities. The success of the company depends upon the effectiveness with which its resources are used to convert the need into an active want to buy its products. The products that a company should sell are, therefore, those that will continue to make the most effective and most profitable use of its overall resources. It is on the achievement of this objective that the product policy should be based.

Chapter 5

Marketing Planning

As with the other chapters in Part 1, this chapter is concerned only with the way in which marketing is used in the overall management of the business. It is concerned with planning the strategy and not with planning the various tactical activities that may be required for its implementation – these latter are reviewed in Part 2.

Planning has been described as the process whereby companies reconcile their resources with their objectives and opportunities. In this sense, an effective marketing plan becomes an integral part of the overall plan for directing and controlling a company's affairs. Indeed, in a fully market-oriented company, the two are virtually synonymous.

There are three inter-related planning aspects in a successful marketing strategy. These are:

Planning the type and varieties of products that are to be produced.

Planning the markets and sectors of a market in which those products are to be sold.

Planning the ways in which the needs of the prospective purchasers in those markets are to be converted into an active want to buy the company's products.

In writing about a marketing plan, it becomes almost inevitable that these three aspects are treated separately in some sequential order. Nevertheless, they should not be regarded as three separate stages in which one stage is completed before the next stage is commenced. There is considerable overlapping in the planning of the three aspects. The determination of the most suitable products will be influenced by the markets in which those products would have to be sold and by the factors that are influencing the buying decisions of the purchasers in those markets. Similarly, the determination of the most suitable markets will be influenced by the factors that will convert the needs of the purchasers in those markets into a want to buy the products. This interrelationship must always be taken into account throughout the planning operation. It should be regarded as one single operation and not as a combination of three separate stages.

The first aspect, the selection of the most suitable types and varieties of products, has already been covered in the previous chapter. This included passing references to the need for examining the various sectors of a market and the different buying motives in those sectors. This chapter deals with the second and third aspects and the evolution of the final plan.

MARKET SEGMENTATION

A 'market' consists of a group of purchasers who have certain common characteristics (see Chapter 2 – Defining the Market). However, no two of these purchasers are ever completely identical. There can be differences in their requirements, both in quality and quantity, and differences in the things that are influencing their buying decisions. Because of these differences, a product or selling approach that may be eminently suitable for some of these purchasers may not be equally suitable for others.

If the total market consists of only a few purchasers, as in the aircraft industry, each purchaser can be regarded individually both as to his requirements and as to the things that influence his buying decisions. If necessary, different products can be designed for each and a different service can be provided in order to meet these individual differences and secure favourable buying decisions. However, this becomes impracticable if there are a larger number of purchasers and is impossible in a mass market. Nevertheless, account must still be taken of these differences if a successful marketing plan is to be prepared.

The purpose of market segmentation is to determine the differences among purchasers which may affect the choice of market area or marketing methods. The market is divided into sectors or segments in such a way that the purchasers in each segment, while not being exactly identical, are of a similar nature and are influenced by similar buying motives. This not only enables the most suitable segments to be selected in rela-

MARKETING PLANNING

tion to the company's resources, but the products and approach can be specifically designed in the most suitable way for each of the selected segments. (Market segmentation is sometimes known as 'Sectoring the Market'. For all practical purposes the two terms are identical.)

There are two factors that have to be taken into account in dividing the purchasers in a total market into appropriate segments:

a. Differences in product requirements;
b. Differences in the things that influence buying decisions.

These two may be quite unrelated. For instance, a tablet of toilet soap might be produced that would be equally suitable for every household in the country, but the kind of things that influence one housewife's choice of toilet soap can be very different from those that influence another's. Hence, an advertisement that may have an extremely effective impact on some purchasers may have no impact at all on others. Similarly, an attempt to produce a product or create an image that is universally suitable for every purchaser can easily result in its having no major impact on any of them.

Example of Market Segmentation[1]

A straightforward example of segmentation may be provided by taking a simple, universally used product – the paint-brush – and examining its market. The purchasers of paint-brushes are divided almost equally between trade buyers on the one hand and domestic users on the other. This provides the two main segments in which both the product requirements and buying motives are likely to be different.

Each of these segments is then examined separately to discover whether all the purchasers in that segment have the same product requirements and are influenced by the same buying motives. This shows that the trade buyers must be further divided between the large contracttors, who buy in substantial quantities directly from the manufacturer, and the smaller but very much greater number of local builders and decorators who buy their paint-brushes from a builder's merchant. In the

[1] This example is included solely to demonstrate the principles of segmentation. Market conditions are continually changing and the findings quoted are not necessarily still correct at the present time. In practice, it is essential that up-to-date information should be used in preparing any aspect of the marketing plan.

domestic user segment, women constitute a higher proportion of the purchasers than might be expected. In general, a woman's requirements and motives when she is buying a paint-brush are very different from those of a man.

The total market therefore divides into four segments. The requirements and buying motives in each of these segments can be summarized as follows:

> Large Contractors: The buyer is remote from the painter who uses the brush. He is unlikely to be able to judge the quality of a paint-brush himself. He is looking for brushes of reasonably good quality at the lowest price he can obtain and will probably reject a highly priced, top quality brush. He buys in large quantities directly from the manufacturer and may seek quotations from several suppliers.
>
> Local Builders and Decorators: The buyer is better able to judge the quality of the brush. He is less concerned with price than with buying a high quality brush that will have a long life and continue to give a good finish. He will be conservative in his choice and when he has found a brand that meets his requirements he will be reluctant to change.
>
> Male Domestic Purchasers: The buyer is prepared to pay for a good quality brush and can be persuaded not to buy a cheap brush in which the bristles are likely to come out. However, he is unable to judge the quality of the brush himself and is guided solely by its appearance and what he is told by the salesman. He will therefore buy a brush that has an appearance of quality and can be influenced by advertising or other promotional activities.
>
> Female Domestic Purchasers: A woman buyer is unlikely to be very much concerned about the quality and life of the paint-brush. She will probably be buying the brush for some particular job and will not want to spend time on cleaning it thoroughly with the result that it will be unsuitable for further use. She therefore wants a cheap brush and price is an important consideration in her choice. She is likely to be attracted by a brush that has a long, brightly-coloured handle. (Perhaps because she thinks that, with a long handle, the paint is less likely to get on her hands; perhaps for psychological reasons.)

Since no two purchasers are identical, segmentation must always contain some degree of generalization and overlapping. For instance, some women will, of course, be influenced by the same motives and buy the same brush as a man, and vice versa. However, this does not materially effect the most suitable marketing plan.

Market segmentation therefore shows that, even with a simple product like a paint-brush, a single quality and style of brush and a single selling policy cannot be equally effective throughout the whole market. A manufacturing company first has to decide whether its resources and skills are better suited to some segments of the market than others and whether it should confine itself to those segments. In this example, if it decides to embrace all four segments, this can only be done effectively with four different ranges. Only very small differences may be necessary between some of the ranges but nevertheless these small differences are important. For instance, a brush of the same quality and basic design would be equally suitable for the local builder and for the male domestic user. The only difference might be that the handle of the domestic brush would have a high gloss finish with its name in gold lettering in order to give it the required appearance of high quality. (The quality must, of course, be in the brush itself as well as in its appearance if sales are to be maintained.)

In those cases where a company decides to produce a low-priced range of products as well as a high quality range at a higher price, it will have to consider the effect of the cheaper range on the sales of its better quality products. The poorer performance of the inferior range can easily damage the image for good quality in the more expensive products. In order to avoid this difficulty, it is often advisable to market each range under a different brand name.

If the segments of a market overlap, as in the case of the paint brush, no specific indication of the segmentation is revealed to users. For instance, as far as the purchasers are concerned, there would be nothing to show that the cheaper range was primarily intended for women. Indeed, any such indication might deter male buyers who wanted a cheap brush and cause them to buy a competitor's product.

Segmentation in a Consumer Market
The oldest and still the most common form of segmentation in a consumer market is to divide the purchasers into socio-economic groups

according to the occupation and income of the head of the household. The six socio-economic groups usually used for the British market are as follows:

Social grade	Social status	Typical occupation of head of household
A	Upper middle class	Higher managerial, administrative or professional
B	Middle class	Intermediate management
C1	Lower middle class	Junior management, supervisory and clerical staff
C2	Skilled working class	Skilled manual workers
D	Working class	Semi and unskilled workers
E	Those at lowest levels of subsistence	State pensioners or widows (no other earner in household), casual or low grade workers

A likely income level is usually included in the classification of each of these groups. However, with rising incomes, these figures quickly become out of date and have to be adjusted each year. (The current figures can be obtained from the Readership Surveys that are regularly carried out for the Institute of Practitioners in Advertising.) The annual earnings in Groups C1 and C2 are likely to be in the same range.

The pattern of the consumer market in Britain has, however, changed considerably in recent years and there are many situations today in which the social status of the head of the household has little or no significance in relation to product requirements and buying motives. The typist who comes from a Group C household may be buying the same product for the same reasons as the managing director's daughter. Some of the purchasers in Group B may be buying the same television receiver as some of the purchasers in Group D. In all such cases, some other division of the market is necessary.

Typical divisions to be considered when segmenting a consumer market are as follows:

Sex: The paint-brush example provided an illustration of the very different factors that can influence a woman when she is buying the same product as a man. This is sometimes overlooked, although there can be few products where some differences do not occur.

It is also important not to assume that the majority of purchasers are always of the same sex, for example, that paint-brushes are bought almost entirely by men. Even though the user may be of one sex the purchaser may be of the other. Many products used only by men are purchased for them by women.

Age: There are a large number of products where age groupings have today become very much more significant than socio-economic groupings. Teenagers are influenced by very different factors from those that influence buyers in their middle twenties. At one time, the young newly-married housewife continued to buy the same products as her mother – today many of her purchases are likely to be the same as those of others in her age group rather than her socio-economic group.

Family Earnings: The Government-sponsored 'Family Expenditure Survey' has now been running for several years. This shows that, because of the increase in the number of working wives and the higher earnings of teenagers living at home, the pattern of expenditure is related to the total family income rather than to its social group. For example, the head of the household is a manual worker in 53 per cent of those homes in Britain where the total family income exceeds £1,500 a year. Many of these families are living in council or rent-controlled houses at a comparatively low cost. Their disposable income for the purchase of durable and consumer goods is often considerably higher than that of many families in the managerial group with a number of young children.

When using different levels of family earnings for market segmentation, it has to be remembered that, over a period of a few years many families move from the middle earnings group to a higher group and then drop back to a lower when the younger wage earners get married and leave home. The structure and numbers in each group may be constant over time, but the actual households in the group will vary.

Number and Age of Children: Much of a household's expenditure is influenced by the number and age of the children in the family. A woman with several young children spends her money in a very different way and is living almost a different life from the woman with no children who may, perhaps, be going out to work. Between these two extremes, there is the household in which there are older children some of whom may be self-supporting. There is an obvious difference in the product requirements of purchasers grouped in this way; however, there can also be considerable difference in the factors which are influencing buying decisions for a product that is common to all groups. For example, a toothpaste advertisement that may be very effective for one group may have little or no impact on another.

Hobbies and Recreation: With rising standards of living, an increasing proportion of the family income is spent on occupying leisure hours. Families can be grouped according to the broad nature of their hobbies and recreations – gardening, boating, motoring, camping, active and non-active participation in sports, etc. This again not only influences their product requirements but can also influence their buying decisions on common products.

Many other such groupings are possible and careful research is often necessary to determine the most suitable groupings in segmenting the market for a particular product. However, all the above have been concerned with physical differences between the purchasers. In some situations, differences in personality characteristics can be just as, or even more, significant in segmentation. For instance, there are the non-conformists who prefer to buy a product in a different form rather than follow the popular trend. These purchasers sometimes provide a useful segment for the small company that finds it difficult to compete with the larger producers in a mass market. The buyer's attitude to selling price is another form of this segmentation: there are those buyers who are always on the look-out for a bargain and for whom a low price is the principal attraction; whereas there are others who are more interested in other aspects and for whom the price is not a major consideration. Moreover, there are those for whom a high price is in itself an attraction because of their assumption that it will ensure that they are getting a better product. These groupings are often unrelated to the financial status of the purchaser – the millionaire who watches every penny is not an entirely fictitious character. There are many situations in which a

MARKETING PLANNING

company's most suitable policy is to concentrate on one or other of these segments and to create an image associated with that segment.

Geographic Segmentation
National differences are usually so great that each country must be regarded as a separate market rather than as a segment of a single market. However, geographic segmentation within a country will be necessary in those cases where there are significant differences in the product requirements or buying motives in different parts of the country.

There is, however, another aspect of geographic segmentation. It may sometimes be advisable, particularly for a small company, to concentrate the company's promotional and selling resources in a particular area rather than dissipate them over the whole country. This may enable the company to make an impact in that area which is as big as or even bigger than that of its larger competitors who are selling over a much broader front.

Segmentation and the Marketing Strategy – Summary
The purpose of market segmentation is to enable the company to decide what types and varieties of products it should sell and to whom and how it should sell them. The most profitable decisions cannot be reached unless the market has been systematically analysed and divided into its appropriate segments.

This segmentation enables the company to decide:

a. Whether the company should cover the whole market or whether its resources will be more profitably employed if it selects and confines itself to certain particular segments.
b. How its products should be designed, presented and sold, for each of the selected segments, in order to win the maximum number of favourable buying decisions from the prospective purchasers in that segment.

A market is not static and inert. It consists of people whose requirements, whims and prejudices are constantly changing. Moreover, unlike the company's internal activities, the changes cannot be moulded

MARKETING AND HIGHER MANAGEMENT

or directed by decisions taken in the board-room. It is the company itself that must adapt and change to meet the changing conditions. The analysis and segmentation of a market should never be regarded as finite, but must be kept under continual review and the company must be prepared to make radical alterations to its plans, sometimes at short notice.

MARKETING STRATEGY

The first aspect of the marketing plan was concerned with the products; the second with the prospective purchasers. The third aspect is concerned with bringing the products and purchasers together. The objective is to convert a prospective purchaser's latent need into an active want to buy the company's product rather than some other product of a competitor.

This part of the plan goes back to the basic analysis of buying motives described in detail in Chapter 2. As was shown, the purpose of this examination was to determine which of the ten basic factors are playing the most important parts in influencing a purchaser's choice when buying a particular product. This will govern the way in which that product should be designed, presented and sold. The ten basic factors that can influence a buyer's decision are again summarized here for convenience:

1. The fitness of the product for the buyer's purpose.
2. The buyer's personal opinion of the product's design and appearance (as distinct from its intrinsic fitness for his purpose).
3. The selling price.
4. The availability of the product to the buyer or, where applicable, the time required for its delivery to him.
5. What the buyer knows from his own experience or has heard from others about the supplier's reputation for the consistency in quality of its products and for their reliability in use.
6. Where applicable – what the buyer knows from his own experience or has heard from others about the reliability of the supplier's delivery date promises.
7. Where applicable – what the buyer knows from his own experience or has heard from others about the speed and effectiveness of the after-sales service provided by the supplier.

8. Where applicable – the credit facilities provided by the supplier.
9. The predisposition to buy the product that has been created in the buyer's mind by advertising or other promotional activities.
10. The persuasion exercised by a salesman.

Examples were given in Chapter 2 which showed that the relative importance of each of these factors varies considerably with different products and that this variation can completely alter the nature of the marketing plan.

The product analysis must, of course, be carried out separately for each segment of the market. If there are intermediaries between the company and the user, it must be carried out in relation to the buying decisions of both the distributors and the ultimate purchasers. The following check list can be used:

Factor 1 – Fitness for Purpose
 a. What is the nature of the need that the product is satisfying and what is the precise purpose for which it is bought by the user? Is it quite certain that this purpose is known? (See Chapter 2.)
 b. In relation to the other factors, how important is the fitness of the product for the buyer's purpose in influencing his choice between competing products?
 c. If it plays only a minor part, can it be safely ignored in making the marketing plans?
 d. If it plays a significant part, how does the product compare in this respect with similar products of competitors?
 e. What are the factors that make one product better fitted for a customer's purpose than another?

Factor 2 – Design and Appearance
 a. In relation to the other factors, how important is the appearance of the product or its packaging in consciously or subconsciously influencing a buyer's choice between competing products?
 b. If this plays only a minor part, can it be safely ignored in making the marketing plans?
 c. If it plays a significant part, what are the features in the product's design that are influencing the buyer's decision? (See Chapter 2.)

d. How does the product compare in each of these features in relation to similar products of competitors?
   e. For how long will it be possible to continue to sell the product in its present form? What plans must be made to ensure that the product will be appropriately altered before sales start to fall? (See Chapter 4.)
   f. During the next five to ten years, is the demand for this type of product likely to increase or to decline?

Factor 3 – Selling Price
   a. Is the product being sold in the most suitable price range? (For example, might it be better to improve the product's acceptability and sell it at a higher price?)
   b. How does the price/quality relationship of this product compare with other products in the company's range? In this respect, does it affect the company's image or the sale of its other products?
   c. How important is the selling price in influencing a buying decision? (For example, would an alteration of 5 per cent in the selling price have an appreciable effect on the quantity sold?)
   d. How does the selling price compare with the selling prices of similar products of competitors?
   e. Where applicable – how does the distributor's discount compare with the discount on competitors' products?
   f. What steps have to be taken to assess the relationship between price and volume in order to determine the most profitable selling price? (See Chapter 3.)

Factor 4 – Availability
Company's Direct Customers.
   a. If delivery is made from stock, can adequate stocks always be maintained and are they suitably located?
   b. If delivery is not usually made from stock, might this be feasible? If not, can the production control procedures provide acceptable delivery dates that can be met?
   c. If it is an existing product – does the volume of the demand ever exceed the output? If so, how often does this occur and for how long? If it is a new product – is this likely to happen?

MARKETING PLANNING

Sales through Distributors.
   d. Might it be feasible and economic to sell directly to the user or consumer? (See Distribution Planning.)
   e. If there is more than one intermediary, for example, a wholesaler and a retailer, might it be feasible and economic to bypass one of these intermediaries?
   f. What are the most suitable outlets for selling the product to the user? For example, in addition to any existing or conventional outlets, are there any others that might be used? (For example, selling hosiery in self-service grocery stores.)
   g. In what proportion of the appropriate outlets does the product sell or would the product have to be sold in order to provide an economic sales volume? (See Chapter 3.)

Factor 5 – Reputation for Quality and Reliability
   a. In relation to the other factors, how important is a company's reputation for quality and reliability in influencing a buyer's choice when purchasing this type of product?
   b. If it plays a negligible part, can it safely be ignored in the marketing plans?
   c. If it plays a significant part, has the company an existing image that is associated with some particular price/quality segment? If so, does the product come within this segment?
   d. What is the company's present reputation for the quality and reliability of its products? For example, how frequently does the company receive complaints about faults in its products or – where applicable – what proportion of the company's products are, on average, rejected on inspection by the customer?
   e. How does the company's reputation in this respect compare with that of its competitors?

Factor 6 – Reputation for Delivery
   a. In relation to the other factors, how important is a reputation for a quick and reliable delivery service in influencing a buyer's choice between competing products. (For example, is this a situation in

which a broken delivery promise could cause annoyance or irritation to a customer?)
  b. If it plays only a minor part, can it be safely ignored in the marketing plans?
  c. If it plays a significant part, what is the company's present reputation in this respect? (For example, how often are complaints received from customers about late delivery? In the previous twelve months, what proportion of the deliveries have been made after the quoted delivery date?)
  d. How does the company's reputation for the speed and reliability of its delivery promises compare with that of its competitors?
  e. If a particularly quick and reliable delivery service could be provided for the product, could this constitute a *major* factor in influencing a buyer's choice, for example in supplying materials or components to industry.

Factor 7 – After-sales Service
  a. Is this a situation in which some form of after-sales service is normally provided by the supplier? If so, to what extent does the efficiency of this service influence a buyer's choice between competing products?
  b. Where applicable – what is the company's present reputation in this respect and how does it compare with that of its competitors?
  c. If an after-sales service is not normally provided by other suppliers, would the provision of such a service have any effect in influencing a buyer's choice?
  d. In either of the above cases, if a particularly quick and efficient after-sales service could be provided for the product, could this constitute a *major* factor in influencing a buyer's choice?

Factor 8 – Credit Facilities
  a. Is this type of product at present being sold on hire purchase terms and, if so, are there any variations in these terms between competing products that may affect the buyer's choice?
  b. If the product is not at present being sold on hire purchase terms, is it the kind of product where this might be feasible?

MARKETING PLANNING

   c. Is it the kind of product that might be let out on a rental basis instead of being sold outright?
   d. If there are intermediaries between the company and the ultimate purchaser, to what extent do the credit terms that are offered to the distributor by different companies influence his buying decisions?
   e. Could better credit facilities, in one form or another, be used as a *major* selling feature for the product either to intermediaries or to the user?

Factors 9 and 10 – Promotion and Salesmanship
For the purpose of this check-list, these two factors can be combined. They must, of course, be treated individually at a subsequent stage in planning the selling strategy.
   a. When the prospective purchaser has been fully informed about all the factual information that he wants to know about the product, to what extent will his *buying decision* be influenced by any advertisements he has seen or by the persuasion of a salesman? (In this context, it is important to distinguish between the two roles of conveying information and influencing a buying decision – see Chapter 2.)
   b. What is the relative importance of the part which these two factors can play in relation to the other factors that are influencing the buyer's decision?

MAKING AND USING THE BUYING FACTOR ANALYSIS
The case examples of footwear in Chapter 4 (p. 92) and paint-brushes in this Chapter (p. 113) have already provided some indication of the way in which the Buying Factor Analysis provides the basis for planning the strategy. One of the most prevalent dangers in almost any aspect of marketing is the assumption that the beliefs and opinions of customers are well known. The producer is naturally an expert in his product – he knows the things that the customer *ought* to be taking into account in making a buying decision; he knows what is important and what is unimportant in that context. There is almost inevitably a subconscious tendency to assume that the customer will react in the same way. Because of this, it is essential that any preconceived opinions or snap judgments

should be rigorously avoided in carrying out a Buying Factor Analysis. The analyst must always begin with the assumption that he knows nothing at all about the customer's attitude to the product. In the absence of such an approach, it is unlikely, in the footwear example, that the factors influencing a man's choice when he was buying shoes would have been discovered. Paint brushes had been sold to domestic users for very many years before this approach drew attention to the obvious but important difference between the male and female purchasers.

Some form of Market Research (see Chapter 8) will be required if reliable information is to be obtained about purchasers' buying motives. However, it should not be assumed that this will necessarily have to be some highly elaborate or costly operation; a fairly simple study will often provide the required information. The research will, of course, have to be very much more extensive with those consumer goods where there is little difference between competing brands and where the choice is mainly influenced by subconscious motives of which even the purchaser is quite unaware. In these situations, motivation research and interviews in depth may be necessary.

The analysis, if it is properly carried out, will show clearly and specifically what are the principal factors influencing a purchaser's decision when buying that kind of product. With some products, the decision may be mainly influenced by the design and appearance of the product; with others it may be the price, the service that is provided, the effect of advertising, or one or more of the other factors already mentioned. Usually it will be some combination of several of these factors. The results of this analysis provide the basis for the entire marketing strategy; they will show what must be done in order to design, present and sell the product in such a way as to win the maximum number of favourable buying decisions from the prospective purchasers in the selected market.

It is worth emphasizing at this point that there are many situations in which the effect of advertising or the persuasion of a salesman play only a small part in relation to other far more important factors that are influencing the buyer's decision. They will therefore play only a correspondingly small part in the marketing strategy. There are many products where the overall marketing plan should be much more closely concerned with the design or production departments than with the sales department.

PLANNING THE METHODS OF COMMUNICATION

It was pointed out in an earlier chapter that it would be quite impossible for a company to sell its products if the potential purchasers of those products were unaware of their existence and purpose. Every company must, therefore, establish some method or methods of communicating this essential information to the prospective purchasers in its selected markets. In addition, this communication may also be able to play some part in influencing a purchaser's decision to buy the company's product rather than some competitive product.

Communication with prospective purchasers can be carried out either visually, by advertising and display, or by word of mouth, as at a selling interview. These form the two main divisions of the many different methods of communication available. The choice of the most effective method, or the most effective combination of methods, requires careful planning. Among other things, this choice will depend on what part, if any, the communication can be made to play on its own in securing an order and on the channels of distribution through which the goods will pass from the producer to the ultimate user or consumer.

For example, with products that are sold through a self-service store, neither the producer's nor the retailer's salesman can be used to convey information to the user or to influence the buying decision. The role of the producer's salesman is limited to that of getting the goods on to the retailer's shelves, although even this is often largely governed by negotiations at a higher level with the central buyers of large multiple organizations. Under these conditions, the producer must rely entirely upon visual communication through advertising and display to secure the user's order.

The position is completely reversed in the case of such products as capital equipment sold to industry. In this context, the salesman provides the principal and most effective means of communicating with the prospective user. Advertising, if it is used, can play only a minor and subordinate role, perhaps in helping to obtain an interview for the salesman or in providing information about the product. It cannot perform the final act of securing the user's order – this must be done by the salesman.

In both these examples, the selection of the most suitable methods of communication is comparatively simple. However, the majority of situations lie somewhere between these two extremes and various alternatives may be possible. For example, two of the alternative plans that are open to a company manufacturing domestic dishwashers are as follows:

a. The company can employ a sales force to call on retail distributors to persuade them to stock and sell its dishwashers. In this case, it can use advertising to inform prospective users about its products and to try and create a favourable predisposition to choose one of its own models when a buying decision is being made in the showroom. The user's order will be secured by the distributor's salesman.
b. It can use advertising to persuade prospective users to return a coupon asking for a salesman to call. In this case, it will employ a sales force to call on those prospective users who have returned the coupons. The salesman's objective will be to secure the user's order. (It will be noted that the fact that the prospective purchasers have returned a coupon indicates that they already have a favourable predisposition to buy the product.)

This example shows that the following are all directly related to one another:

The size and objective of the sales force.
The nature, extent and objective of the advertising.
The physical channels of distribution between the producer and the ultimate purchaser.

None of these functions should ever be planned separately, since they are all part of one single plan. For instance, a particular channel of distribution might be selected because this would enable the most effective use to be made of advertising.

In this dishwasher example, the main features of the marketing strategy would be the same for either of the two selling plans. In both cases, the principal factors that will in the long run influence purchasers' buying decisions are:

The appearance and performance of the dishwasher.
Its suitability to meet the varying needs of different households.
Its reliability.
Its selling price.

The important difference between the two plans lies in the communications between the producer and the user. In the first plan, the activity is initiated by the producer's sales force which is used to persuade distributors to stock and sell the product. By this means, the producer can ensure that its product is one of the models that is available and on display when a prospective purchaser enters the showroom of one of its distributors in order to buy a dishwasher. The company's advertising may be one of the factors that have induced some of those prospective purchasers to enter the showroom and it may have created a favourable predisposition to choose the company's model. However, the actual buying decision will be made in the showroom after seeing other models that are on display and after listening to the distributor's salesman.

In the second plan, the activity is initiated by the producer's advertising. This leads to the visit of the salesman who provides a direct and personal link between the producer and the user at the moment when the buying decision is being made. This has certain obvious advantages. The disadvantage is that the company's product will not be seen by those prospective purchasers who go to a showroom or retail shop to buy a dishwasher.

One of the most significant differences between these two plans is in the use and purpose of the producer's advertising. In the first plan, the advertising has an indirect objective and its effect cannot be precisely determined; it *may* have induced some of the prospective purchasers to enter the showroom and, even though some other model is eventually chosen, it *may* have fulfilled its purpose of creating the initial predisposition to buy the company's product – the fact that another model was chosen may have been due to what happened in the showroom and not to any defect in the advertising. On the other hand, if a sale is made, it may have been the effect of a competitor's advertising that caused that purchaser to go to the showroom to buy a dishwasher.

In the second plan, advertising is used for a quite different and more specific purpose. Its sole objective is to obtain the names and addresses of prospective purchasers. As this is its purpose, its effectiveness can be easily and directly measured in terms of the number of enquiries received in relation to the advertising cost. In this way, the relative effectiveness of different designs and styles of advertisement can be quickly and easily discovered without the use of any elaborate research techniques. Similarly, by keying the coupon to each of the various advertising media that are used, the relative effectiveness of each medium can be directly measured in terms of the number of coupons received from that medium for a given advertising expenditure. The total expenditure can be adjusted month by month to provide only a sufficient number of leads to keep the sales force fully employed, so that unnecessary wastage in advertising expenditure is avoided. Particularly when larger advertising expenditure is involved, this ability to obtain a simple and direct control over advertising costs with one selling plan may be an important factor in choosing between alternatives.

There are, of course, many situations that are very different from those illustrated in this dishwasher example. However, in every case, the determination of the most suitable selling and distribution plan depends upon analysing the communication objectives and relative costs of each of the alternative plans that could be employed. These are discussed in fuller detail in the sections that follow.

ADVERTISING

Advertising can be defined as any inanimate means of communication between a company and the potential users or distributors of its products. The means or 'media' that are used for conveying the communication include the following:

Postal communication (direct mail)
Newspapers
Periodicals
Trade and technical journals
Television
Radio
Billposting
Merchandising and display
Public relations, etc.

When considering the incorporation of advertising into a selling and distribution plan, the two essential preliminary requirements are:

a. To define the *exact purpose* which the advertising is intended to achieve (the Advertising Objective).

b. To define the people, in precise and specific terms, with whom the communication is to be made.

Companies that spend very large annual sums on advertising are unlikely to embark on any campaign without first having taken these two preliminary steps. However, these steps are just as essential in preparing any selling plan in which advertising is to play a part. The extent of this part, and the sum involved, does not affect the need for this action if an effective and economic plan is to be evolved.

Advertising Objectives
It might be said that the objective of any advertisement for a product is to increase the sales of that product. However, in preparing the selling plan, it is necessary to define *how* the advertisement is expected to achieve this result. In other words, it is the specific objective of the advertisement itself as distinct from the other selling activities that must be precisely defined.

Within the overall selling plan, advertising can be used for a variety of quite different purposes. These purposes can be divided into two main categories. In the first, the purpose of the advertisement should be to get the reader or viewer to take some positive action directly as a result of seeing the advertisement without any other stimulus, as in a mail order advertisement. If this action is in the form of some direct contact with the advertiser, it is referred to below as a 'Direct Action' objective; if it is to take place with some other party, and not directly with the advertiser, the objective is shown as a 'Directly Associated Action'. In the second category, the purpose of the advertisement should be to convey information and create a favourable impression; thus supporting some other action rather than creating the action on its own.

Some typical examples of the immediate purpose for which an advertisement can be used in each of these categories are as follows:

Direct Action
To persuade a prospective purchaser (user or distributor) to order a particular product by mail or telephone.
To persuade a prospective purchaser to send in an enquiry – this may be about a particular product or for some more general information.

To persuade a prospective purchaser to send in a request for a salesman to call.

To persuade a prospective purchaser to supply his name and address in order to provide a lead for some subsequent action.

To persuade a suitable candidate to apply for employment.

Directly Associated Action

To persuade a prospective purchaser to select or ask for the advertised product in a self-service store or retail shop. (Note that, in this category (for example, cigarettes, detergents, etc.), the objective is to secure a sale entirely by visual means. Neither the advertiser's nor the distributor's salesmen will have played any part in influencing the user's buying decision.

Sales Force Support

To assist salesmen in obtaining an interview and selling the company's products by conveying information about the existence and purpose of the products.

To assist salesmen in obtaining an interview and selling the company's products by creating a favourable impression of the company and its products in the minds of prospective purchasers.

'Selling Out' Support

To create a favourable predisposition to buy the advertised product in the minds of prospective purchasers when buying that type of product from a distributor or retailer. (Note that, in this category, the distributor's salesman or some other factors at the point-of-sale may be influencing the eventual buying decision – see the Dishwasher example.)

To create a favourable predisposition to buy an 'end product' in which the advertiser's raw materials or components are used.

Recruitment Support

To attract suitable recruits by creating a favourable impression of employment with the company. (Note the distinction between this form of advertisement and the direct action objective of persuading a candidate to apply for a particular appointment.)

Financial Support
To attract capital investment by creating a favourable impression of the company or by other means.

In preparing the selling and distribution plan, the part that any advertising is to play and the precise purpose for which it is to be used should be defined in some such terms as those given in the above examples. This aspect must be planned in conjunction with the part that is to be played by the sales force, which must be defined in similar terms. For instance, which of these two activities will play the larger part in influencing a buyer's decision? Which, if either, will be used for the final act of securing the order from the ultimate user? (In some situations this activity will, of course, have to be left to the distributor.)

Some advertising objectives that may be economically attainable under certain conditions may be quite unattainable under others. Therefore, in planning the objective, it is important to consider whether the proposed objective could, in fact, be economically attained in the planned situation. For instance, it has been shown that when selling cigarettes, the user's order is not obtained by a distributor's salesman, but directly by means of visual communication between the manufacturer and the user. However, there are many products for which the manufacturer's or a distributor's salesman performs the act of securing the user's order. Nevertheless, an attempt is still sometimes made to use advertising under these conditions as if its purpose was directly to sell the product or obtain an order. Such advertising is likely to be unsuccessful or to be a very expensive way of securing an eventual order. For example, in selling domestic products such as carpets or cookers through retail distributors, the direct objective of any advertising should not be to obtain an order, but to create a favourable predisposition to buy the advertised product in the minds of prospective users when the buying decision is being made on the retailer's premises. This will require a different advertising strategy from that used by the cigarette or detergent manufacturer. There is little doubt that considerable sums are wasted on advertising every year through failure to define its specific objective or because of its use for an objective that is not economically attainable with the particular product and channel of distribution.

It has already been seen, in the dishwasher example, that the control of advertising expenditure and the measurement of its effectiveness is very much simpler if the advertising is being used for a 'direct action' objective. There its purpose is to produce some specific action. As there are no other variables, the amount of action that results from the advertising is a direct measure of its achievement. If the action occurs with another party and not directly with the advertiser (a directly associated action), the advertiser will, of course, have to take appropriate steps to find out about this action if the same degree of control is to be obtained. For example, a cigarette manufacturer will need to know about the movement of his products from the retail outlets to the user. Because of the time lag through the channel of distribution, the manufacturer's own sales would not be a sufficiently accurate measurement for this purpose. (See Retail Audits – page 167.)

If advertising is being used for one of the support objectives, its ultimate achievement will be reflected in the volume of sales obtained. However, there will be a time lag between cause and effect. Moreover, in any particular period, there are many other factors that may have caused an increase or reduction in sales. The volume of sales will not, therefore, provide any direct and immediate measurement of achievement. Nor will it enable the effectiveness of a particular advertisement or advertising medium to be determined. This does not, of course, mean that an adequate measurement and control of advertising effectiveness cannot be obtained. It will, however, require the use of rather more elaborate research techniques since the immediate objective of the advertising is to influence an attitude of mind towards the company or its products. Its effectiveness will be shown by the extent to which this objective has been achieved. (See Advertising Research, page 190, and the Relationship between Advertising Costs and Sales Volume, page 75.)

It will usually be necessary, in preparing the selling and distribution plan, to consider the method or methods that are to be used for conveying the visual information. This can be by direct mail, press advertising, television, point of sale display, billposting, or some other appropriate medium. The most suitable method will depend, not only on the people to whom the information has to be conveyed, but also on the advertising objective. (For example, in the plan to sell dishwashers directly to the user, the objective of the advertising was to persuade the readers to return a coupon. Television advertising would obviously be unsuitable under these conditions, although it might have been used with the alternative plan of selling through retail distributors.) It is, however, unnecessary at this stage to prepare a detailed media plan. This is a routine operation to be handled by the advertising manager or other appropriate executive in conjunction with the advertising agent. (See Advertising Research, page 196.)

Merchandising and Display
The word 'advertising' has been used throughout this section in its broadest sense to cover all forms of visual communication between seller and buyer. This includes the label and package of the product and its display at the point where it can be seen by a prospective purchaser, which may be at an exhibition or at the usual point of sale – for example, a retail shop. With some products, this form of visual communication can play an important part in influencing a buyer's decision and should be planned just as carefully as any other form of advertising.

In selling consumer goods and household products, this activity is sometimes described as 'merchandising' which, in this sense, has been defined as 'obtaining maximum persuasion at the point of sale without personal salesmanship'. (In its more correct but less commonly used sense, merchandising embraces all activities concerned with the place and method of selling the merchandise – this includes distribution channels and pricing policies as well as packaging and display at the point of sale). Staff employed by the manufacturer for the specific purpose of arranging for the display of goods and promotional material at the retail outlets are, in some industries, described as 'merchandisers'.

The growth of self-selection and self-service stores has increased the importance of the part that is played by this form of communication in influencing a buyer's decision. Moreover, because buyers are becoming increasingly attuned to it, the effect of its impact seems to be increasing in all forms of retail selling. It is particularly important with those products which may be purchased on impulse, through seeing them on display, rather than as a premeditated purchase. In these cases, it is visual communication that alone directly secures the user's order. (For example, a high proportion of the sales of paperback books are not premeditated purchases; many of them are bought on impulse through seeing them on display at a bookstall, perhaps while waiting for a train.) This has led to the pre-packaging and display of even such things as nuts and bolts in an ironmonger's shop and has resulted in greatly increased sales.

This form of visual communication should always be carefully and imaginatively examined as part of the selling and distribution plan in all those cases where it might be appropriately used.

Visual Aids for Salesmen

Such things as pamphlets, brochures and catalogues carried by a salesman are another form of visual communication between the company and its customers. As before, this communication can perform two functions: it can carry out the basic function of conveying information about the products and it can also play a part in influencing a decision to buy those products. The design and appearance of this material must inevitably project an image of the company in the mind of the buyer. A company can hardly expect to project a favourable image if its sales literature is badly designed and badly printed on poor quality paper. In the same way, untidy and 'dog-eared' documents are likely to reflect a similar image of the salesman's company. This is mainly a subconscious effect on the mind of the buyer, and it is only in the very worst cases that it would be consciously recognized.

The presentation aspect is also important to letters, invoices, accounts and other documents that are sent out by the company. These are merely another form of visual communication with the company's customers. They should therefore be regarded in the same way as any other communication or advertisement that is designed for a supporting objective to assist the sales force. They not only convey information but, by projecting some image of the company, they also have an influence on a buying decision. This influence may be favourable or it may be unfavourable. The first requirement is to ensure that none of these communications is having an unfavourable effect through carelessness or lack of attention. Consideration can then be given as to how this form of visual communication can be used to project the most favourable image of the company and its products.

THE COMPANY'S IMAGE

A company's image might be described as the predominant overall impression of the company in the minds of the buyers of its products.

There are few situations, if any, where this impression does not play some conscious or subconscious part in influencing a buying decision. With certain branded products, the brand name takes the place of the maker's name and, in this context, 'brand image' should be substituted for 'company image'.

Whether this overall impression is satisfactory or unsatisfactory will depend first and foremost on the company's achievement in relation to those aspects which the Buying Factor Analysis has shown to be the principal features in influencing a decision to buy the company's products. For example, a reliable delivery service may be extremely important to an industrial buyer. If one of his suppliers is frequently failing to meet its delivery promises, this will affect his *predominant* overall impression of that company and it will have a poor image regardless of how good it may be in other respects. Meeting the requirements of the Buying Factor Analysis in the design of the company's products and services is, therefore, an essential pre-requisite to projecting a good image.

However, a buyer's overall impression of a company is not formed only in relation to the extent to which its goods and services are satisfactory. One company may have an image associated with the production of high quality goods in the higher price range, whereas another company's image may be of a particularly dynamic and progressive organization. These are only two of the many different images that a company may possess. In a market-oriented company, the nature of this image is deliberately planned and does not come about by accident. It is governed by the product policy and market segmentation that has been adopted in the overall marketing plan. The projection of the required image must be an integral part in planning the communications between the company and the users of its products.

The image is in the mind of the buyer, so that the kind of image formed will depend upon the way in which the company 'presents' itself to its customers in all visible evidence of its existence. This includes the style and design of its advertisements, packaging, sales literature, letter headings, accounts, and all other external documents. It applies to the appearance of its vehicles on the road and of its factories and offices in those cases where they are likely to be seen by a significant proportion of the company's customers. Each of these, individually, may play only a very small part in influencing a buyer's decision and,

MARKETING AND HIGHER MANAGEMENT

for this reason, some of them may seem to be unimportant. Nevertheless, it is their combined, cumulative effect which influences the kind of image of the company that is formed in the mind of the buyer. For this reason all aspects must be planned and co-ordinated to project the one single required image.

As far as possible, all visible evidence of the company should be immediately recognizable as of that company. This is aided by the use of a standardized house-colour and the standardized design of all visual communications. In recent years, the manufacturers of breakfast cereals have shown that a package can still retain instant brand recognition even though the printed matter on a substantial area of its surface is frequently changed. It is the general style and design that portrays the company's image and not the subject matter that is conveyed.

Good design that will project the right image of the company requires skill and experience. It is rarely successful if it is based on the opinions of industrial executives who can hardly be expected to be experts in this field. However, good design is not expensive. It may cost a little more than leaving the work to a local printer but, even for the smaller company, this will be a negligible amount in relation to the money spent on other ways of promoting and selling the company's products. If required the Council of Industrial Design is always able to advise an industrial company on a suitable designer for its particular requirements.

THE SALES FORCE

Procedures for planning the operations of the sales force are discussed in Chapter 12. As far as the overall marketing plan is concerned, it is normally only necessary to consider whether the company will sell directly to the users of its products with its own sales force, or whether it will use intermediate distributors to sell to some or all of these users.

The most suitable plan will depend upon the relative cost and effectiveness of the alternative channels of distribution that could be used. (See Dishwasher example, page 128.) In general, a smaller and less costly sales force will be required if some part of the selling operation is left to a distributor, but this must be compared with the cost of the discount that would have to be paid to the distributor. The essential requirement is to determine the number of call points that would have to be visited by the company's own salesmen in relation to each of the alternative methods of selling and distribution that might be used. In selling directly to the user, this is, of course, the number of users in the selected market or market segments. Or, if distributors are used, it is the number of distributors that would be required to cover these users. This information can usually be obtained with sufficient accuracy from comparatively simple desk research. (See Market Research, Chapter 8).

The number of salesmen required to cover the call points in a particular channel of distribution will depend on:

a. The number of call points.
b. The frequency with which these call points must be visited.
c. The average number of calls per week that can be made by a salesman under the particular selling conditions.

In practice, there are likely to be considerable differences in the above between one sales territory and another. This must, of course, be taken into account in planning the deployment of the sales force – see Chapter 12. However, for the purpose of the marketing plan, overall averages are sufficiently accurate. For example:

Total number of call points to be covered	4,000
Average call frequency required	Monthly
Average calls per call point per year	12
Therefore, total calls required per year	48,000
Average number of calls per week per salesman	20
Calls per year (say 48 weeks)	960

Therefore, the approximate number of salesmen required to cover 4,000 call points under these conditions is:

$$\frac{48,000}{960} = 50$$

In order to determine the cost of this sales force, an estimate must be made of the approximate annual cost of maintaining a salesman, including all such items as expenses and supervision. If, in this example, this cost is approximately £2,500 per annum, the total cost of the sales force using this channel of distribution to cover the 4,000 call points would be £125,000 per annum, or an average of approximately £32 per call point per annum. This cost can then be compared with the annual cost of the discount that would have to be paid if those call points were covered by a distributor instead of directly by the company's own sales force. For instance, if the distributor received a discount of 10 per cent and if the average value of the sales from a call point exceeded £350 per annum, it would obviously be more economic to sell directly to that call point at a cost of £32 instead of paying a discount of £35 or more to a distributor. Any difference in the cost of transporting the goods must also be taken into account in those cases where this represents a significant item in the total costs.

It should be emphasized that these are approximate costings only for use in considering alternative methods of selling and distribution in the overall marketing plan. For this purpose, precise accuracy is usually unnecessary. A much more accurate approach must, of course, be used when it comes to preparing the detailed plans for the physical distribution of the products and for the deployment and control of the sales force.

As far as this aspect of the overall marketing plan is concerned, the essential requirement is to define and quantify the people or companies who are to be visited by the company's own sales force and to define the precise objective which those visits are intended to achieve. It is on this information that tactical operating plans will be based.

THE MARKETING PLAN – SUMMARY

Successful marketing is not achieved merely by planning and co-ordinating certain aspects of the company's activities. It depends first and foremost on the adoption of a marketing-oriented policy by top management, which must be based on an effective marketing plan for the overall management of the company's affairs.

The marketing plan is, therefore, concerned with policy-making decisions. Its purpose is to determine the most suitable types and varieties of products that the company should produce, to select the markets or market segments in which those products should be sold, and to plan the most suitable procedures and methods for communication between the company and the potential users of its products. The objective of the marketing plan is to obtain the most profitable use of the company's resources and this must be the overriding consideration in every aspect of its preparation. The plan is essentially concerned with profits rather than with sales volume.

All decisions in the marketing plan must be made and can only be made by top management since those decisions govern the company's overall policy and affect the whole of its activities. Responsibility for the execution of the various facets of the plan can, however, be delegated to an appropriate executive or executives (see Chapter 6), but responsibility for the plan itself cannot be delegated. For this reason, it is essential that top management should have a thorough understanding of the principles of marketing and of the factors that must be taken into account in the preparation of the plan as outlined in this and the previous chapters in Part 1.

Chapter 6

Marketing Management

The market orientation of a business is not achieved merely by the appointment of a marketing manager over a marketing department. There are, indeed, several companies – even quite large ones – that are using all the techniques and procedures of marketing with conspicuous success without the word marketing appearing in the title of any one of their executives.

THE ROLE OF THE MANAGING DIRECTOR

It was shown in the previous chapter that marketing starts with the company's overall policy and that the preparation and execution of the marketing plans involve decisions and actions in every department of the company. The responsibility for this can, therefore, rest only with the individual who is responsible for company policy and who has the unified authority and responsibility for the whole of its activities. This is normally the managing director or his equivalent. This means that, whatever the title that may be given to some other executive, it is the managing director himself who should be actively responsible for the company's marketing operations. It is he who must make the final decisions on the marketing plan and ensure that it is effectively carried out. He could not delegate this responsibility to any one individual without also delegating to that individual the managing director's overall authority and responsibility. It is particularly noticeable that, in those companies that are most successful with their marketing, the managing director is personally completely marketing oriented. He, above all others, must fully understand the meaning and purpose of marketing.

However, although the managing director cannot delegate the overall

MARKETING MANAGEMENT

authority and responsibility for marketing, he can of course delegate the responsibility for preparing the marketing plans and keeping them under continuous review. The various aspects of this planning and co-ordinating function can either be delegated to certain senior executives, who also have other responsibilities, or it can be delegated to a marketing director or manager specifically appointed for the purpose. The most suitable structure will depend on the size of the company and the nature of its business.

MANAGEMENT STRUCTURE

As has been shown in previous chapters, there are very big differences between the factors that influence a buying decision for one product as compared with another and, because of this, the nature and extent of the planning activities for successful marketing in one industry may be quite different from those in another. For this reason there can be no standardized pattern for a management structure that would be suitable for every industry.

In deciding upon the most suitable structure, the first thing to consider is the nature of the marketing activities that have to be carried out in the particular company (see Chapter 5). For instance, in selling consumer goods, the marketing activities may be very largely concerned with promotional planning whereas, in other industries, the emphasis may have to be on product design and presentation or on the services provided. The first step, therefore, is to use the Buying Factor Analysis to determine what has to be done. This must be defined before attempting to decide who should carry it through.

When the nature of the activities has been defined, consideration can be given to the most suitable individual or individuals to whom the responsibility should be given for planning and co-ordinating these activities. There are many situations, particularly in the smaller companies, where it would be quite uneconomic to appoint a highly-paid executive for the sole purpose of planning the marketing activities. Marketing may still be carried out effectively and there are various possible ways of delegating responsibility under these conditions depending upon the particular circumstances. One such arrangement is as follows:

1. The responsibility for obtaining information about the market and maintaining a continuing review of the factors that are influencing

customers' buying decisions is given to a market research manager. Or, in those cases where such an appointment would not be economically justified, this responsibility is delegated to the sales manager.

2. The managing director himself retains full responsibility for the actions that must be carried out to enable him to make the following decisions and to keep them under continuous review:

   a. The type and range of products that the company should be producing in order to make the most profitable use of its resources. (See Chapter 4.)
   b. The markets or market segments in which those products should be sold. (See Chapter 5.)
   c. The channels of distribution and methods of communication that should be used between the company and the potential users of its products in the selected markets. (See Chapter 5.)

3. Under the overall control and co-ordination of the managing director, the executives responsible for design, production, sales and finance are given an equal and joint responsibility for:

   a. Deciding what products should be made, how they should be designed and presented, at what price they should be sold, and what quantities should be produced.
   b. Planning the way in which all the actions and decisions in each of their departments will be co-ordinated and directed towards winning the maximum number of favourable buying decisions at an economic cost.

This list is not exhaustive and is given only to illustrate the kind of structure that can be used when no separate marketing manager is appointed. It can obviously be modified or expanded to suit particular circumstances. However, under these conditions, successful marketing is more than ever dependent upon the personal direction of the managing director. He must provide the co-ordination in the senior management team that is so vitally important in the preparation and execution of marketing plans. In some cases, the managing director may be aided in this by the appointment of a personal assistant who is fully trained and experienced in marketing. At the same time, every member of the management team must be alive to the principles of marketing and must understand fully the way in which the activities in his own department will play either an adverse or favourable part in influencing a customer's buying decision.

Although there are some exceptions to the rule, it is generally undesirable to delegate the entire responsibility for planning and co-ordinating the marketing operations to the sales manager. The sales manager's function, like that of the works manager, is an administrative function. He is responsible for the administration and control of the sales force and the whole of the company's selling activities. Like the other members of the management team, he has authority and direct responsibility for executing his part of the marketing plan. Harmonious relations are often difficult to establish if, at the same time, he is given responsibility for planning and co-ordinating the activities of the other members of the team. It tends to suggest interference by the sales manager in departments over which he has no authority.

However, the combination of the marketing and sales management functions in one individual has occasionally been successful in small or medium-sized companies marketing those consumer goods where production is mainly confined to packaging or bottling operations. Under these particular conditions, the Buying Factor Analysis is likely to show that marketing is primarily concerned with product policy and with the company's promotional and selling activities, including the design of the packs. If the product policy is decided by the board, the rest of the marketing function can be combined with the sales management function without causing any serious problems. Nevertheless, the larger manufacturers of consumer goods almost invariably separate the marketing and sales management functions.

A few companies employ a so-called 'marketing manager' who is responsible to the sales manager. However, this individual is fulfilling a quite different function and is, in effect, more likely to be performing the duties of a promotional or merchandising manager.

THE MARKETING MANAGER

In many cases, the nature and extent of marketing activities may make it desirable and economic to appoint a marketing director or manager who is specifically responsible for planning and co-ordinating these activities. He should be directly responsible to the managing director or to the individual who has overall executive authority and responsibility. The marketing manager normally has no line authority over the managers responsible for design, production and sales. In this respect, his position is somewhat similar to that of the financial director or manager. In both cases, there is an overall planning and co-ordinating responsibility without administrative authority.

However, in some cases, the marketing manager may also be given responsibility and authority for the execution of certain aspects of the marketing plan, such as advertising, where this does not cut across the lines of responsibility and authority of the other executives. Occasionally, the sales manager comes under and is responsible to the marketing manager. This is, in effect, a different structure and is similar to that already described in which the marketing and sales management functions are combined in one individual who, in this case, has under him a sales manager to whom he delegates this part of his responsibility. The conditions under which this type of structure can be successful have already been described.

When appointing a marketing director or manager, it is again particularly important that careful consideration should be given to the nature of the planning activities for which he will be responsible, as revealed by the Buying Factor Analysis. As an extreme example, experience in planning promotional campaigns would be of little value in planning the marketing of capital equipment to industry. A background in selling and sales management is by no means essential except perhaps in marketing consumer goods. Little research appears to have been done yet on this subject, but it seems probable that there are many industrial and domestic durable products where the most successful marketing managers would be those with a technical or engineering background. However, the marketing manager must first and foremost be customer-oriented and this is an attitude of mind which is not always easily acquired by those whose previous experience has been mainly of a scientific or technical nature.

The marketing manager must, of course, fully understand the basic concept of marketing and he must have an intimate knowledge of the techniques and procedures that are available for planning and controlling the various aspects of a company's marketing operations.

Imagination, adaptability and enthusiasm are among the most important characteristics that he must possess. He must have a personality that will enable him to win the confidence and co-operation of the other members of the management team so that, without having any authority over their activities, he can ensure that they are all working together and taking the appropriate actions to secure the common marketing objective of the company. These personality characteristics can be much more important than practical experience.

The marketing manager will be responsible for instituting and controlling suitable procedures for keeping the company fully informed about its markets. He will be responsible for preparing recommendations based on this information on the company's product policy, the design of its products, markets and market segmentation, channels of distribution, and the selling and promotional strategy. He must keep the overall marketing plan under continuous review in the light of changes that occur in the market. However, within this overall plan, his primary and continuing responsibility is to plan and co-ordinate all those activities throughout the company that will in any way, either directly or indirectly, influence a purchaser's buying decision. This consideration should define the limits of his planning responsibilities.

As was pointed out in the chapter on financial aspects, the marketing manager must not make the mistake of assuming that his objective is to maximize sales volume, as this could have disastrous results. However, in a progressive company, the marketing manager should be planning for growth at some agreed average annual rate and the objective of all his activities should be to secure and maintain the most profitable use of the company's expanding resources. (See Long Range Planning, Chapter 7).

MARKETING PERSONNEL

The nature and size of the staff, if any, that comes under the marketing manager will depend upon the size of the company and the nature of its products. For example, in larger companies producing mass consumer goods, there may be a marketing director or manager who has under him a market research manager, an advertising manager, and a number of brand managers. Each brand manager is responsible for planning the marketing of a particular brand or group of brands. A brand manager will, of course, have no line authority over the salesmen selling his brand, since this is the responsibility of the sales manager.

In consumer goods organizations, the brand managers will be primarily concerned with packaging and promotional activities. In the case of durable and industrial products, the brand managers may be replaced by product managers. For instance, a company manufacturing domestic electrical equipment may have a number of product managers who are responsible to the marketing manager. One product manager may be responsible for cookers, another for refrigerators, and so on. However, in this case, the product manager in the marketing department will be concerned, among other things, with the design and styling of the products for which he is responsible. He will, therefore, be working closely with his opposite number in the research and development department.

The size of the staff employed on market research also varies considerably from one company to another. In the larger organizations, even if there is no marketing manager there may be a market research department working under a market research manager. The smaller company may have little more than one assistant engaged on this work. However, *every* company needs to know something about its market. The more it knows about its prospective customers, the better it will be able to plan its activities to win their favourable buying decisions. The cost of obtaining adequate information is usually quite small in comparison with the money that is spent on promoting and selling the company's products. But, if the information is correctly used, it can have a substantial effect on the company's profits. The danger is in doing too little rather than too much.

EXTERNAL MARKETING SERVICES

There are certain aspects of marketing in which it may sometimes be more effective and more economic to employ external services rather than use the company's own staff. In market research, for example, much of the information can often be obtained from desk research and, once instituted, this can be done internally. However, field research, requiring the use of interviewers, can usually be done better and at less cost by an outside organization that employs staff who are trained and continually engaged in this work. (See Market Research, Chapter

8). If the company has a marketing manager, he is normally given the responsibility for recommending the use of external marketing services if and when necessary, and for planning and controlling the use of these services. In other cases, this is the responsibility of the managing director.

SUMMARY

In any company, certain specific activities must be carried out in order to prepare and execute an effective marketing plan. The essential requirement is to determine what each of these activities should be in the light of the company's particular marketing situation, and then to make some suitable arrangements for them to be effectively carried out. The overall responsibility for the marketing activities must rest with the managing director. However, he can delegate the responsibility for some or all of these activities, depending on their nature, to one or more of the members of his senior management team or to a marketing manager. In doing this, he must of course ensure that the responsibility given to one individual does not cross the lines of responsibility and authority given to others. Responsibility and authority must always go together. All those concerned in the preparation and execution of a marketing plan must always remember that its objective is not to maximize sales but to secure and maintain the most profitable use of the company's resources.

In the management of marketing, care should be taken to avoid confusing 'planning' with 'doing'. For instance, if a marketing manager is appointed, he does not design the product, he does not even design an advertisement for the product and he does not sell it. But, without careful planning, based on a study of the market, none of these activities can be integrated and carried out in the most effective way to attain the fundamental objective of the company.

Chapter 7

Corporate Long Range Planning

A study of marketing in relation to the higher management of a business would not be complete without a brief reference to the allied subject of Corporate Long Range Planning. It is not part of the marketing function, but the two are closely related and neither can be completely successful without the other.

The ability to adapt to changes in the environment has always been an essential requirement in any form of evolutionary development. The species that have failed to survive are those that were unable to adapt themselves soon enough to changes.

This is just as true in industry as it is in nature. In the long-term, the growth and continued success of a business depends upon its ability to adapt itself to the changes in the economic, social, political and technological climate in which it exists. Today, we can hardly fail to recognize that this climate is changing at a faster rate than ever before. In Britain, social and economic change is evidenced by such things as the changing age structure of the population and the changes in the distribution of wealth. Internationally, political and economic changes in the emerging nations are having a striking effect on world markets. In the field of technology, there can be few companies that are not being affected in some way or another, however remotely, by the development of new processes and new materials.

As has been shown in the previous chapters, an effective marketing and product policy will enable a company to adapt itself to changes in its markets in order to attain its immediate objective. However, changes in the environment will also affect other things besides demand for the company's products. These changes may affect production and clerical methods, material supplies, the availability of labour, conditions of employment, the availability of capital for expansion, taxation liabilities, and almost any aspect of the company's business.

A company's ability to adapt itself to the changes in its environment depends upon the extent to which it has planned for these changes and prepared itself for them in advance. In addition, the company must know where it is going. In the long term, a company cannot continue to be successful if it stands still. Its immediate objective may be to make the most profitable use of its existing resources, but a progressive company must also define the long-term objective on which its policy for the future will be based. In the light of the likely changes in its environment, the company must consider such questions as:

Where do we want to go?

How important is sheer growth?

How important is security for staff and employees?

How important is security for the shareholders?

What degree of risk is acceptable and what should be the return on capital in relation to that risk?

Should we concentrate or diversify?

If we are going to expand, should we expand vertically in the distribution channel or horizontally into other products or other markets?

Should we expand through mergers and company acquisitions or through our own resources?

After the present management has gone, who are the future directors and senior executives of the company and where will they come from?

These are just a few of the many questions that a progressive company should be considering in making its future plans. This is the field of Corporate Long Range Planning. It must embrace every aspect of management and must plan to meet the changes that will occur, not only in the company's markets, but in the overall environment in which it operates.

Long Range Planning, as a specific management function, is a natural development that follows logically from modern concepts of business administration and marketing, to both of which it is closely allied. It is being used extensively by the more progressive companies, although in Britain its use by industry as a whole is still comparatively limited. Managements tend to be pre-occupied with the problems of today and the future plans of many companies do not extend much beyond the next year or two in anything but the haziest terms. Nevertheless, with the increasing tempo of change in the industrial climate, there can be little doubt that Corporate Long Range Planning, coupled with a dynamic marketing policy, will have to be adopted by more and more companies if they are to survive or are to avoid being taken over by their more progressive competitors.

PART 2

Marketing Tools and Techniques

Chapter 8

Market Research

The term 'Market Research' is used to include any activity that is directly concerned with finding out information about a market. These activities range from a simple study and analysis of published statistics to the more elaborate procedures of interviewing and field research. The more that a company knows about the prospective purchasers of its products, the better it is able to plan the design, production and sale of those products to win favourable buying decisions. Market Research is the essential fact-finding operation on which all successful marketing is based.

Many textbooks on marketing include these fact-finding operations under the much broader title of 'Marketing Research'. It is important, therefore, that the meanings of the two terms should not be confused. Marketing Research, as its name implies, is concerned with overall research into the way in which a company sets about marketing its products. Market Research, on the other hand, is solely and directly concerned with finding out information about the market. Thus, the term marketing research embraces all those aspects already discussed in the previous chapters. Market research provides the information on which the various marketing decisions and actions are based.

In planning market research, it is first necessary to define the geographic location of the market to be examined, for example, the home market or some specific export market. Within that geographic market, the objective will be to obtain information about the nature and size of the market for some particular product. This may include finding out such information as:

Who are the people who have a need that could be satisfied at least as well and as economically by the purchase of this product as by any other available means? (See Chapter 1.)

The number of these people and the proportion of them that have the financial ability to satisfy their need by the purchase of the product.

The quantity and frequency of their purchases that would be necessary fully to satisfy their need. Hence, from the foregoing, the size of the potential demand for the product.

The size of the current demand for products of the same type and in the same price bracket. Hence, the share of the current demand being obtained by the company.

The location and distribution of the demand throughout the defined market.

The factors that are influencing the buying decisions of prospective purchasers when buying the product.

The relationship between the selling price and the size of the demand for the product.

The nature and structure of the market for purposes of market segmentation. Differences between product requirements or buying motives of different groups of purchasers.

Where applicable – the number and location of suitable distributors for the product.

The factors that are influencing the buying decisions of distributors.

The movement of goods through the channels of distribution.

The reputation and image of the company in the minds of prospective purchasers.

This list is not complete for all conditions. Its aim, in summary, is to find out who and where are the potential purchasers of the product, how many of them there are, how much and how often they buy, and what are the factors and motives that influence their buying decisions.

It will be seen that some of the information which is sought is of a quantitative nature – it is concerned with numerical facts about the market such as the size and distribution of the demand. Other information is of a qualitative or behavioural nature – why people act in certain ways and the things that influence their buying decisions. Much of the quantitative information can be obtained from statistical studies that come under the heading of 'Desk Research'. Obtaining qualitative information is likely to require observations or interrogations in the field.

Before initiating any form of market research it is particularly important that the purpose and objective of the research should be precisely specified. Failure to do this is a not uncommon cause of much wasteful and useless research. There is often some piece of information that might appear to be useful or interesting superficially. But the purpose of research is to enable some particular decision to be made. Therefore, before seeking *any* item of information, either on its own or as a part of a broader research, the key question must be answered: 'If we had this information, what would we use it for and what would we be able to do about it?' The use that is to be made of the information may also affect the form of research that should be used and the way in which it should be carried out; it will often govern the degree of accuracy that is necessary and this can make a significant difference to the cost. The researcher should therefore be told, not only *what* information is required, but *why* it is required and what use will be made of it. This will enable a skilled researcher to conduct the research and prepare his findings in the most suitable way.

In the past, the findings of market research have sometimes been mistrusted and mistakes have certainly been made. These have been due both to the way in which it has been carried out and to the way in which it has been used. Anything beyond some of the simpler forms of desk research should be conducted only by fully trained and experienced staff. However, it is the higher management of the company which has to initiate and use research. If they are to do this correctly, and if the fullest benefits are to be obtained from this valuable marketing tool, it is necessary to have a broad understanding of the various ways in which information is obtained. A detailed knowledge of the techniques and procedures that are employed by the researcher is, however, unnecessary. Many textbooks solely devoted to this subject are available for those who are directly concerned with carrying it out.

DESK RESEARCH

By far the greater part of all market research carried out by industry is in the form of internal desk research. The methods used for obtaining the information range from the simple examination of published statistics to the more sophisticated mathematical analysis carried out by a skilled statistician.

The procedure adopted must obviously depend upon the type of product and the nature of the information that is sought. Research can be seen at work in an elementary form with those products that are regularly used by every household in the country and for which the *per capita* consumption does not vary significantly in different parts of the market. With these products, the size of the demand in each territory is directly proportional to its population. It is therefore necessary to do no more than refer to the Registrar-General's population statistics to calculate the size of the population within the boundaries of each territory and, hence, the distribution of the demand. The relative share of the total demand in each territory that is being obtained by the company can then be determined.

There are, of course, many products purchased for the home in which the *per capita* consumption varies from one part of the country to another. For example, the distribution of the demand for children's toys in Britain would be quite erroneous if measured in terms of population. In these cases, some other statistics such as the Census of Distribution must be used.

The information that is used in Desk Research emanates from various sources such as government departments, trade associations and appropriate directories. . . . Some industries, both in industrial and consumer goods, are extremely well supplied with statistics. In these industries, comprehensive quantitative information about the market can be obtained from a simple analysis of published data. More commonly, however, there may be no published statistics that relate directly to the particular product or particular market segment about which the information is required.

In these cases, the researcher first has to consider possible sources from which information might be obtained. A considerable amount of information is collected and is available that is not published. For instance, many of the statistics that are regularly published by government departments are, in fact, summaries of more detailed information that has had to be obtained in order to produce the published statistics. This more detailed information is usually available on request. The fact that there is no *published* information about a particular type of product does not necessarily mean that that information does not somewhere exist in some form or another.

Often, it may not be possible to obtain the required information directly. It has to be obtained indirectly from other information that is more readily available. It may be necessary to determine the way in which two or more pieces of related information can be suitably weighted and combined together to provide the required information.

A simple illustration is provided by taking a consumable product that is used only in drawing offices as an example. The objective is to determine the size of the demand for this type of product in each of the company's sales areas. There may be no available statistics that relate directly to the sales of drawing office supplies in general or to this product in particular. . . . However, there is likely to be some relationship between the consumption of the product and the number of draughtsmen employed in each area. The latter is a piece of information that can be obtained from employment statistics. The nature of this relationship is therefore examined. Draughtsmen are employed in many different industries as well as in architects' offices, local authorities and other similar situations. The examination may show that the relationship between the consumption of the product and the number of draughtsmen differs considerably from one industry to another. The employers of draughtsmen must therefore be classified and grouped according to the average annual consumption per draughtsman. Desk Research can be used to determine the distribution of these groups throughout the country. From this information, and from the number of draughtsmen employed, the approximate annual consumption of this type of product in each sales area can be estimated.

In this simple example, it required very little imagination or experience to suggest suitable data that might be used to obtain the required information. However, extensive preliminary research is often necessary to discover suitable and available sources from which the required information could be built up. There are some situations in which some of the basic information that is used may appear at first sight to have no direct connection with the particular product that is the subject of the research. In the more complex situations, the information may have to be constructed from several factors that can vary in relation to each other. This will acquire a detailed mathematical analysis.

Successful Desk Research depends almost entirely upon the knowledge and experience of the research staff. An experienced researcher knows where to look or who to ask and becomes thoroughly familiar with the many likely and unlikely sources from which information can be obtained. This knowledge comes only from practical experience. It is for this reason that anything but the simplest research should be carried out by staff who are fully and continuously employed on this work. In those cases where it would not be economic for a company to employ its own staff, the use of a reputable external research service is not expensive. This is almost certain to be very much more effective than using staff who are normally engaged on other work to try to find some particular piece of information as the need arises.

Many companies do not yet realize the full extent of the information that can be obtained through Desk Research. Because of the specialized nature of a product or the lack of directly related statistics, it is often too readily assumed that it would be quite impossible to obtain certain information. Yet there have been many instances in such situations when an experienced researcher has had little difficulty in finding the answer.

In addition, a well-organized research department will have immediately to hand the various records, statistics, directories and other information that relate directly or indirectly to its industry. There will be a constant flow of incoming information, culled from many sources, and management is provided with a continuous information service about its markets.

FIELD RESEARCH

All market research starts in the field. The statistics that are used in Desk Research stem from Field Research that has been carried out by others. The censuses of population that were carried out throughout the Roman Empire are one of the earliest examples of organized field research. The purpose of these censuses was to obtain information that was used for trade as well as for political and military purposes. The basic principles have changed little since the time of that particular census which has gone down in history as coinciding with the dawn of the Christian era some 2,000 years ago.

Field research takes many different forms and can be used equally as well to obtain information about either industrial purchasers or domestic consumers. It may be carried out for an individual company or, on a syndicated basis, for a group of companies who subscribe to its cost and share its information. It is also carried out for professional institutes, trade associations, government departments and other organizations.

Similarly, it may be carried out as a single operation to obtain certain information, or it may be a continuing operation to reveal trends and changes that occur.

The information is obtained either by observation or by interrogation. Observational studies in the field are comparatively simple to arrange but only a limited amount of information can be obtained in this way. Nevertheless, it is not always realized how much can be discovered about the behaviour and attitudes of purchasers by watching their actions and listening to their conversation while their buying decisions are being made. An intelligent observer stationed at the point of sale can often detect reactions of which the purchasers themselves are not consciously aware and can provide valuable information about unexpected factors that may be influencing a buying decision. Simple observational studies can also be used to obtain certain quantitative information, such as the number and type of people who pass a particular site at various times throughout the day.

In interrogational research, some form of questionnaire is usually employed. The questionnaire may be sent through the post or the questions may be asked over the telephone or at a personal interview. A postal questionnaire has the advantage that the research is cheaper to carry out and that it is more convenient for the respondents who can answer the questions at their leisure. However, the response ratio is likely to be low unless the research is concerned with some subject in which the respondents themselves are interested and would like to know the findings. A low response ratio is not, in itself, a serious disadvantage as this can be overcome by sending out a much greater number of questionnaires than the number of responses necessary to obtain reliable information. However, there is a danger that the responses that are received may not constitute a representative sample. Some people are prepared to take the trouble to answer and return a questionnaire, others are not. The type of people who do not reply may represent an important segment of the market whose answers might have been different. For this reason, caution has to be exercised in drawing conclusions from the answers received. Another disadvantage of the postal questionnaire is that it does not provide the opportunity that is given by a skilled personal interviewer for observation of the respondent's reactions in order to judge the reliability of answers given. Nevertheless, there are many situations in which a postal questionnaire can be safely employed to provide reliable information.

The telephone can sometimes be used successfully to obtain information about industrial purchasers. Usually, a large number of calls have to be made and very careful preliminary planning is necessary. The required information has to be converted into the form of questions which the respondent is likely to be able to answer accurately on the telephone, from memory, without reference to records or other information. Reliable information cannot be obtained if there is any resentment to the telephone call on the part of the respondent. This is avoided if the approach is properly planned and is conducted by a skilled researcher.

In industrial research, postal and telephoned questionnaires are sometimes used to supplement personal interviews that have been carried out with a smaller number of the more important purchasers. This extends the size of the sample and enables the information from the personal interviews to be confirmed or amended.

The personal interviews that are used in field research take several different forms. They extend from the outdoor questioning of passers-by to the meeting that has been arranged by prior appointment with a buyer or senior executive of a large organization. In industrial research, the interviewer must be of the same status as the respondent so that they can talk on equal terms. He has to have an adequate knowledge to be able to discuss the purpose of the project and any product technicalities that may be involved. This is not so important in consumer research where personality and intelligence are the principal requirements.

Certain kinds of information can, of course, be obtained by the company's own salesmen. However, for most research operations, the relations at the interview have to be very different from those that exist between a buyer and a salesman. We all subconsciously react quite differently to a situation in which we suspect that we might be expected to buy something. On many projects, if unbiased and unprejudiced information is to be obtained from the respondent, it is preferable that the interviewer should not be associated in the respondent's mind with any one particular supplier. This, of course, presents no difficulty if an outside market research organization is used.

SAMPLING

In any market research operation, the people about whom information is to be obtained must be defined. It is, of course, usually unnecessary to interrogate each one of these people individually. A suitable sample is selected that will provide the required information with a sufficient degree of accuracy for the purpose for which it will be used. Great care has to be taken to ensure that the constitution of the sample is exactly the same as the constitution of the whole.

The industrial manager need not be concerned with mathematical procedures for determining the size of the sample that is necessary to obtain a given degree of accuracy. However, the size of the sample that has been used for some particular piece of research may sometimes appear to be very small in relation to the size of the whole and this may cause him to have doubts about the validity of the information. It should therefore be understood that, in sampling, the number in the sample is not governed by the number in the whole. This can be illustrated by assuming that a total population is made up of many different groups of people in such a way that the characteristics of all the people in each group are the same. There are, of course, likely to be considerable differences in the number of people in each group and some may be extremely small. Since the characteristics of the people in any one of these hypothetical groups are identical, all the people in that group would give the same answer to a question that was put to them. Thus, in reply to a particular question, all the people in some of the groups might answer 'Yes' and all the people in the other groups would answer 'No'. A sample is selected in such a way that the proportion of people in each group in the sample is the same as in the total population. (See Figure 8.1.)

When the question is put to this sample and 40 per cent of them give a 'Yes' answer, it follows that 40 per cent of the total population would give the same answer. If the sample has been correctly selected, it would make no difference to the results whether the total population consisted of one million people or fifty million. The only requirement is that the proportion of each group in the sample must be the same as in the

MARKETING AND HIGHER MANAGEMENT

Fig. 8.1

whole. The sample must be large enough to ensure that this is achieved with the required degree of accuracy and *it is this alone that governs its size*.

In practice, most of the information that is required about domestic consumers can be obtained from samples of less than 5,000 people. There are some research operations in which an extremely small sample can be used with complete safety. It is, of course, essential to ensure that homogeneity is achieved *in relation to the particular information that is sought*. For instance, in a political survey, increasing the size of the sample by a further 1,000 people would reduce its accuracy if those people all happened to be manual workers. A large sample could, therefore, be less accurate than a small one.

QUESTIONNAIRES

A previously prepared questionnaire is necessary in almost all forms of field research. The responses may be entered either by the interviewer or by the respondent, as in a postal questionnaire. The design of the questionnaire is usually the most important part of the entire operation and the validity of the information that is obtained depends very largely upon the skill of its designer.

MARKET RESEARCH

On the surface, the preparation of a list of questions to obtain certain information may seem to be a comparatively simple undertaking. However, a questionnaire prepared on this assumption is unlikely to produce reliable information. Apart from the fact that it cannot be assumed that every respondent is going to answer every question correctly or honestly, some of the more elementary mistakes that can be made are as follows:

An ambiguous question may be asked that cannot be understood by the respondent or to which he gives an entirely different answer from that which was intended. An unusually bad example is taken from a postal questionnaire that was sent to industrial buyers by a company producing electric welding equipment. Its purpose was to obtain information about the market for welding electrodes and one of the questions asked was 'How do you buy your electrodes?' . . . The writer of the question obviously knew the kind of answer he intended, but the respondent does not know whether he should reply that he buys them packed in cardboard cartons, that he buys them from a local merchant, or that he buys them by the gross. Each of these answers would be an equally correct reply to the question. However, in this example, the mistake would have become obvious from the replies. The greatest danger is in asking an ambiguous question where it is not apparent from the respondent's answer that he has misunderstood the intention. In this case, the answer given will be accepted and used although it is quite incorrect.

Another common mistake is to ask an indecisive question. As far as possible, each piece of information that is sought has to be converted into a question, or series of questions, that can be answered only by a 'yes' or a 'no'. For example, a respondent should not be left to express an opinion in his own words, but must be given a number of different opinions and asked to say with which of these he agrees. The straightforward positive or negative reply not only ensures a much more reliable answer from the respondent but, without it, it may be difficult to analyse the replies and collate the information from a large number of questionnaires.

A third mistake arises from failure to consider whether the majority of respondents would, in fact, be able to give an *accurate* answer to the question when it was put to them at a personal interview or over the telephone. (Or, in a postal questionnaire, whether the accurate answer could be given without going to a certain amount of trouble.) This is a particularly dangerous mistake for two reasons. First, the respondent will be irritated if he is asked questions to some of which he does not know the answers and an irritated respondent is an unreliable respondent. The second and more important reason is that his answer may be a guess, or that he may give an unconsidered reply, rather than saying that he does not know. In these cases, the information provided by the replies will be of little value and may lead to entirely erroneous conclusions being drawn from the research.

However, even if these more elementary mistakes are avoided, it still cannot be assumed that every respondent is going to give a true and reliable answer to every question asked. To allow for this, a skilled researcher takes various precautions. First, he endeavours to convert the information that is sought into the form and type of questions to which a respondent will *want* to give a correct answer rather than an incorrect or misleading answer. Secondly, he takes it for granted that some proportion of the replies that are received will be incorrect or inaccurate. Steps are always taken, therefore, in any properly designed field research operation to detect the unreliable answers that are received. For example, check questions are often included which are designed in such a way that the answer given by the respondent to a check question provides a guide to the reliability of the answers given by that respondent to one or more of the other questions. Check questions are also often included to check that the respondents constitute a fully representative sample of the total. Finally, when the completed questionnaires are received, the overall pattern of the answers given to the various questions is analysed. Any divergencies from this pattern in the replies of any of the respondents are carefully examined. This examination may lead to the answers given by some of those respondents being completely disregarded as being of doubtful reliability. Care has, of course, to be taken to ensure that this action does not affect the homogeneity of the sample, and some of the satisfactory respondents may also have to be discarded in order to preserve the balance.

The preparation of a questionnaire is not, therefore, something to be undertaken lightly, even for the simplest field research operations.

Considerable skill and care is necessary if reliable information is to be obtained.

CONSUMER PANELS

In appropriate situations, information is often obtained by setting up a panel of people who constitute a fully representative sample of the users or consumers of the product. Changes in the overall demand and in the share being obtained by individual companies can be kept under continuing review by obtaining periodic information from the members of the panel about their purchases. Housewives' Panels and Farmers' Panels are typical examples.

Once the panel has been set up, it can also be used as a quick and economic way of obtaining *ad hoc* information. For example, the members of the panel may be asked to select which they prefer out of three or four products that have been sent to them in plain cartons that are unmarked except for an identifying letter or number. The particular advantage of speed and economy results from the fact that a representative sample is already in existence and the preliminary stages of a normal field research operation are therefore unnecessary.

The establishment of the panel is usually carried out by an independent organization and the cost is shared by a number of companies who subscribe to the service.

DISTRIBUTION RESEARCH AND RETAIL AUDITS

A procedure that is similar in principle to the above is commonly used for obtaining information about the movement of consumer goods from retail outlets to consumers. This information is particularly important in view of the time lag which exists through the normal channels of distribution. It may be weeks or months before a change in the demand for a company's products is reflected in the orders received at the factory. Moreover, when the change in these orders does eventually occur, its size is likely to be magnified. For example, a 5 per cent decline in the purchases made by consumers may have been going on for many weeks although distributors have still been placing their normal monthly orders. However, because of the decline, wholesalers' and retailers' stocks will have been slowly rising. When they become aware of this, they may reduce their next order by as much as 50 per cent and it may be several months before the manufacturer is able to gauge the true extent of the decline. Exactly the same problems will, of course, arise if sales are increasing.

Distribution research is normally carried out by an independent organization for companies who subscribe to the service. In its most common form, a representative sample of retail outlets is selected. The type, size and regional location of the retail outlets in the sample is, of course, in exactly the same proportion as in the total market. These outlets are visited at regular intervals by 'auditors' who carry out a complete stocktaking of all brands of the particular types of products with which the research is concerned.

These 'auditors' also examine invoices and record the quantities that have been received since their previous visit. From this information, the volume of sales of each brand can be determined.

Subscribers are therefore kept informed about the size and changes in the share of the market being secured by each of their competitors as well as by themselves. Regional variations are also revealed. This form of field research is usually referred to as a 'Retail Audit'. It is used by most of the larger manufacturers of consumer goods for the mass market.

Similar services are also available in Britain for household durable products. However, in this case, the sample consists of households and not retail outlets. These households are regularly visited by 'auditors' and an inventory is maintained of the contents of each room in each household in the sample. Any additions to the inventories indicate the type, make and quantity of household articles that are being purchased. The only difference between this procedure and the use of a Householder's Panel is that the provision of the information is not left to the members of the panel but is obtained from inspection. It inevitably costs more than the use of a panel but it could be argued that the information may be more reliable.

MOTIVATION RESEARCH

In answering questions in a questionnaire, respondents can, of course, only provide information which is known to them, or which they think is known to them and believe to be true. However, as has been pointed out elsewhere, a purchaser is not always *consciously* aware of some of the things that may be influencing his or her buying decision or, in some cases, even the real reason why the purchase is being made. This information could not, therefore, be obtained merely by asking a direct question. For example, if smokers were asked why they chose one brand of cigarettes rather than another of the same type, the answers from some respondents would be useless and from others would be no more than guesses and, therefore, of no practical value.

However, by framing *indirect* questions which the respondent can readily answer without guessing, it is often possible to obtain information about these subconscious motives. Considerable skill is, of course, required in designing the questions and some knowledge of psychology is usually necessary. In the more straightforward cases, these questions can be asked in the ordinary way at a normal personal interview. In other cases, it may be necessary to observe the respondent's reactions to the questions and the interview has to be conducted by a trained psychologist. These interviews are, of course, much longer and probe in much greater depth than in the normal type of interview used in field research. However, a smaller sample is usually sufficient and therefore fewer interviews have to be carried out.

There are, of course, many products for which the more advanced forms of motivation research are quite unnecessary. At present, such sophisticated techniques only become economically practicable in those cases where it is the unknown subconscious motives that play the major part in influencing a buying decision. However, there are few industrial or domestic products where some simple form of motivation research cannot be used to advantage. It may reveal some quite unsuspected factor that is having an effect on purchasers' decisions. Because of the vital importance of this information to successful marketing, there can be little doubt that in the not very distant future there will be a considerable extension in the use that is made of motivation research by industry as a whole.

SUMMARY

An intimate knowledge of the market is an essential prerequisite to successful marketing. However, it is a knowledge that must be based on facts and not on intuitive guesses or personal opinions. Obtaining adequate information is just as essential and just as economically practicable for the small business as it is for the large industrial organization.

Much of the information can usually be obtained from Desk Research. The cost of any Field Research that is necessary is generally very small in relation to the value of the sales turnover that is involved. However, care has to be taken to ensure that the research is carried out correctly if reliable information is to be obtained. Incorrect information may cause more damage than no information at all.

When using market research, it is important that its purpose and limitations should be understood. It can be used to obtain factual information about what is happening in the market at present and what has happened in the past. It will not, on its own, provide any reliable information about what is going to happen in the future. Mistakes have sometimes been made in trying to use it for this purpose. What Mrs Brown and Mrs Jones bought today and what they bought last week are matters of ascertainable fact. What they are going to buy next week is not factual information and, if they were asked what they were going to buy, no reliance whatever could be placed on their answers. Similarly, the opinions that they hold today are not necessarily the opinions they will hold tomorrow.

It is the function of the market forecaster to try and predict what is going to happen in the future. However, in order to make his predictions, he must, among other things, have reliable information supplied by market research about what has happened in the past. The two functions should not be confused: market research and market forecasting should always be regarded as quite separate.

Chapter 9

Market Forecasting

In the literature of marketing there seems to be no universally recognized distinction between Market Forecasting and Sales Forecasting. It might be logical to assume that a market forecast is a prediction of what is going to happen to the total demand in a particular market and that a sales forecast is a prediction of a company's own sales. In practice, this distinction between the two titles is rarely made and both terms are freely used to cover all forecasting activities.

However, regardless of whether these two aspects of forecasting are given different titles, the distinction between them is important in preparing the forecast. There are certain kinds of change, such as a change in purchase tax, that will affect the total demand for a product; there are other kinds of change, such as some activity of a competitor, that may make no difference to the total demand but will affect the share of that demand that is obtained by the company. Confusion can arise and mistakes can occur if this distinction is not remembered both in making and in using a forecast.

In an established market, the size of the demand for a product next year will be the same as the size of the demand for that product this year unless something happens to cause it to change. Forecasting, therefore, depends fundamentally on a study of the likely incidence and effect of *changes* in market conditions.

The changes that can alter the size of the demand for a particular product can be grouped into three broad categories:

a. A change in the number of potential users.

b. A change in the financial ability of potential users to purchase the product.

c. A change in the needs and desires of potential users.

A change in the *share* of the demand that is secured by a particular company will be caused either by action taken by the company itself or by action taken by its competitors.

Some of the changes may be easily foreseen while others may be quite unpredictable. For example, a change in the number of potential users rarely occurs suddenly or unexpectedly, but is more likely to follow a predictable trend. A change in the general economic climate can usually be foreseen, but it may be impossible to predict accurately a change in taxation that may affect the demand for the product. Some of the changes in users' needs follow recognizable trends. For example, the demand for rivets is being steadily superseded by the use of welding; but other needs may be influenced by factors that are entirely unpredictable, such as the difference between a mild and cold winter. Similarly, a change in the share of the demand may be due to some action of a competitor that it would have been quite impossible to foresee. However, a skilled forecaster, like a skilled chess player, can often predict the likely moves of an opponent.

FORECASTING PROCEDURES

The methods used in forecasting range from little more than intelligent guesses based on experience, to highly sophisticated mathematical procedures. As with so much else in marketing, the situation that confronts the forecaster differs very widely from one industry to another.

The more elaborate procedures that have to be used in some industries are quite unnecessary in others. For example, some industries have a comparatively stable market in which, apart from normal seasonal variations, only small changes occur from one year to another. In these situations, forecasting is not only relatively simple but it is also very much less important to the company than it is in those industries where large changes can occur and where the company's profits are governed to no small extent by the accuracy with which it has been able to forecast the demand. In such industries, forecasting becomes an important activity. The large changes make precise forecasting more difficult but, because of the effect on profits, every possible step has to be taken to reduce the margin of error.

The most suitable procedure has to be selected for the particular conditions. The following is a brief description of the more common methods which are used either on their own or in some suitable combination.

Field Surveys of Buyers' Intentions

It has been said that forecasting is 'the art of anticipating what buyers are likely to do under a given set of conditions'.

It might appear from this that the most reliable way of making a forecast is to obtain the information from the buyers themselves by carrying out a survey of their buying intentions. In practice, this has certain limitations. The buyer can only say what he or she would do 'under a given set of conditions'. Therefore, it is first necessary to predicate the conditions. Moreover, it is not every buyer who is prepared to disclose what his intentions would be under those particular conditions.

However, even if correct intentions can be obtained, it is necessary to consider what reliance can be placed on the information. What a buyer *intends* to do and what he or she actually does when it comes to making a buying decision may be entirely different. For instance, when considering the purchase of products for the home, the stated future intentions of buyers are often expressions of wishful thinking without due regard to practicality or financial ability to make the purchase. The real decision may not be made until it comes to the moment of choosing between, say, a continental holiday or new furniture for the living-room. Nevertheless, there has been some evidence in the United States to show that, if a large enough sample of householders is selected, the errors tend to balance out and the information has some value as a guide to trends in the overall demand for domestic products during the next six or twelve months. Little reliance can be placed on a buyer's expressed intentions with regard to choice of make or brand.

Surveys of buyers' intentions are, however, sometimes used in the marketing of industrial equipment and can provide useful information. For instance, information can be directly or indirectly obtained about the intended capital expenditure in various industries, about projected new construction or about new equipment that will be required in replacement and expansion programmes. It may also be possible to obtain information from the buyers about likely changes in the using industry that might otherwise be unknown to the forecaster.

A knowledge of the buying intentions of leading distributors may also be useful in forecasting the demand for certain products that are not sold directly to the user.

Ordinary market research procedures are used in carrying out a survey of buyers' intentions (see Chapter 8, Field Research). For reasons of economy, the survey is sometimes combined with a questionnaire seeking other kinds of information. Personal interviews are usually more reliable although they may be confined to the larger industrial buyers or distributors and supplemented by postal or telephoned questionnaires.

The value and reliability of this method of forecasting depends upon the extent to which the buyers themselves have clear and planned intentions for their purchases and are prepared to disclose those intentions. In practice, its use is mainly confined to industrial products where advanced planning is required on the part of the user and to new products where there is no previous data on which a forecast can be based.

Specialists' Opinions

A practice that is more common in the United States than in Britain is regularly to obtain information and advice from external specialists who have expert knowledge of some environmental condition that can affect the demand for the company's products. These include leading economists, bankers, parliamentarians and experts in certain markets or fields of technology. They are usually paid a retaining fee for their services.

A more common form of this method is to subscribe to and use the periodic social, economic and business forecasts that are prepared by various bodies such as the Economist Intelligence Unit and other research organizations. Background information of this kind is extremely useful to the forecaster in many industries.

Trend Projection

By far the most common method of forecasting is to use what has happened in the past as a guide to what is likely to happen in the future.

In its simplest form, this consists of no more than plotting the monthly sales for the last few years on a graph and extending the line forward to the future. However, a sales graph is usually an irregular line owing to fluctuations in sales from month to month. It is therefore necessary to determine the mean sales trend over the past few years.

A seasonal fluctuation in sales occurs to a greater or less extent with almost any product in response to variations in demand throughout the year. This is the first and often the most important fluctuation that has to be removed in order to establish the mean sales trend. The most common way of making this adjustment is to use 'Moving Annual Totals' for plotting the sales graph. A monthly moving annual total (M.A.T.) is simply the total sales for the preceeding twelve months. This is illustrated in the following example which shows a monthly tonnage sold over two years converted into moving annual totals for the last twelve months:

	YEAR A	YEAR B	
	Tons per Month	Tons per Month	M.A.T.
Jan.	129	122	1787
Feb.	128	129	1788
March	154	152	1786
April	172	181	1795
May	183	197	1809
June	172	178	1815
July	156	162	1821
Aug.	110	108	1819
Sept.	143	156	1832
Oct.	164	167	1835
Nov.	161	163	1837
Dec.	122	120	1835

It will be seen that the individual monthly sales have varied considerably and do not provide a clear picture of what is happening. The use of moving annual totals in Year B has eliminated the effect of seasonal variations and reveals the sales trend very much more clearly.

This or some other method of removing the effect of seasonal fluctuations provides a mean sales trend which is sufficiently accurate as a basis for forecasting in many situations. However, it takes no account of periodic or other variations that do not regularly recur. To cater for these, various mathematical procedures have been developed for analyzing the shape of the sales curve and determining a mean trend that is likely to continue.

In practice, these procedures are only used when an accurate analysis of a fluctuating trend can be relied upon, by itself, to provide a useful guide to the future.

A forecast that is based solely on some forward projection of a past trend assumes that what has happened in the past is going to continue in the future. If the market has been relatively stable and there has been little fluctuation from the mean trend for several years, this may be a reasonable basis for making a short-term forecast. For example, such direct projection can sometimes be used with certain basic raw materials. However, there are many products for which it would be unsafe to make this assumption and it could never be used as a basis for long-range forecasting.

The next step, therefore, is to examine the past trend over several years and to determine the causes of each of the changes that have occurred. As pointed out in the introduction to this chapter, the causes of a change in demand can be grouped into certain broad categories and it is this analysis of the past trend that provides the basis for the future projection. When the factors that have caused a change have been determined, consideration is given to whether and when any of these factors are likely to occur again in the future.

Even the most detailed examination of a past trend will not, however, reveal some new factor that may arise which has not previously occurred. For example, there was for many years a very large and expanding demand in Britain for woman's fully fashioned nylon stockings. The demand followed a trend that was accurately predictable from considerations of economic conditions and changes in the age structure and purchasing power of the population. Nevertheless, quite suddenly, the demand began to fall and was replaced by a demand for seamless stockings – these had previously been in existence for many years with a declining demand at the bottom end of the price range.

In little more than a year, the vast national sales of fully fashioned stockings dropped away and a considerable amount of costly machinery and highly skilled labour became redundant. No examination of what had happened in the past could have predicted this large and sudden decline.

This and many similar examples illustrate the danger of placing too much reliance on complex mathematical or computerized procedures for forecasting sales. A detailed analysis of what has happened in the past provides the forecaster with valuable information about the way in which a company's sales are affected by changes in market conditions. It will reveal, for example, the effect on sales of a change in purchase tax or, more generally, the extent to which the sales of certain products are influenced by changes in economic or other conditions. But, in preparing the forecast from this information, the forecaster has to consider:

a. Whether the causes that are bringing about a current upward or downward trend will continue.

b. Whether and when some change that has occurred in the past will occur again in the future.

c. Whether some new change may occur in the future that has not previously occurred in the past.

d. Whether some action may be taken by competitors that will affect the company's share of the demand.

An analysis of past events is therefore an important part of most forecasting operations but it can rarely be relied upon, by itself, to give an accurate prediction of future sales.

Market Testing
When a new product is launched on the market there is, of course, no previous information directly related to that product that can be used for forecasting sales. It may be possible to make a reasonably accurate estimate of the *potential* demand (see Chapter 1, page 17) but this is likely to be many times greater than the volume of sales that will be obtained initially. A somewhat similar situation arises when an existing product is launched in a new market.

Under these conditions it may be necessary to carry out a preliminary market test in order to be able to make a reliable sales forecast. The normal procedure in carrying out these tests is to market the product to a small representative sample of purchasers before launching nationally. With a domestic product, a suitable test area is selected in which the constitution of the population is approximately the same as in the country as a whole. Any advertising that will eventually be used to promote the product must, of course, be proportionately represented in the test area if meaningful information is to be obtained. For this reason, one or other of the smaller commercial television areas is commonly used in Britain for carrying out these tests.

Similar tests are also used to forecast the effect on sales of a contemplated change in the method of marketing. For example, a company may be proposing to spend £100,000 on promoting the sales of an existing product that has not previously been nationally advertised. It is likely to be quite impossible to predict the effect that this will have on sales without trying it out in practice. A small test marketing operation will show whether or not the proposal is justified before the company has committed itself to considerable advertising expenditure. Such market tests, carried out under carefully controlled conditions, are being used increasingly for predicting the effect on sales of a change in the product or in the way in which it is promoted.

However, market tests will only provide information that relates to the immediate future. They are of no value in long-range forecasting.

USING SALES FORECASTS

When a company is preparing financial budgets for control purposes, it is sometimes assumed, perhaps only subconsciously, that it should somehow always be possible to make a precise forecast of the volume of sales that will be obtained by the company during the next twelve months. Yet, in practice, a sales forecast can never be more than a prediction that is based on certain assumptions which may or may not prove to be correct.

It has been pointed out that some of the changes that can affect a company's sales are more easily predictable than others and that some changes can occur which are entirely unpredictable. Therefore, at best, the forecaster can only assume an average situation from the most reliable information available and some margin of error is inevitable in *every* sales forecast.

However, in most situations the forecaster should be able to make a reliable estimate of the extent of this margin provided no major and entirely unpredictable change occurs. With some products, the margin may be very small, whereas with others it may have to be quite substantial. Ideally, therefore, a sales forecast should never be given as a single absolute figure, but rather as functioning within certain limits (expressed as a plus or minus percentage). If this procedure was more widely adopted there would be much less misunderstanding and misuse of sales forecasts by production and financial managers.

Whether or not the margin is stated, the fact that some margin inevitably exists should always be taken into account by those who use the sales forecasts. Production, stocking and financial control procedures should be planned to be sufficiently flexible to provide an adequate margin for the company's particular marketing situation and this is particularly important in relation to budgetary control. In those situations where the company has a very stable market, it may be possible to produce a forecast with an extremely small margin of error with the result that the revenue, expenditure and profit can be precisely controlled to a pre-arranged plan. This cannot be done successfully for products that have a more fluid market where the control must be correspondingly more flexible.

It is possible to adhere strictly to a budgeted sales revenue, even if the demand cannot be closely predicted, by fixing the budgeted revenue at or below the lower limit of the margin of error in the forecast and restricting the output to that level. In other words, the budget and output are planned on a minimum forecast that can be achieved with reasonable certainty and which is, therefore, below the mean expectancy of the demand. Full responsibility can then be given to the sales department for ensuring that the budgeted revenue is maintained. Some companies have done this and have obtained perfect budgetary control, although they may not always have realized that they were achieving it in this way.

However, there are dangers in adopting this policy in a competitive market, particularly in those situations where the margin of error in a forecast must inevitably be wide and in which, as a result, the company will normally be operating appreciably below the maximum potential of its products. A company that is not exploiting the demand for its products to the full is missing opportunities, and it may be indirectly handing business to its competitors and helping them to expand. Sometimes, by failing to meet the full demand that has arisen, the company may be causing ill-will among its customers through delays in delivery. The ability to adhere strictly to a rigid budget of expenditure and obtain a planned profit may, therefore, be a short-term benefit that will eventually be lost as more and more business passes to competitors who are endeavouring to secure every profitable sale that they can.

If a company is fully to exploit its market and make the most of its opportunities it has to be flexible in every aspect of its activities. Without a forecast, any planning would be impossible. But those who use the forecast should always recognize and understand its inevitable limitations.

Chapter 10

Product Planning

The types and varieties of products that a company should market in order to make the most effective use of its resources are normally subjects for policy decisions at top management level. This has already been discussed under Product Policy in Part 1 (Chapter 4).

This chapter is concerned with the routine planning operations for ensuring that the selected products are designed and presented in the most suitable way to win favourable buying decisions. This requires complete collaboration between the design and marketing functions.

FITNESS FOR PURPOSE

In Chapter 2, the fitness of the product for the buyer's purpose was indicated as the first of the ten basic factors that influence a prospective purchaser's buying decision. It was pointed out that, for this reason, it is important that the precise purpose for which a product is being bought by the purchaser should be clearly understood. In many cases this is self-evident, although there are some instances in which even the buyers themselves would find it difficult to define the exact reason for their purchase. It was also pointed out that the purpose for which the product is purchased by the buyer is not always the same as the purpose for which it will be used by the user. Obvious examples are seen in articles like electric shavers and the more expensive fountain pens, many of which are bought for the purpose of presenting them as gifts. This has to be taken into account in the design and packaging of these articles even though the eventual user may quickly discard the attractive presentation cases in which they are sold.

Every product specification should, therefore, start with a definition of the precise purpose or purposes for which the product will be purchased and used. A procedure should be instituted for keeping each of the existing products under regular review as to its continuing fitness for the buyer's purpose in comparison with the similar products of competitors.

PRODUCT DESIGN

The design and appearance of the product, or its packaging, is often one of the most important factors in influencing a buying decision. For this reason, product design may have to be one of the principal aspects of a company's marketing operations. There have been many instances where time and money spent on trying to influence a buying decision through promotional and selling activities would have been very much more effective if it had been devoted to altering the product's design or appearance instead.

In this particular context, design is not something that should be viewed in any abstract or aesthetic sense. The prospective purchaser's buying decision is influenced solely by his own personal opinion of the product's design and appearance. It is with *this* opinion that the marketing aspect of design is concerned.

'GOOD DESIGN' IS DESIGN THAT SECURES CONTINUING SALES FROM THE PARTICULAR PURCHASERS FOR WHOM THE PRODUCT IS INTENDED.

In the design of any product there are certain specific features which, to a greater or lesser extent, will influence the buyer's decision. The first step in the marketing examination of an individual product is to analyse and specify the particular influencing features in that product. For instance, when a buyer is choosing between alternative television receivers within a given price range, his or her choice may be influenced by such things as:

The size of the screen
The quality of the picture in comparison with other models
The size of the cabinet
The shape and proportions of the cabinet
The veneer and colour of the cabinet
The frontal appearance of the receiver
The position and lay-out of the controls

The shape of the control knobs
The type of channel-change control
The general standard of finish, etc.

Based on an analysis of this type, the suitability of the company's own product in comparison with competitors' products can be examined for each of the influencing features. This will show the particular strengths and weaknesses in the design of the company's product. The analysis is concerned only with the features that may influence a customer's decision and these are not necessarily the same as those that govern the product's performance. For example, to the engineer, the freezing mechanism is the most important feature in the basic design of a domestic refrigerator whilst the rest is merely a food storing cabinet in which this mechanism is installed. The majority of purchasers, however, give little or no thought to the freezing mechanism. It is something that they take for granted and its design is unlikely to play any immediate part in influencing their choice between one model and another.

An analysis of the influencing features must also consider that the purchasers themselves are not always consciously aware of some of the things that may be affecting their buying decisions. For instance, when choosing a refrigerator, the buyer will open and close the doors of the various models on display. Although the buyer may not realize it, the sound and action of the door-latch mechanism may be influencing the choice. A model with a poor mechanism is likely to produce an adverse reaction. These subconscious influencing features occur in many products: they include the design of the label on a bottle as well as the colour of the paint or the shape of the control levers on a machine tool.

Attention to these important details is the essence of successful marketing and gives a company an edge over its competitors. As with so much else in marketing, this requires an intimate knowledge of the whims, fancies and opinions of the purchasers for whom the product is intended. In making the product examination, the investigator and the designer have to be extremely careful not to be prejudiced by their own opinions, or those of their colleagues, as to what constitutes good design in the product. This is a common mistake that has occurred in many products ranging from the design of a dust-cover on a novel to the interior lay-out of a car.

For the majority of products this examination of the influencing features does not require any very elaborate or extensive research – see the case example of the paint-brush manufacturer on page 113. Its significance will depend upon the importance of the part played by the design and appearance of the product in comparison with the other factors which are influencing a buying decision for that product. There are some consumer goods where it is the buyer's subconscious reaction to certain aspects of the design of the product or its pack that plays a major part in influencing the choice of brand – see Chapter 2. In these cases, some form of Motivation Research is likely to be necessary in order to produce the most suitable design.

The market-oriented company will have some organized procedure for ensuring that this analysis and examination of the influencing features is effectively carried out. The form of this procedure must inevitably vary widely depending on the nature of the product and the size of the company. However, in every case, it has to be a continuous procedure in which each of the company's products is regularly reviewed. The fact that a product is right for the market today is no guarantee that it will continue to be right for the market tomorrow. Sooner or later the demand for every product in its existing form must begin to decline. It was shown in Chapter 4 that an alteration to the product that is made only when it is eventually forced on the company by declining sales is always an alteration that is made too late. As a broad guide, every product should be reviewed at least once a year even if only to make sure that an alteration to some aspect of its design is not yet necessary. (See the Life Cycle of a Product on page 95.)

QUALITY AND RELIABILITY

There have been many instances where Market Research has shown that the personal opinions of a company's customers about the quality or reliability of its products were playing a very much greater part in affecting their buying decisions than had previously been supposed. However, some industries are affected to a greater extent than others and the relative significance of this factor must always be examined in preparing a company's product plans – see Chapter 5.

This consideration is particularly important in those cases where the degree of quality or reliability in an article is related to its production

PRODUCT PLANNING

costs and the price at which it must be sold. Under these conditions, the right balance must be obtained and it is sometimes too readily assumed that price is more important than quality or reliability. For example, in the face of rising costs, some products have been redesigned in order to keep them within approximately the same price range. This may have been achieved by such things as reducing the thickness or quality of materials used in their production or other similar economies that result in a reduction in the standard of reliability. Breakdowns or failures become more frequent than in the earlier models which they replaced.

The problem of obtaining the right balance between price and reliability is complicated by the fact that the effect on sales of a change in selling price is immediate whereas the effect of a change in reliability cannot be fully determined until a considerable time after it has occurred. For instance, a reduction in selling price that is accompanied by a reduction in reliability may initially produce an increase in sales. The product is still being purchased on the company's established reputation for the reliability of its products. It may be many months before the reduced reliability begins to have any effect on sales which may eventually drop to a lower level than those of the previous model. A similar effect occurs in the reverse direction if the reliability and price are increased. A considerable time must always elapse before the full effect of the change becomes apparent.

The situation is sometimes further aggravated by the assumption that sales volume or turnover is the basis on which the balance should be struck between selling price and reliability, the objective being to obtain the balance which will secure the maximum sales revenue. However, it was shown in Chapter 3 (Selling Prices) that the effect of a change in selling price on sales revenue is very different from its effect on profits. A reduction in selling price that increases sales revenue may reduce the profits, an alteration that reduces the sales revenue may increase them. Hence, an increase in selling price that is necessary in order to increase reliability, or to maintain the standard in the face of rising costs, could increase or maintain the profit even though the sales revenue is reduced. Any alteration must, therefore, be based on the product's contribution to fixed costs and profits and not on the sales revenue.

It will be seen that the problem of finding the right balance between selling price and reliability is not one that can be solved easily or quickly. Yet, in practice, it often receives remarkably little attention beyond, perhaps, considering the initial effect on sales. As has been shown, this initial effect can be completely misleading. If a company has a satisfactory reputation for the quality and reliability of its products, the introduction of a cheaper product to a reduced standard of reliability may appear to be extremely successful and profitable for many months after it has been launched. Similarly, new designs are sometimes introduced which enable production costs to be reduced and which appear to be fully acceptable to the market, they may even result in a temporary increase in sales. The 'improved' design is hailed as a success. When, some time later, sales begin to pass to a competitor, the real cause may not even be realised.

In order to determine the most profitable standard to adopt for a particular product, it is first necessary to determine the true extent to which the company's reputation for quality and reliability is affecting the buying decisions of the prospective purchasers *in the segment of the market for which that product is intended.* It has to be remembered that, when a purchaser is choosing between competing products, he has no means of judging whether the particular product he selects is, in fact, going to be reliable when he puts it into use. He will be consciously or subconsciously basing his decision on what he knows from his own experience, from having bought that company's products in the past, or on what he has heard from others about them.

The significance of this factor must be considered in relation to the extent to which the purchaser's decision is also being influenced by the selling price. For instance, in the purchase of a domestic refrigerator, neither price nor reliability is one of the major factors that influence the buyer's choice. However, the majority of purchasers take the reliability of the refrigerator for granted and, of the two, the price is the more important. Sales would probably be lost if the cost of greater reliability had to be reflected by a significant difference in the selling price. The position may be very different with products that, because of their nature, are much more prone to failure than a refrigerator and where a manufacturer can more easily acquire a poor reputation for reliability.

Care may have to be exercised in carrying out the research and interpreting any information obtained from the users themselves. This is an area in which there can be considerable differences in the needs and opinions of different users. It could be said that every purchaser wants

PRODUCT PLANNING

quality and reliability, but that not all of them are prepared to pay for it. Market segmentation may be necessary and, as shown in the paint-brush example (page 113), different standards may be required for different segments of the market.

However, quality and price are not necessarily related. There are many situations in which it would be both unnecessary and unprofitable to raise the selling price in order to cover the cost of providing better quality or greater reliability. If the market investigation has shown that a company's reputation for quality and reliability is a significant factor in influencing a buying decision, then an improvement in this respect may enable the company to obtain a greater share of the market. Therefore, although any additional cost that is incurred will have reduced the contribution per unit, the total number of units sold will be increased and the most profitable selling price for the product may remain unchanged – see the sections on Costs and Selling Prices in Chapter 3. In this sense, the cost of improved quality and reliability can be regarded in the same way as any other promotional and selling cost which has a direct effect on sales volume. With all these costs, the determination of the most profitable expenditure depends on knowing the effect which each is having on the volume of sales obtained. However, it must not be forgotten that, as has been shown, a considerable period of time may elapse before an alteration in the standard of quality or reliability is fully reflected in the share of the demand that is obtained. Initially, any additional cost incurred in improving the standard may have to be regarded as an investment.

There can be few marketing situations in which quality or reliability does not play some part or other in affecting the user's attitude towards a company and its products. Customers can very easily become irritated by receiving goods with even comparatively minor faults that have slipped through inspection. Failures and breakdowns in use are a frequent source of intense annoyance although only a small proportion of the users affected may take the trouble to complain to the manufacturer.

A company's policy towards quality and reliability is not something that can be decided lightly. Considerable research is sometimes necessary and it can be one of the most complex aspects of marketing. Its importance is not confined to products of a mechanical nature, but it applies to almost any article or service. This has been demonstrated in recent years by companies like Marks and Spencer, whose success has been due in no small way to a policy of setting out deliberately to build up a high reputation for quality in relation to selling price in every article that is sold. It is recognized that the inclusion of even one faulty line could affect this image. There are other companies where, through insufficient attention to this important aspect of marketing, a lowering of standards has brought a short-term increase in profits but has been followed by a steady decline in the company's fortunes.

THE PRODUCT MIX

In a range of products, some products are likely to be more profitable to a company than others. Therefore, a change in the product mix may affect the total profit earned by the company. The composition of the product mix is primarily governed by the relative size of the demand for each product. Any alteration in the needs and requirements of the market may, therefore, alter the mix and affect the company's profits – see Chapter 1, The Nature of the Potential Demand.

To a lesser extent, the product mix can also be influenced by the proportion of the total promotional and selling effort that is devoted to each product. By moving the emphasis from one product to another, it may be possible to increase the overall profit. However, careful consideration is always necessary before attempting to do this. The 'most profitable' products are not necessarily those in which there is the greatest difference between unit cost and selling price. Placing the emphasis on these products could merely result in dissipating the selling effort and reducing the overall profit. Reference should be made to the section on the Relative Profitability of Individual Products in Chapter 3, where this aspect of Product Planning is fully discussed.

SUMMARY

In modern industry, considerable attention is given to increasing efficiency in the production, selling and administrative aspects of a business. Nevertheless, no matter how efficient a company may be in these respects, its success must ultimately depend on its products. Over the years, the most successful companies have always been those that have consistently continued to produce the right products at the right

PRODUCT PLANNING

price in the right form for their selected markets. The 'right' products are those that exploit the company's strengths and make the most effective use of its resources – see Chapter 4. The 'right' price is the price which, in the long-term, will provide the maximum contribution to the company's overheads and profits – see Chapter 3. The 'right' form is the design, appearance, quality and reliability that will influence prospective purchasers to buy those products rather than some other equivalent products of a competitor. All of these depend upon an intimate knowledge of the things that are consciously and subconsciously influencing the buying decisions of prospective customers. Effective product planning depends on effective market research and is an integral part of successful marketing.

Chapter 11

Advertising Research

In preparing an overall marketing plan, it is necessary to decide what part, if any, is to be played by advertising and how much should be spent on it. This has already been discussed under Marketing Planning in Chapter 5. For this purpose, it is necessary to be able to make some reliable assessment of the relationship between advertising expenditure and sales volume. The general nature of this relationship is shown in Figure 3.8 on page 74.

Advertising research is basically concerned with examining the effectiveness of advertising expenditure. If a given sum of money is devoted to advertising a particular product in a particular market, there are a number of factors that will govern the effectiveness of that expenditure. Of these, the most important are:

a. The design of the advertisements themselves and their effectiveness in attaining their intended objective. (For objectives, see Chapter 5, page 131.)

b. The selection of the media in which the advertisements are displayed.

c. The time of the year and the frequency at which the advertisements appear.

It was shown in Chapter 5 that, by a process of trial and error, it is comparatively simple to determine the effect of each of these factors when the advertising is being used to achieve a 'direct action' objective. For example, in Mail Order advertising, the replies received from one style of advertisement or from one advertising medium can easily be compared with those received from another by the use of some simple

ADVERTISING RESEARCH

keying procedure. Relative effectiveness can be directly measured by the number of orders received for a given cost. However, some other method must be adopted if the advertising is being used for one of the 'support objectives', such as creating a favourable predisposition to buy the product from a distributor or from the company's own salesmen.

TESTING THE DESIGN OF THE ADVERTISEMENT

Several methods are used for determining the relative effectiveness of different styles and designs of advertisement when this cannot be measured directly by the number of replies or orders received. The more elaborate methods provide the more reliable information but are inevitably more costly to carry out. The greater accuracy is obviously more important for those companies which are spending very large annual sums on advertising and where many thousands of pounds of this expenditure could easily be wasted. Under these conditions, the cost of even the most elaborate research is likely to be small in relation to the advertising expenditure involved. In other situations, much simpler methods may be quite adequate.

A procedure that is often used in this and in many other aspects of marketing is similar in principle to that commonly used in scientific research when probing into the unknown. An hypothesis is postulated and tests are carried out, under carefully controlled conditions, to determine whether or not the hypothesis is correct. Similarly, in Comparative Research, various alternatives are proposed and tests are carried out to determine which of the alternatives is the best. In other words, the research does not set out to find the solution to a problem but merely to discover whether a possible solution is correct, or to discover whether one alternative is better than another. When this technique is applied to Copy Testing in advertising, research will not reveal the ideal design for an advertisement but will show that one design is likely to be more effective than another. This is not only valuable in itself but it also leads to a better understanding of the kinds of design that are best suited for particular situations.

The research is usually carried out by the company's advertising agent. The following are merely brief descriptions to illustrate some of the methods more commonly used.

Copy Theme Testing

Copy Theme testing is also sometimes referred to as Concept testing. Its purpose is to test the basic theme or 'copy platform' to be used in the advertisement. In its simplest form, a specimen card is prepared for each of the alternative themes to be tested. The card usually has an illustration of the product without any reference to a maker's or brand name; the picture is accompanied by a simple statement of the basic idea to be used as the copy theme. The cards are shown to a representative sample of purchasers who are asked quite simple questions such as: 'Which of these do you think you would be most likely to buy?', or 'What is your reason for preferring that one?'

Although the questions may be simple, considerable care is taken to ensure that the answers do, in fact, relate to the theme and not to chance or some other factor. For example, the same basic theme is often expressed in two different ways, half the respondents being shown one presentation and half the other. This ensures that the idea behind the theme is being tested and not merely the particular words that have been used.

Quite small samples are usually adequate for these tests and no very great cost is incurred in carrying them out. However, rather more elaborate and more costly variations of this basic method are sometimes used.

Press Copy Testing

Similar methods to those used for testing the theme are also used for testing the completed design. Alternative advertisements, in the form in which they would appear in the press, are shown to a representative sample of users who are asked questions about them. The same procedures are used for carrying out the tests and similar precautions are taken for ensuring reliability.

Simple tests of this nature do not, of course, do any more than show differences in reaction to different advertisements. They are useful for choosing between alternative designs but they do not reproduce the conditions under which an advertisement would be read or indicate the extent to which, under those conditions, it would subsequently affect the actual buying decisions of potential customers. Other tests must be used for this purpose.

Keyed Replies and 'Hidden Offers'

Reference has been made to the more exact measurement of achievement that can be obtained from the number of replies received from alternative advertisements that have a 'direct action' objective. It is sometimes possible to simulate this situation in other forms of advertising. This is done by including in the alternative advertisements something that will induce the reader to return a coupon or send in a reply, perhaps by offering to supply a free sample or provide further information about the product. Considerable care has, however, to be taken to ensure that the relative number of replies received from each advertisement is measuring effectiveness in relation to the real purpose of the advertisement and not in relation to the offer. For example, if the advertisements are designed in such a way that a free trial offer is a predominant feature, the replies received will provide little indication of the extent to which the design of each advertisement has achieved its true objective of creating a favourable predisposition to buy the product. The offer must be a minor or subordinate feature and is often referred to as a 'hidden offer'; the fact that a reply is received should indicate that the advertisement has created the required impact on the reader.

Split-run Copy Testing

The accuracy of the measurement that is obtained from the number of keyed replies received from alternative designs of advertisement will depend upon the extent to which all other variable factors have been removed. For example, the test would obviously be useless if the alternative designs were displayed in different media. However, even if the same medium is used, it is likely that a different number of replies would be received from *the same* advertisement if it appeared at different times or on different days in the week. For an exact comparison, the two alternative advertisements under test would have to appear simultaneously in the same place in the same medium on the same day, so that half the readers would see one of the advertisements and half the other. This can be achieved with certain newspapers and periodicals that provide a 'split-run' service for advertisers. Each of the two advertisements appear in alternate copies in every bundle coming off the printing presses. There are, however, only a limited number of publishers who have the facilities for providing this service.

With some other publications it is possible to arrange for half the issue to carry one advertisement and half the other. This is often adequate but is not as exact as a split-run, because the copies are not inter-mixed and there may be uneven geographical distribution of the two advertisements. Local differences may be having some effect on differences in the number of replies received from each advertisement.

Test Market Copy Testing

As its name implies, this method consists of mounting two different campaigns in two different test markets, or test areas, and comparing the effect of each on sales in the two areas.

This method of copy testing has certain attractions in that the results are measured in terms of sales actually achieved – the ultimate purpose of the advertisement. However, in practice, it is often far from easy to ensure that all extraneous variables have been eliminated. For instance, if an exact comparison is to be obtained, the proportions of each type of customer in the two areas must be identical. But if the constitution of the two markets is known, it may be possible to make a statistical adjustment for any differences in order to obtain an approximate comparison. The share of the demand that is being obtained in each area before the test is commenced must also be approximately equal.

The advertising media used for the test must obviously have an identical coverage of the potential purchasers in each area. This may be difficult to arrange in the case of press advertising since national media cannot be used for the test; local publications must be used in each area and these may have very different characteristics. For this reason, this method of testing is generally more useful for poster and television advertising. It is particularly well suited to television where two of the commercial television areas can be selected for making comparative tests of two different types of advertisement.

Because of the time lag between consumer purchases and factory sales, it is often necessary when dealing with consumer goods to use retail audits in order to obtain a true comparison of the effect on sales in each of the test areas. (See Retail Audits in Chapter 8.)

Attitude Studies

When an advertisement is not being used to attain a 'direct action' objective, one of the problems that always presents itself is the selection of the most suitable criterion for measuring its effectiveness. The methods so far described have relied either on the simulation of a direct action objective or on the volume of sales obtained. However, although the ultimate purpose of the advertisement may be to increase sales, there are many other factors besides the advertisement that will affect a company's sales. The presence of these other variables may cause a measurement that is based on sales to be quite inaccurate and misleading. For instance, it has been shown in an earlier chapter that, although an advertisement may have been completely successful in attaining its required objective of creating a favourable predisposition to buy the advertised product when the prospective purchaser enters a retail shop, other factors (which have nothing to do with the advertisement) may cause some other product to be selected when the buying decision is made. Alternatively, if a sale is made, it may have been the result of a competitor's advertising, which motivated the purchaser to go to the shop to buy that type of product. Moreover, sales volume is rarely, if ever, static. In a test period, even if there had been no change at all to the advertising, there would almost certainly have been some change in the volume of sales obtained.

The advocates of the use of Attitude Studies for the determination of advertising effectiveness point out that the specific purpose of an advertisement is to generate a more favourable attitude to the product advertised; therefore it is the extent to which the advertisement has changed this attitude that is the true measure of its effectiveness. The objective of these tests is therefore to discover the attitude of users to the product both before and after exposure to the advertisement.

The tests take various forms. In general, they use the sampling and questionnaire techniques of market research. Questionnaires are designed to discover the respondent's 'predisposition to buy'. The more elaborate attitude studies use the psychological approach and depth interviews of Motivation Research.

The important departure in this method, as distinct from some of the previous methods of copy testing that have been described, lies in the fact that these tests are not concerned with the respondents' attitude towards the advertisement but with their attitude towards the product.

Pre-testing Television Commercials

Considerable research has been carried out in recent years on the development of copy-testing methods and on improving their accuracy. Much of this research has been concerned with television advertising, where the cost of preparing the film has to be added to the cost of time on the air. In view of the high costs that are often involved in the use of this medium, it is particularly important that there should be some reliable means of testing the effectiveness of an advertisement before it is put on the air rather than waiting until after it has been seen by viewers – and the cost has been incurred – before trying to discover whether it has been effective.

One of the methods most commonly used is to invite a representative sample of users to attend a private cinema performance. Between the films, various advertisements are screened as in a normal performance, which will include the advertisements under test. Questions are put to the audience before the start and after the end of the performance, which are designed to discover whether and to what extent the trial advertisement has changed their attitude towards the product.

In order to avoid the cost of preparing an expensive film that may be rejected on these tests, a television camera and video tape recorder are sometimes used to produce a mock-up version on tape of the proposed film. This can be produced very cheaply in a small studio using a film projector and suitable scenes from a film library to provide the background. It has the big advantage that a number of different ideas can be tried out at very little cost before embarking on the production of the film.

Although, superficially, these tests with an invited audience may appear to be comparatively simple and elementary, considerable research and carefully designed procedures go into ensuring the validity of the results obtained. In some of these tests, specially designed equipment is used to measure the viewer's subconscious reaction to the advertisement which supplements or replaces the information obtained from the answers to a questionnaire. Much experimental work is still being carried out in this field.

MEDIA SELECTION

The second factor that governs the effectiveness of the money spent on advertising a product is the selection of the media in which the adver-

ADVERTISING RESEARCH

tisements are displayed. The cost of advertising in any particular medium is, of course, broadly related to the number of its readers or to the number of people who will see an advertisement shown in or on that medium. The effectiveness of the expenditure therefore depends upon the proportion of those people who are potential purchasers of the advertised product or who are in a position to influence a buying decision. For example, two companies with quite different products may be advertising in the same medium. In the first company, only 10 per cent of the people who see its advertisement in that medium are potential buyers of its product. The type of product advertised by the second company is regularly purchased by 30 per cent of the readers or viewers, so that much less of its advertising expenditure is being wasted in displaying the advertisement to people who do not buy the product. Some wastage is almost inevitable, but the object of effective media selection is to minimize this wastage.

As with Copy Testing, the selection of the most economic media presents no serious difficulty if the advertisement is being used to attain a 'direct action' objective. For example, in Mail Order advertising, the number of orders obtained per £100 of expenditure in different media can be quickly discovered. However, as before, some other method must be adopted if the advertisement is being used for a supporting objective.

Perhaps the simplest method, although one that is not always practicable, is to simulate a direct action objective as in Copy Testing. An offer of some kind is included in the advertisement and the number of keyed replies received per £100 of expenditure in different media is compared. In this case, it is not so important that the offer should be 'hidden'. The objective is not to test the effectiveness of the copy but to test the effectiveness of the medium in reaching prospective purchasers of the product.

This method is particularly suitable for industrial products where readership information about the appropriate medium is less readily available. An offer can be included to supply a brochure or to provide further information about the product. Not all potential purchasers will, of course, reply. However, the number of replies received from each medium is usually a reliable guide to its *relative* effectiveness. The possible inclusion of Direct Mail as one of the alternative media should not be overlooked in carrying out these tests.

The most commonly adopted method for consumer products is based on the use of Readership Surveys. These provide information about the readers of the various media that are available, or about the audiences of commercial television companies. The Readership Surveys that are regularly carried out for the Institute of Practitioners in Advertising provide a wealth of statistical information about the readers of the majority of newspapers and periodicals published in Great Britain. The total number of readers of each publication is shown and is analysed for such things as sex, age, socio-economic group, marital status, number of children, the ownership of certain products such as cars, lawn-mowers and so on. Geographical and other analyses are also included.

If the potential purchasers of the product have been precisely segmented and defined (see Chapter 5), the Readership Survey will indicate selection of the medium that will reach the greatest number of potential purchasers at the lowest cost. Because of the many variables and the large number of media that might be suitable for a particular product, this can sometimes be a somewhat complex operation and, in these cases, computers are being used increasingly for this purpose.

There is, however, a further and less easily quantifiable factor that has to be taken into account in media selection. This could be loosely defined as the effectiveness of each publication as an advertising medium. A simple calculation will show the advertising cost per thousand readers in each medium. From the readership analysis, this can be converted into a cost per thousand potential purchasers. But the advertising effectiveness of two media may be different even though the cost per thousand potential purchasers is the same. For example, if an advertisement is placed in a daily newspaper, there is only one day during which it is likely to attract the attention of a potential purchaser. If the same advertisement is placed in a household weekly, there are seven days during which that issue will be in the living room and during which its pages will be turned over by the potential purchaser. Therefore, the advertisement stands a very much greater chance of attracting the reader's attention.

Similarly, the majority of readers of newspapers and similar publications do not set out consciously and intentionally to read the advertisements. The advertisement has to attract and divert the reader's attention from the editorial content. However, there are other publications, such as Good Housekeeping and Ideal Home, where many readers will deliberately study the advertising pages; occasionally the magazine may even have been purchased for the primary purpose of examining the advertisements for some particular product that the reader is proposing to buy. Here, again, this factor would not be taken into account in a selection that was based solely on the cost per thousand readers.

There is no simple means of giving a numerical value to this factor in order to rate one publication in relation to another. In fact, within limits, it is quite likely to vary from one product to another. However, most advertising agents, from their experience, are able to place an empirical value on this factor when advising their clients on media selection.

OTHER CONSIDERATIONS

There are many other subordinate factors to be considered in planning an effective advertising campaign. They include such things as the following:

> The size of the advertisement. Is a large advertisement in one issue likely to be more or less effective than two smaller advertisements in two issues at the same cost? (Or, in television, is one 30-second advertisement likely to be more or less effective than two 15-second advertisements?)
>
> Will a more expensive advertisement in colour be proportionately more or less effective than an advertisement in black and white?
>
> Should the advertising be spread uniformly throughout the year or should the same expenditure be concentrated into certain shorter periods? – In general, concentration into shorter periods is likely to have a much greater impact than spreading the same expenditure more thinly throughout the year. There are, however, some exceptions.
>
> If there are seasonal fluctuations in the demand, what is the most effective time of the year for advertising? – The results obtained per £ of advertising will always be higher during a period when demand is rising than when it is declining. However, this approach inevitably magnifies the peaks in the sales curve, and it may sometimes be more economic to use the advertising expenditure less effectively during a decline in order to smooth out the peaks and troughs.

MARKETING AND HIGHER MANAGEMENT

SUMMARY

There are some companies that give a minute and critical examination to every item of their costs with the noticeable exception of their advertising expenditure which receives much less careful consideration. This may be because, unlike the other items, the board or the company's accountant has no way of knowing, even approximately, how much should be spent or whether the money is being spent effectively. The expenditure is sometimes treated almost as if it were a fixed overhead that has to be carried or is even regarded as some kind of luxury that can be reduced or dispensed with when profits start to fall. It is only true, however, that every pound spent on advertising is being completely wasted unless it is *contributing* to the company's profits by increasing sales. Advertising used correctly can be an extremely effective and profitable tool of marketing. However, it is possible that there may be some truth in the frequent statement that industry as a whole wastes more money on advertising than on any other activity. It is not *how much* is spent, but *how* it is spent that is the primary cause of this wastage.

A company has a right to expect and will receive advice from an advertising agent on every aspect of its advertising in the same way as the company itself would advise its own customers on the use of its products. However, apart from any special work, an advertising agency's costs have to be recovered from the commission which it receives from the advertising media for the sale of space. Therefore a company that is spending £10,000 a year on advertising cannot logically expect to receive more than one tenth of the time and attention that the same agent would give to another client spending £100,000. Moreover, as in the purchase of *any* commodity, it would be extremely unwise to leave the decision to the supplier or his agent as to the price that should be paid or the quantity that should be purchased. Companies that spend large annual sums on advertising usually employ experienced advertising managers who are responsible for the profitability of this aspect of their business. The cost of employing an experienced specialist solely for this purpose would obviously be uneconomic on a small advertising budget. However, the individual who is responsible for authorizing the expenditure should at least be familiar with the various procedures that have been described in this chapter and should ensure that appropriate methods are used for checking the effectiveness of the expenditure which he is authorizing.

Chapter 12

The Function of the Sales Force

The organization and control of a field sales force comes within the province of sales management rather than marketing. However, the adoption of the marketing philosophy suggests that there is a need for a complete reappraisal of the traditional concepts on which the planning and control of a company's sales force are commonly based.

In practice, little research seems to have been done on this subject and the purpose of this final chapter is merely to suggest some lines of approach.

THE ROLE OF THE SALESMAN

It is evident from an elementary consideration that the persuasion exercised by a salesman is only one of the many factors that govern the sales volume obtained. Depending on the product and on the distribution plan that has been adopted, the part that is played by the company's salesmen in influencing sales volume may be large or it may be extremely small. (See Chapter 2.)

Yet, when it comes to planning and controlling the activities of a sales force, it has usually been tacitly assumed that the volume of sales obtained from a territory is solely and directly related to the skill and effort of the salesman in that territory. For example, controls for examining the performances of salesmen are usually based, either directly or indirectly, on the sales volume obtained. The same basis is not infrequently used for the remuneration of salesmen. However, there are many situations in which any such basis would be no more realistic than attempting to measure the consumption of electricity by the number of appliances that have been switched on. Rough and ready measures of this kind do not stand up against scientific management.

The volume of sales that is obtained from a particular territory in a given period depends on:

1. The size of the potential demand. (In many industries this may vary considerably from one time of the year to another.)
2. The share of the demand that is obtained by the company.

It was shown in Chapter 1 that the size of the potential demand for a particular product depends on:

a. The number of people who have some need that could be satisfied at least as well and economically by the purchase of the product as by any other available means.
b. The proportion of those people who have the financial ability to satisfy their need by the purchase of the product.
c. The quantity and frequency of their purchases that would be necessary to satisfy their need.

The activities of a salesman do not, therefore, play any part in influencing the size of the potential demand in his territory. This depends solely on the particular products he is selling and on the environmental conditions in which he is selling them. Variations that occur from one time of the year to another are entirely unrelated to the salesman's efforts.

Similarly, it was shown in Chapter 2 that the persuasion exercised by a salesman is only one of ten basic factors that may be influencing the share of the potential demand obtained. For example, with nationally advertised consumer products, a small change in advertising is likely to have a very much greater effect on sales than any variation in the skill and effort of the company's salesmen. There can be few industries in which the sales volume is not affected by changes that occur in one or other of these influencing factors. The changes can, of course, be brought about either by the company's own activities or by those of its competitors.

No market ever remains completely static. In view of the changes that can occur both in the size of the demand and in the factors that influence the share of that demand which is obtained, it would be quite illogical to assume that every variation in sales volume is always due to a variation in the skill and effort of the company's salesmen. It follows, therefore, that controls based on the sales volume achieved each month can, at best, provide no more than a very rough guide to the performance of the sales staff and may even be completely misleading for this purpose.

EFFECT OF SKILL AND EFFORT ON SALES

The foregoing considerations are fairly generally recognized, although their effect rarely seems to be applied in practice to the planning and control of a sales force. However, even if the extraneous variables that affect sales are taken into account, there is often a further underlying assumption that, if everything else remained constant, the volume of sales obtained by a salesman would be directly proportional to his personal skill and effort. In other words, if there was nothing else affecting sales, a 10 per cent increase in the skill and effort of the salesman should produce a 10 per cent increase in his sales. This underlying assumption is fundamental to many of the sales controls and financial incentive schemes that are used in industry.

But the relationship between the skill and effort of a salesman and the monthly volume of sales that he obtains varies considerably from one kind of selling situation to another. For example, the one may be almost directly proportional to the other in the case of a door-to-door salesman selling brushes or encylopaedias. With zero effort, for example, if the salesman stayed at home, there would be no sales; how much he sells will depend only on how long and how skilfully he works. At the other extreme, if a company is selling a nationally advertised consumer product through retail outlets, a variation in the skill and effort of its salesmen would have a very much smaller effect on its sales.

There is little practical data so far available on which to base an examination of the relationship between the performance of a salesman and the sales that he obtains in the many different situations that occur in industry. It seems likely that, under some conditions, this may be a curvilinear rather than a straight line relationship. Some possible examples are illustrated graphically in the following diagram where 'K' is the volume of sales that would be obtained by a salesman of 'average ability'. It is assumed that all other variables affecting sales remain constant.

Fig. 12.1

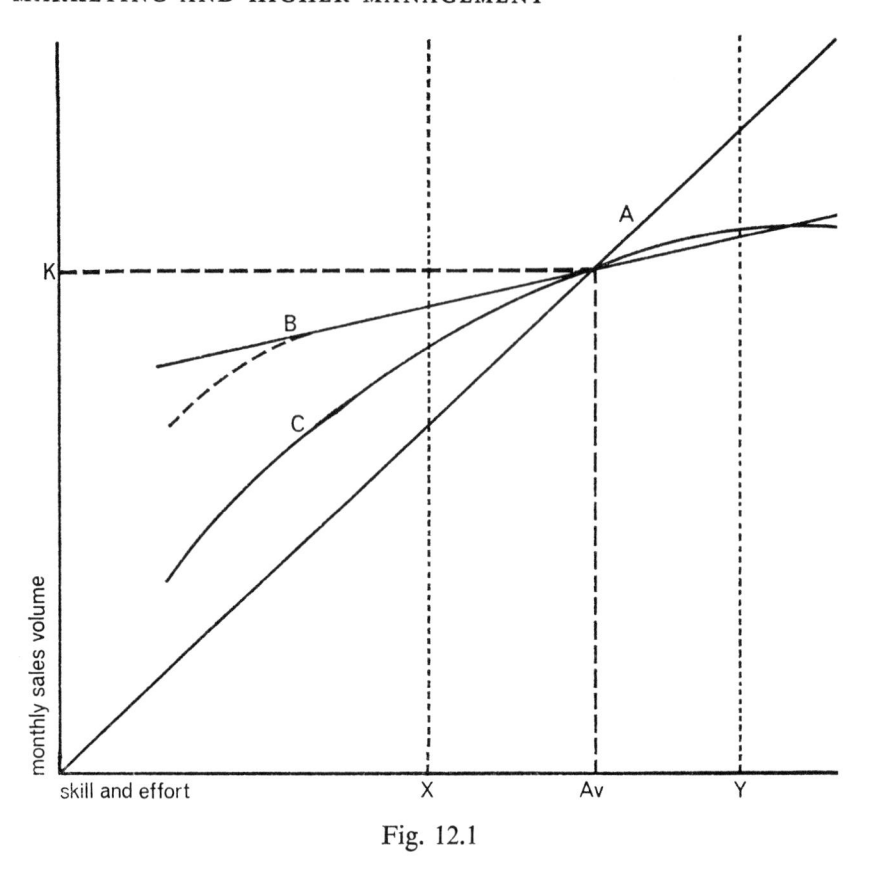

Line 'A' is the directly proportional relationship that is typical of a straightforward manual operation where the output is directly proportional to the skill and effort of the operator. It seems likely that door-to-door salesmanship has a relationship of approximately this nature.

Line 'B' might represent a situation in which the company's salesmen play only a very small part in influencing the buying decisions of the eventual consumers. A similar relationship might occur if a high proportion of a company's business is in the form of repeat orders from existing customers.

Line 'C' represents a situation in which, beyond some maximum point, any further increase in the skill and effort of the salesman would not produce any further increase in sales from the territory.

It seems likely that in practice there must often be some saturation point beyond which no further increase in sales would be obtained. Most lines may, therefore, tend to flatten off as this saturation point is approached, as in Line 'C', even though they may have earlier followed a straight line relationship. From a practical point of view, consideration need only be given to the situation that lies within the normal range of variations in skill and effort in a company's sales force. This might be in the area between lines 'X' and 'Y' in the diagram.

There are several points that emerge from the variable nature of this relationship between performance and sales under different conditions. For example, it is apparent that the difference between employing a mediocre and a good salesman has a very much greater effect in some industries than in others. In a typical sales force, the skill and effort of the poorest salesman might, for example, be 25 per cent below the average and that of the best salesman 25 per cent above. In some situations (Line A), this would make a difference of 67 per cent in the sales from their territories (75 to 125), whereas in another situation the same variation in performance might make a difference of less than 10 per cent in the sales. For the same reason, the importance and effect of training salesmen to improve their skill and effort will be very much greater in some industries than in others.

In practice, the existence of these differences in the relationship between performance and sales is masked by the many other variables that are affecting the sales obtained by each salesman. It is undoubtedly for this reason that such a relationship is rarely observed or taken into account. Nevertheless, evidence of its existence can be seen by the fact that the difference between the sales achieved by the best and worst salesman in a sales force is very much greater in some industries than it is in others. For example, in the sales forces of jobbing printers there are often very wide differences between the sales of the best and worst salesman. This suggests that, in this situation, sales are almost directly proportional to skill and effort. On the other hand there are many cases where, after all the factors that are affecting the sales in each territory have been fully taken into account, the differences between the results achieved by each salesman are comparatively small.

This variable relationship between performance and sales in different industries is obviously of particular significance in relation to performance measurements. In order to be able to make these measurements accurately, it is necessary to be able to isolate the effect of small variations in the skill and effort of a salesman from all the other variables affecting the sales obtained from each territory each month. This presents fewer difficulties and is likely to be achieved more accurately in those situations where performance and sales are almost directly proportional (Line A). Variations in performance are directly reflected by variations in sales. However, in a high ratio situation (Line B), the effect of a variation in the salesman's skill and effort from one month to another can easily be concealed by much larger variations in sales occurring from other causes. Very much greater precision is therefore necessary in the procedure for detecting differences in performance if an accurate measurement is to be obtained.

THE MEASUREMENT OF SALESMEN'S PERFORMANCES

At present, no completely reliable and effective method of measuring the skill and effort of salesmen seems to have been developed. The degree of accuracy in the methods that are commonly used varies considerably. Under suitable conditions, the better methods provide a useful and reliable guide, but there are few situations, if any, where it would be possible, for example, to say quite precisely that the skill and effort of one salesman was 5 per cent higher than that of another. Most existing control systems provide a guide to performance rather than a measurement. Even so, there are probably still many cases where the personal opinion of a sales or area manager provides a more reliable guide to individual performance than any control figures produced by the company. Such opinions and judgments can hardly provide a reliable basis for effective management and control.

In order to 'measure' performance, it is first necessary to define and establish some standard against which the results can be compared. This is, indeed, the basis of all systems of measurement.

The selection of the standard to be used is quite arbitrary and is a matter of convenience. For example, the average length of a man's 'foot' is merely a convenient standard on which to base an accurate measurement of distance. In the measurement of human performance, a convenient standard and the one that is most commonly used can be defined as: 'The achievement that can be regularly attained by a skilled performer of *average* ability'.

When applying this to a salesman as a measurement that is to be based on sales volume, the standard can be defined as, 'the volume of sales that would be obtained from a salesman's territory if it was being operated by an effectively trained and motivated salesman of average ability'.

This fundamental standard should not be confused with the so-called 'Sales Targets' that are used by some companies and which are consciously or subconsciously fixed in relation to the salesman who is in the territory and on the past volume of sales that he has obtained. This can never provide any true measurement of the relative skill and effort of each salesman for comparing performances. The standard for each territory must be based, not on the salesman who happens to be in the territory at the time, but on the volume of sales that could reasonably be expected if it was being operated by a salesman of average ability. The sales obtained by the salesman each month can then be compared with this standard to provide a measurement of performance. This will show the true differences between one salesman and another as well as any variations that are occurring in the performance of each salesman from one month to another.

In order to comply with the definition, the standard must take account of all variations that occur in the sales volume for any reasons whatever, which are not due to variations in the skill and effort of the salesmen. The accuracy of the measurement depends entirely upon the accuracy with which this can be achieved and, as mentioned above, this presents many problems.

Apart from differences in the skill and effort of the salesmen, the factors that affect the volume of sales obtained from a territory can be grouped into two categories:

a. The local differences between one territory and another that cause a difference in the relative size of the demand for the company's products, for example, differences in the number of potential users. These factors differ from one territory to another, but do not vary significantly from one month to another within each territory.
b. Variations in the size of the demand from one month to another. These can be due to seasonal fluctuations, changes in the products, and all other variable factors that are outside the salesman's control.

Territorial Differences in the Demand

The differences in the relative size of the demand in each of the territories can usually be determined without any great difficulty by market research. The extent of the research that is necessary will, of course, vary considerably from one industry to another.

However, the volume of sales that can be obtained is not necessarily directly proportional to the size of the demand in each territory. The extent to which the attainable sales is influenced by the size of the demand depends on the intensity of the sales coverage. For example, in a hypothetical situation in which *every* potential purchaser was being regularly visited by a salesman at optimum frequency, the volume of sales that could be obtained with a given degree of skill and effort would be directly proportional to the size of the demand for the company's products in each territory. At the other extreme, perhaps in selling some piece of capital equipment, the salesman may be visiting only a small proportion of the total potential purchasers in his territory each month. Any differences between the total number of potential purchasers in one territory as compared with another may make little or no difference to the attainable sales.

The intensity of the sales coverage in each salesman's territory is inversely proportional to the number of potential customers in that territory and it can be conveniently expressed in terms of 'salesmen per 100 outlets'. In these terms, the coverage in each territory will normally, of course, be less than unity and is expressed in decimals. The nature of the relationship between sales coverage and the share of the demand that can be obtained is shown graphically in the following diagram.

In theory, if all purchasers were identical, the relationship would follow the dotted line. The sales obtained for a given degree of skill and effort would be directly related to the number of purchasers called upon up to the point at which every potential purchaser was being regularly visited at the optimum frequency of calling. Beyond this point, no further increase in the intensity of the sales coverage could produce any further increase in sales. However, in practice, purchasers are never identical in their buying habits and some may have a bigger potential than others. Below the saturation point, it is usually the purchasers with the larger potential who are more intensively covered. The smaller purchasers are either omitted or visited less frequently. Increasing the sales coverage therefore results in a curve of 'diminishing returns'.

Fig. 12.2

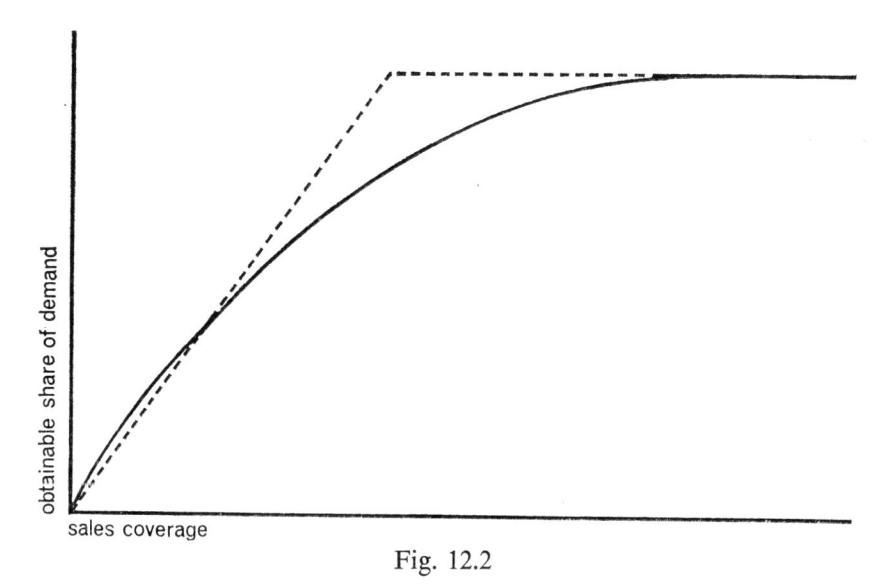

If a company is marketing the kind of products that are consumed or sold by the purchasers on whom it is calling, much of the salesmen's time is likely to be spent on regularly repeating calls on the same customers and there may be a high intensity of sales coverage. This is the type of situation that often occurs in selling consumable products to industry or in selling to wholesale and retail distributors. It would rarely, if ever, be economic to operate at or near the saturation coverage (see Chapter 3) and, in this situation, most companies have a sales coverage that is somewhere along the curved part of the relationship shown in the diagram. However, if the company is selling products that are retained by its customers for their own use, the salesmen are unlikely to be calling on exactly the same people each month and there is usually a very much lower intensity of sales coverage. Many such companies are operating on the straight line part of the relationship and the relative size of the potential demand in one territory as compared with another may make little or no difference to the attainable sales.

It follows that, in setting accurate standards, the allowance that must be made for differences in the size of the potential demand will vary according to the intensity of the sales coverage in each territory. In any particular selling situation it is therefore necessary to know the relationship between coverage and sales in that situation. One method that is adopted for determining this relationship is to use the sales that have been obtained from each territory during the last twelve months to draw the graph shown in the last diagram. The procedure can be seen in an elementary form by taking as an example a company selling a consumable product, where the relative size of the demand in each territory is directly proportional to its population. (For the purpose of performance measurements, it is not necessary to know the *absolute* size of the demand in each territory.) Simple research will determine the total population and number of outlets in each territory. The relative share of the demand obtained in each territory during the past twelve months can be expressed as 'sales per 1,000 population'. Similarly, the sales coverage can be expressed as 'salesman per 100 outlets', for example, in a territory having 500 outlets the coverage is 0·2. These provide the two ordinates for the graph and a point is plotted for each territory. Starting at zero, a mean line is drawn through the plotted points. This shows the extent to which the share of the demand that is being obtained is influenced by the sales coverage under those particular conditions. This provides the factor that must be used to allow for differences in sales coverage between one territory and another in establishing the standards for each territory.

The use of some such procedure is not uncommon for determining the extent to which sales are affected by variations in the intensity of sales coverage. The method appears in various guises and it is sometimes treated under the heading of 'Operational Research'. The example given was used only to illustrate the principle. In practice, there are few situations in which the demand for a product is directly proportional to the population in each territory or in which any comparably simple basis could be used. Several different factors may have to be taken into account and extensive research is often necessary. Nevertheless, in most situations this is an entirely practicable and feasible procedure.

As has been shown, there are some situations in which the intensity of the sales coverage is comparatively low and will, therefore, have little or no effect on the attainable sales volume. A simple examination will usually show if this situation exists and it is of course unnecessary to use any elaborate methods for accurately determining the relative size of the demand in each territory.

It is significant that situations in which there is a low intensity of sales coverage are often likely to coincide with those in which the sales volume is almost directly proportional to the skill and effort of the salesman – see the previous section of this chapter. The two situations might coincide, for example, in selling specialized equipment to industrial users. In both situations any errors will have less effect on the accuracy of the measurement. Hence, if the two coincide the difficulties in establishing reliable measurements based on sales volume are considerably minimized. However, the converse is equally applicable. Situations in which there is a high intensity of sales coverage, for example, in selling consumer goods, are often likely to coincide with those in which many of the variations that occur in sales volume are due to factors entirely unrelated to the skill and effort of the salesman. Therefore, when the two situations coincide, not only is it a more complex problem to obtain the necessary data but also the data must be obtained with a smaller margin of error, if a reliable measurement is to be made.

Seasonal and other Variations in the Demand

The second group of factors that have to be taken into account in the measurement of performance are those that can cause the sales volume to vary from one month to another. These include any normal seasonal fluctuations in demand as well as all other variations which are due to factors outside the salesman's control.

It was shown in Chapter 9 that, in determining a sales trend, the effect of seasonal fluctuations can be removed by the use of 'Moving Annual Totals' – see page 175. These are sometimes used for the same purpose in the control of sales performance. The standard sales volume for each territory is expressed as an *annual* figure and the moving annual total at the end of each month is compared with this figure as an index of achievement. This procedure undoubtedly has much to recommend it as a general control of sales. However, in the measurement of personal performance, it has to be remembered that a monthly moving annual total merely removes the effect of any variation in sales volume that occurred in the same month in the previous year. That variation may or may not have been due to a seasonal variation in the demand; it may have been wholly or partly due to some other circumstance that occurred during that month.

It is also important to bear in mind, when using this method, that any variation in sales that has occurred during the month will be reflected in terms of annual sales. For example, if the average monthly sales were £10,000, a 10 per cent drop of £1,000 from one month to another due to a non-recurring variation might be shown in the moving annual total as a drop from £120,000 to £119,000. In other words, the full extent of the drop is shown but, unless this is recognized, it might appear to have been a decline of less than 1 per cent.

However, seasonal fluctuations in the demand are only one of the many factors that can cause a variation in sales volume from one month to another. For example, in an expanding economy, demand for the products of many companies is increasing. A 10 per cent increase in sales from this cause does not represent any increase at all in the skill and effort of a salesman. Similarly, in the 'fashion' industries substantial changes can occur in sales volume that are due to the design of the products and not to any variations in the individual performances of salesmen. In many industries, such things as production faults, delivery delays, advertising and the activities of competitors can cause a very much greater variation in sales than is ever caused by variations in the skill and effort of salesmen. In practice, the skill of the salesmen and the effort which they put into their work do not normally vary very widely from one month to another. But it is these comparatively small changes that have to be measured and that must, therefore, be isolated from all the other changes which may have occurred.

So far, even in the design of more advanced control and incentive schemes, little serious attempt seems to have been made to cater for these changes in market conditions that are outside the salesman's control. Further research is needed in this area in order to devise practical methods for obtaining a reliable measurement of the personal performances of salesmen.

A possible line for research may be provided by the fact that most of the variable factors in this category are likely to have a uniform effect on sales throughout the whole market and, apart from any special local conditions, will have proportionately the same effect in each territory. For example, if some seasonal or other variation in the demand has reduced a company's total sales by 10 per cent in a particular month, then the extent by which the decline in each territory was more or less than 10 per cent would indicate a local variation which, if there were no other factors, could only be due to a variation in the skill and effort of the salesman. For this purpose, the various factors that affect the sales

THE FUNCTION OF THE SALES FORCE

achieved in each territory can be regarded as falling into one or other of the following categories:

a. Differences in the local conditions between one territory and another.
b. Differences in the market conditions between one month and another.
c. Differences in the skill and effort of the salesmen.

Market research can be used to determine the factors that cause a difference between one territory and another. If the effect of the common variables that have affected sales in all territories can be screened out, the variable factor that remains is the difference in the personal performance of each salesman.

One of the many possible practical applications of this principle has already been tried out in certain companies. Market research is used to determine what *proportion* of the company's total sales would be obtained from each territory if they were all operated by salesmen of average and equal ability. In other words, a standard is set for each territory which is expressed, not in terms of sales volume, but as a percentage of the company's total sales. This standard is determined in the usual way (as previously described) and is based on the extent to which the sales in each territory are affected by the relative size of the demand, the intensity of the sales coverage and by any other local conditions outside the salesman's control.

The actual sales achieved each month in each territory are expressed as a percentage of the total sales for that month. The 'achieved percentage' is compared with the 'standard percentage' to provide the measurement of performance. For example, if the standard for a territory is 5 per cent of the total sales and if the sales achieved are also 5 per cent this would represent a standard performance on the part of the salesman and could be expressed as a performance of 100. However, if the sales achieved were 6 per cent of the total, this would represent an above average performance and could be expressed as a performance of 120. The figures on which the standard and achieved percentages are based can, of course, be in terms of monetary value, weight sold, contribution to profit, or any other suitable unit.

If the market research is correctly carried out there should usually be no serious difficulty in establishing the 'percentage standards' with adequate accuracy. The standards will have to be adjusted from time to time but, over a period of twelve months, there are unlikely to be any substantial changes in the local conditions that govern the relative volume of sales attainable from each territory. The standard is not, of course, affected by seasonal fluctuations or by any other common factor that may cause a variation in the demand for the company's products. Nor is it affected by any change in selling prices. If there is a large regionalized sales force, with a number of territories in each region, it would be preferable to express the standard for each territory as a percentage of the regional total and not of the national total.

Under suitable conditions, this particular application of the basic principle undoubtedly provides a very much more accurate measurement of performance than is commonly achieved through conventional measurements based on the volume of sales obtained. It achieves the objective of screening out the effect of all variations, however caused, that are common to a particular market or geographical region. It also has the advantage of being simple to operate and easy for the salesmen to understand. Nevertheless, it has certain limitations and weaknesses. Of these, perhaps the most important is that this particular method cannot be used for a small sales force with less than seven or eight salesmen. For example, if there were only two salesmen, and if one of those salesmen increased his percentage by increasing his effort, this would automatically lower the percentage recorded for the other salesman even though there had been no change in his own performance. This is an inherent inaccuracy of percentage standards in this context. However, the resulting margin of error rapidly diminishes as the number of salesmen increases. In the larger sales forces the effect is so small that it can be ignored.

Another weakness in this application of the principle is that, by removing the effect of *all* common variables, the effect of any overall change in the performance of the sales force is also removed. For example, an overall increase in performance resulting from improved supervision and control would not be directly revealed in the individual measurements of performance. However, this does not affect the accuracy in measuring the relative performance of each salesman and the ability to obtain a true comparison between the performance of one salesman and that of another. In practice, a high degree of accuracy in the relative measurement of individual performances is very much more important for control purposes than a similar accuracy in measuring the average overall performance which can usually be determined by other means.

Expressing the standards in terms of percentages also has the disadvantage that if, for some particular reason, the standard for one territory has to be altered, the standards for all the other territories have to be adjusted accordingly so that the total remains at 100. For example, if some change occurs that will have a significantly greater effect in some parts of a region than in others, the standards for all the territories in the region would have to be adjusted whether or not they had been affected by the change.

Because of these limitations, the use of percentage standards does not provide a universally applicable procedure for removing the effect of the common variables that are outside the salesman's control. There are probably many situations in which percentage standards could be safely used to provide extremely reliable controls that are very much more accurate than anything that has previously been obtained. But, before they are adopted, care must obviously be taken to ensure that the situation is one that is within the limits for which this method is practicable.

This approach is based on the recognized principle of segregating those variables that have some common characteristic from the remaining variables. Apart from the use of percentages, there are many possible applications for this principle as an accurate measurement of skill and effort.

The Time Lag between Performance and Results
There is a further factor that cannot always be ignored in the measurement of a salesman's performance. This is the interval that may elapse between a change in the selling activities and its effect on sales. For example, if a skilled salesman is put into a new territory that has not previously been covered, or into one that has not been fully developed, it may take him many months to build up the sales in that territory. If an accurate standard has been fixed for the territory it will have been based on the level of achievement that could eventually be obtained by a skilled

MARKETING AND HIGHER MANAGEMENT

salesman of average ability. Therefore, during the period of development, a comparison between this standard and the results actually achieved each month would not, by itself, provide a true indication of the skill and effort of the salesman.

The situation might be as shown in the following diagram where, at the present time, the sales achieved are at 50 per cent of the standard for the territory.

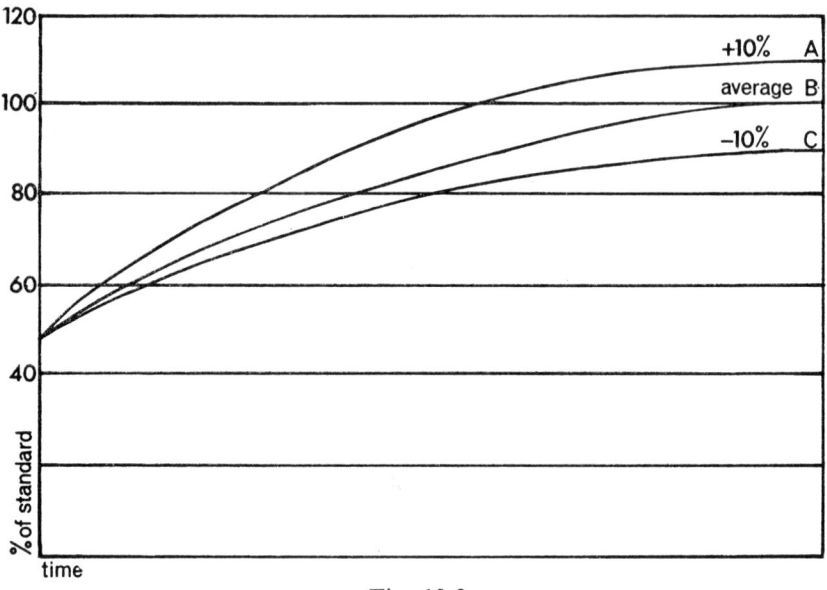

Fig. 12.3

If an accurate standard has been set, and if the salesman is of 'average ability', the sales would eventually reach 100 per cent of the standard and would follow line 'B' on the diagram. However, if his performance was 10 per cent above or below average, the sales would follow either line 'A' or line 'C'.

Under these conditions, since the time scale is indeterminate, it is doubtful whether a completely accurate measurement of performance could ever be made during the period of development. However, a progressive company may be reorganizing its sales force and changing the boundaries of its territories from time-to-time. This time lage effect may, therefore, be occurring frequently but variably in one or more of the territories. In these cases it is desirable to have some reliable form of performance control, particularly if a bonus or commission payment is also involved. This can be achieved by basing the performance control on two separate factors. It will be seen from the diagram that the difference between curves A, B and C is in their rate of increase. Therefore, at any particular moment in time, the two factors that must be taken into account are:

a. The level of attainment in relation to the standard for the territory.

b. The change that has occurred in the level of attainment each month.

For example, in considering a territory in which 60 per cent of the standard is currently being obtained with a high rate of increase, it is quite possible that this percentage may represent a considerably higher performance on the part of the salesman than that of a salesman in another territory who is obtaining 80 per cent of his standard with little or no increase (line 'A' as compared with line 'C' in the diagram).

This dual measurement has been applied in many companies where there is a fluid situation in order to provide a more reliable performance control. It forms the basis of the PA Duplex Incentive Scheme which is used in many industries: the bonus payment is in two parts, one part depending on the achievement in relation to the standard and the other on the rate of increase in sales in the territory. This has a further advantage in that it provides a very strong additional incentive for a salesman to increase his sales. Moreover, it overcomes the difficulty that is sometimes encountered as a result of the drop in earnings that might be suffered by a highly skilled salesman if he is put in to develop and expand a territory in which there has previously been a poor performance. Under this system, his opportunities for earning bonus in the new territory are just as great as in one that is already fully developed. It is merely the proportions that he receives from each part that will be different.

SUMMARY

It is by no means a simple matter to introduce any system that will provide a reliable measurement of the performance of salesmen. A minor obstacle that may sometimes have to be overcome is what might be called an attitude of mind on the part of management towards the controls used in the sales department. In the past, it has usually taken not much more than a few hours to design simple sales records and to fix some kind of sales target for each territory. Any control system in which it might take several weeks of research to establish accurate standards is often regarded as being something that would be far too elaborate and complicated to be considered. Nevertheless, whatever system is used, a considerable amount of research will always be necessary if reliable standards are to be established and an effective measurement of performance is to be obtained.

It could be argued that simple controls based on the sales obtained by each salesman have been used for many years and have generally been considered adequate. However, such controls can never provide more than a rough guide to the actual degree of skill and effort displayed by each salesman. The advantages to be gained from having accurate work measurements on the shop-floor is generally recognized. If a company is to continue to be successful, it is probably even more important that the controls used in the sales department should be at least as accurate as those used in production.

The cost of introducing effective sales controls is unlikely to be any more than the comparable cost of using modern methods of work measurement in the production departments. In most cases the cost may be very much less. Moreover, once the initial research has been carried out, very little work is involved in adjusting the standards from time to time as conditions change. The cost of this maintenance work is likely to be almost negligible in comparison with the equivalent cost of maintaining a work study department to keep production standards up-to-date.

There is also an urgent need for more accurate performance measurements in those situations where the salesmen receive some form of commission or bonus as a financial incentive. In any part of a business, the only purpose in having a financial incentive is to provide an inducement to the employees to improve their skill and effort. It follows that the incentive cannot be fully effective in achieving this objective unless the payments that are made are directly proportional to the relative skill and effort of each employee and are not affected by any variations outside his control. Few conventional commission schemes for salesmen fulfil this requirement and the true motivating effect of the commission payment is often small in relation to its cost.

In recent years, as discussed in this chapter, a certain amount of research has been carried out on improving the reliability of performance measurements in the sales department. Some progress has been made towards establishing more accurate yardsticks or standards on which these measurements should be based. As a result, some companies have very much more effective sales controls than others. However, as yet, no entirely satisfactory method seems to have been developed that could always be relied upon to provide an accurate measurement of individual performances each month regardless of any changes that may have occurred.

In theory, there are no insurmountable difficulties to be overcome in devising a procedure that will provide an accurate measurement of skill and effort. The problem, in this respect, is different from that of obtaining an accurate sales forecast where some future event may be entirely unpredictable. A performance measurement is concerned only with the event after it has already occurred. In essence, the problem is concerned with the isolation of one particular variable – the skill and effort of the salesman – in a situation in which there are many different variables. Some of these are variable in relation to time but fixed in relation to place, others are variable in relation to place but fixed in relation to time. A few, of which skill and effort are the most significant, vary in relation to both time and place. One of the possible lines of approach to the solution of the problem has been suggested in this chapter and there are undoubtedly several others.

Glossary

Account Executive

An executive on the staff of an advertising agency who provides the personal contact between the agency and the client. An agency may have a number of account executives each of whom handles a particular group of clients.

Account Opener

A salesman who is given the specific task of opening new accounts which are subsequently passed over to other salesmen for servicing.

Activity Sampling

A Work Study procedure employing discontinuous as opposed to continuous observations, e.g. recording, at regular intervals throughout the day, the particular activity on which a salesman is at that moment engaged.

Advertising Appropriation

The money allocated to advertising in a sales budget period.

Advertising Research

Embraces all those activities and procedures which are concerned with the determination of the effectiveness of advertising expenditure and with the way in which an advertisement should be designed and presented – see Chapter 11.

Agent

A person who does not trade on his own account but acts on behalf of others. Unlike a Factor (q.v.) he does not take legal possession of the goods which he is selling. Hence, he has no legal responsibility for the goods and cannot be sued by a customer in relation to them. (In a few cases the legal definition is disregarded and the term 'agent' is loosely applied to a distributor).

GLOSSARY

AIDA

A well-known mnemonic, used in training salesmen, to indicate the correct sequence for a selling interview or selling letter. The initials stand for: Attention, Interest, Desire, Action. It is sometimes extended to AIDDA to include: Attention, Interest, Desire, Decision, Action.

Alternative Close

The practice, in closing a selling interview or letter, in which the prospective purchaser is offered alternative lines of positive action rather than a choice between acceptance and refusal. For example, in closing a telephone conversation seeking an interview: 'May I call and see you next Wednesday or would one day in the following week be more convenient to you?'.

Attitude Studies

A form of Market Research to discover the attitude of users or consumers to a particular product or to a company as a whole. When used in Advertising Research they provide a means of assessing the effectiveness of an advertising campaign by examining the attitude of consumers towards the product both before and after being exposed to the campaign.

Audit (Market)

See Home Audit, Retail Audit and Pantry Check.

Back Selling

A term sometimes used in selling materials and components to industry. It refers to those selling activities which are specifically concerned with developing the sales of the *customers'* products in which the company's materials or components are used. For example, the promotion of textile goods, made from synthetic fibres, by the chemical manufacturer who produces the basic material. Back selling is analogous to Selling Out (q.v.) in consumer and durable goods.

Banded Packs

Used to secure consumer trial or increased sales by banding two or more articles together. The articles may be the same, e.g. two articles at a reduced price, or a related article given free or at a reduced price, e.g. toothbrush and toothpaste.

Branded Goods

Goods which, as an integral part of the marketing strategy, carry a symbol, name or design which identifies them and distinguishes them from competitors' products. (Note that the fact that a product carries a label with the manufacturer's name does not, by itself, mean that it comes within this category).

Brand Image
The impression of the brand that has been created in the minds of potential purchasers. With many consumer products this impression plays a leading part in influencing a purchaser's choice.

Brand Leader
The brand which is currently securing the greatest share of the demand for that particular product. (See also: Market Leader and Price Leader.)

Brand Loyalty (or Brand Allegiance)
It can become a habit for a purchaser to continue to ask for and buy a particular brand. This brand allegiance is much stronger with certain types of products (e.g. petrol) than with others. Action that will create brand loyalty is therefore an important aspect in the promotion of many products.

Brand Manager
An executive in a company manufacturing branded goods who is responsible for planning the marketing of one or more of the brands sold by the company. He is usually responsible to the marketing manager and has no line authority over the salesmen selling his brands.

Break-even Analysis
A study of the relationship between volume and profit and of the volume that must be sold before the company starts to make a profit. If a small change in volume makes a significant change in profit, the company is said to be in a 'Volume Sensitive' situation. If a small change in costs would make a bigger difference to the profit than a small change in volume, the company is said to be in a 'Cost Sensitive' situation. These factors have an influence in determining the most suitable marketing strategy for the company.

Budgetary Control
A comparison of forecast cost and income objectives with the actual results achieved, at sufficiently short intervals to allow remedial action to be taken.

Buying Group
A voluntary association of retailers and/or wholesalers who, while trading independently in all other respects, combine to purchase collectively in order

to secure favourable bulk terms. These groups are sometimes referred to as Retailer Co-operatives.

Call Frequency

The frequency at which repeat calls are made by the salesmen on the same customer, e.g. 'a monthly call frequency'.

Call Point

A customer or prospective customer to be visited by a salesman, e.g. 'there are 200 call points in Smith's territory'.

Calling Rate

The average number of calls that a salesman is able to make in a given period (e.g. a week) in a particular territory.

In all repetitive calling situations, planning the size and most economic deployment of the sales force will depend upon the determination of:
  (a) the optimum Call Frequency for various types of customer;
  (b) the number and distribution of Call Points; and
  (c) the Calling Rate under various territorial conditions. (See Repetitive Calling.)

Capital Goods

A term applied to plant and equipment purchased by industrial users, but excluding consumable tools such as files. (All purchases that the buyer charges to a capital account.)

Censuses of Production and Distribution

Two separate censuses which are carried out from time to time by the Registrar-General. The Census of Production shows the number of persons employed analysed by occupation, by industry and by town throughout England and Wales. The Census of Distribution shows the monetary value of sales, the number of wholesale and retail outlets and the number of persons employed in these outlets, analysed by product groups and by town throughout Great Britain. In many industries one or other of these censuses can provide useful background information for determining the nature and distribution of the demand.

Chain Store

A unit of a group of retail stores all of which trade under the same name and offer the same general range of merchandise. There is no universally applicable distinction between a Chain Store and a Multiple Store. See Multiple Store for a more precise definition. (Also see Voluntary Chain.)

Channels of Distribution

The means and stages through which the goods flow from the producer to the ultimate user or consumer. The most commonly used channels of distribution can be classified as follows:

(a) Producer – User (Direct distribution)
(b) Producer – Merchant – User
(c) Producer – Retailer – User
(d) Producer – Wholesaler – Retailer – User

In some industries the terms Factor and Distributor are used. (See these terms for definitions.) Planning the most suitable channel or combination of channels is often an important feature in an effective marketing strategy.

C.I.F. (Cost, Insurance and Freight)

A term used in exporting to indicate that the price quoted includes the cost of goods, insurance in transit, and freight charges to a named destination, e.g. '£25 per ton C.I.F. Singapore'. (Also see F.O.B.)

Commission

See Financial Incentives.

Control Questions

Questions, the answers to which are already known, which are included in a Market Research Questionnaire as a check on the validity of the information revealed by the other questions.

Consignment Stocks

A term used to describe stocks of goods, or spare parts, which are held by a distributor for local sale but which remain the property of the manufacturer in stock.

Consumer Goods

A broad description for goods which are not used for the purpose of trade or industry and which are consumed or discarded after initial use. (Cf. Durable Goods.)

Consumer Durables

A contradictory term that has little to recommend its use. It has the same meaning as Durable Goods (q.v.).

Consumer Panel

A representative sample of consumers who are constituted as a continuing panel to report on the purchase, use or acceptability of products that are referred to them.

GLOSSARY

Consumer Research

That part of Market Research which is concerned with finding out information about domestic users or consumers of a particular product.

Conurbation

A geographical area consisting of a group of towns which together form a more or less self-contained social and marketing unit. The six standard conurbations used for statistical purposes by the Registrar-General and Board of Trade are:

> Tyneside
> West Yorkshire
> Greater London
> West Midlands
> S.E. Lancashire
> Merseyside

Co-operative Advertising

Local advertising carried out by a retailer or other distributor in support of a nationally advertised product, the costs being borne partly by the distributor and partly by the manufacturer. (There is no connection with Co-operative Societies.)

Copy (Advertising)

The words used in an advertisement or, in a more general sense, the design and lay-out of the advertisement.

Copy Theme (or Copy Platform)

A statement of the theme that is to be used in designing an advertisement or series of advertisements in order to obtain the required objective.

Copy Testing

Procedures for testing the effectiveness of an advertisement's design. The procedures range from simple tests of recognition and remembrance to elaborate methods for measuring the relative impact of alternative advertisements. Some form of Copy Testing is usually employed in all major advertising campaigns.

Coverage

See Sales Coverage.

Credit Rating

A rating of the credit-worthiness of customers and prospective customers. Individual credit ratings are liable to change and an effective credit rating system requires continuing review. The rating can be carried out by the company itself or the company may subscribe to an organisation that provides a credit rating service.

Credit Store

A retail store, usually handling a variety of products, which conducts the principal part of its business by selling on extended credit terms as opposed to cash sales or giving normal credit to account customers.

Critical Path Analysis

The use of a Network Analysis (q.v.) to determine which are the critical activities that will control the overall time required to carry out a project, e.g. launching a new product on the market.

Customs Union

A union formed by a group of countries that have agreed to abolish customs tariffs between themselves and to set up common tariffs on all goods entering their countries from the rest of the world (e.g.: The European Economic Community). Also see: Free Trade Area.

Demography

The study of population statistics. A term sometimes used in Market Research.

Desk Research

A branch of market research in which the information is obtained by statistical investigation as opposed to research carried out in the field.

Direct Mail

The use of a letter or circular delivered directly to the prospective customer as a medium for conveying a sales message.

Discount House or Store

A retail department store offering goods for sale at below average prices. The lower prices are usually achieved by reducing the expenditure on service coupled with stocking only those goods which provide a high rate of stockturn or a high yield in relation to the space occupied.

Distribution

A term that has varying shades of meaning in different contexts. In its broadest sense, it covers all those activities concerned with the movement of goods as opposed to those concerned with their production. In its more common industrial sense, it refers to the channels and methods used by a company for the distribution and sale of its products. (In a narrower sense, it is occasionally used to describe the extent of a company's coverage of its market in a particular area.)

Distributor
An independent intermediary who stocks and sells the goods of one or more producers. The term embraces merchants, wholesalers, retailers, etc.

Diversification
Planning the entry into a different market (market diversification), or the introduction of a different type of product (product diversification). Diversification can be carried out by using the company's own resources, or by the acquisition of a company already operating in that market or by making that product.

Dumping
Selling at lower than normal prices for such purposes as unloading surplus stocks. Some countries (e.g. Canada) have anti-dumping laws which prohibit the sale of imported goods at lower than the normal price in their country of origin.

Durable Goods
A term used to describe goods which are not used for the purpose of trade or industry and which are purchased to provide continuing use or enjoyment. (In contrast to Consumer Goods which are consumed or discarded after initial use.) Clothing, footwear and textiles are, however, not usually referred to as Durable Goods. Also see 'Hardware'.

Econometrics
The measurement of economic data. It is concerned firstly with identifying the variables in a system, next with discovering their relationship with one another and finally with building an econometric or mathematical model such that a change in one variable will reflect the changes which will occur in some or all of the others. An econometric study comes within the broad field of Operational Research (q.v.).

Ego Drive
A term used in examining those innate characteristics that cause one individual to become more successful as a salesman than another. It can be loosely described as instinctive self-motivation. See 'Empathy'.

MARKETING AND HIGHER MANAGEMENT

Elasticity of Demand

The relationship between a change in selling price and the resultant change in demand. For example, if a 1 per cent reduction in price increases the demand by more than 1 per cent, the demand is said to be elastic; if it increases the demand by less than 1 per cent, the demand is said to be inelastic. The selling price which will provide the maximum annual contribution to overheads and profit cannot be determined without first determining the elasticity of demand for the product. (See Optimum Selling Price.)

Empathy

Empathy and Ego Drive (q.v.) are considered by some authorities to be the two inherent personality characteristics that are necessary in an individual if he is to become a successful salesman. Empathy is defined as 'the power of projecting one's personality into, and so fully understanding, the object of contemplation'. Loosely it can be described as an instinct to feel as another person feels without necessarily agreeing with that feeling. (Empathy therefore differs from sympathy.) Tests have been developed in the United States for measuring a candidate's empathy and ego drive, these tests are also commercially available for use in the U.K.

Exponential Smoothing

A method of determining the *trend* in the demand when making sales forecasts. The purpose of exponential smoothing is to endeavour to smooth out the effect of some temporary fluctuation in the demand that may not have any lasting effect on the overall trend.

Export Credit Guarantee Department (E.C.G.D.)

A branch of the Board of Trade which provides insurance against non-payment for goods delivered overseas.

Factor

An individual or company that distributes and sells goods produced by another. Unlike an Agent (q.v.) a Factor buys the goods from the producer and has legal possession prior to selling. He is therefore legally responsible to his customers for the quality and reliability of the goods he is selling.

Field Research

That part of Market Research which entails going out into the field to make observations or ask questions in order to obtain the required information.

Financial Incentive

An additional payment in the form of bonus or commission that is given to salesmen as an incentive for skill and effort. In an effective incentive scheme, the financial reward must be solely related to the relative skill and effort of each salesman and must not be affected by factors or conditions which are outside his control. Many conventional commission schemes are extremely weak in this respect and, as a result, their motivating effect is very small in relation to the cost incurred in the payment of commissions. Some method and procedure for measuring the relative skill and effort of each salesman is essential if an incentive scheme is to be fully effective. (See Standard Sales Volume.) In those cases where it would not be practicable to institute such a measurement it is generally preferable to dispense with any form of commission or bonus based on sales volume and to use other methods of motivation.

Fixed Costs

Those elements of the costs which are not affected by a change in volume *that is within the limits of the situation under examination.* (See Variable Costs.) A knowledge of the relationship between the fixed and variable costs in a particular situation has an important bearing on the determination of the most suitable marketing strategy.

F.O.B. (Free on Board)

An exporting term indicating that the price quoted includes transportation to, and loading at, a named port, e.g.: '£20 per ton F.O.B. Southampton'. (Also see C.I.F.).

Franchise

Broadly means the permission granted to a distributor to stock and sell the company's products. There are often certain conditions, laid down by the producer, to which the distributor must agree before being granted the franchise. These may include an undertaking not to sell the products of a competitor. The producer may undertake not to grant a franchise to another distributor in the same locality.

Free Trade Area

A group of countries that have agreed to abolish customs tariffs between themselves but do *not* have a common external tariff to the rest of the world. (e.g. The European Free Trade Area.) A Free Trade Area should not be confused with a Customs Union (q.v.).

General Agreement on Tariffs and Trade (GATT)

An international agreement concerned with customs duties and intertrading between the participating nations. One of its purposes is to avoid situations such as that in which Country A gives financial incentives to its producers to export to Country B; and in retaliation Country B raises the customs duty on goods imported from Country A; the only result would be a general raising of tariff barriers.

Hard Selling and Soft Selling

Terms used to describe two alternative selling procedures. In 'hard selling' the approach is conducted quite blatantly and stridently to try and force the prospective customer to buy. In 'soft selling' a more indirect approach is used to try and lead the prospective customer to the point where he will want to buy. The two terms are, however, somewhat vague and are sometimes given slightly different interpretations.

Hardware

A Board of Trade product grouping which covers ironmongery, cutlery, china, glassware, radio and electrical goods, but excludes furniture and musical instruments.

Hidden Offer

A term used in advertising research when some form of returnable coupon is being used as a means of measuring the relative effectiveness of one advertisement or one medium as compared with another. The 'offer' is something which will be supplied when the coupon is sent in. It is 'hidden' only to the extent that it is not boldly displayed and does not appear to be the principal purpose of the advertisement—this is to try and ensure that it is the real message of the advertisement, and not the offer, that has attracted the respondent. The relative effectiveness of different advertisements or of different media is measured by comparing the number of coupons or enquiries received from each.

Home Audit

A form of market research which is used to find out about the purchase of articles for the home. A representative sample of homes is selected for this purpose. An 'auditor' visits each home at regular intervals and maintains a complete inventory of all the articles in each room. From this, he can discover the purchases that have been made since his last visit. From this sample, each manufacturer's share of the total sales of a particular article can be determined. This form of research is carried out on a syndicated basis for a number of companies who subscribe to the service.

House Account

An account which is serviced directly by the central sales administration and not by a local salesman or area office.

GLOSSARY

House Style

The image of a company that is projected through the design, colouring, lettering and appearance of all visible evidence of that company, e.g. letter headings, stationery, catalogues, vans, advertisements, etc. A good house style requires complete co-ordination in the design of all these items in such a way as to project the required image.

Housewife Panel

A representative sample of housewives who are constituted as a continuing panel to report on the purchase, usage, or acceptability of products that are referred to them.

Image

The impression of the company (company image) and/or its brands (brand image) that has been created in the minds of potential buyers. There are many products where the purchaser's decision is considerably influenced by the name of the maker and by the opinion that he has formed about a particular company. The factors which govern a company's image are therefore often among the most important factors that influence a buying decision.

Impulse Buying

The act of making a purchase on impulse (often through seeing it displayed) as opposed to a premeditated purchase. There are a number of products where a substantial proportion of the total sales results from impulse buying. In preparing the marketing plans for a product it is important to determine the extent to which sales are influenced by impulse buying, as this will govern the most suitable methods for promoting and selling the product. It can also govern the design of the product and the selection of the most suitable channels of distribution.

Industrial Goods

Products or materials which are used for the purpose of trade or industry. They may be capital goods (q.v.), consumable tools, equipment, component parts, or raw materials.

Journey

A planned sequence of calls carried out by a salesman. (Not applicable to all forms of selling.)

Journey Cycle

The period of time required to make a complete journey covering the planned call-points in a territory. Hence, the elapsed time between calls on any one customer, e.g. a four-week journey cycle. This is only applicable in those situations where a salesman is working on a planned sequence of calls.

Logistics of Distribution

A study of the planning and movement of goods from their point of origin to the user or consumer.

Loss Leader

A product which is sold at an uneconomic price for the specific purpose of stimulating sales of other products or of attracting customers into a retail shop.

Mail Order

The method of distribution in which purchases are made through the post – as distinct from placing the order with a salesman or buying at a retail outlet. The customer may be activated to place the order by means of an advertisement or through the distribution of catalogues.

Mail Order House

An establishment that conducts the whole or the principal part of its business through mail order.

Market

A 'market' is a group of potential purchasers who have some common characteristic. It is this common characteristic – and not the products that they buy – that defines a particular market (e.g. the teenage market). Defining the market is one of the first steps in planning a marketing operation.

Market Diversification

Planning to sell to a different group of potential purchasers from those who constitute the company's existing market or markets. This may be through product diversification (q.v.) or through finding new markets or new usages for an existing product.

Market Leader

The company which is securing a larger share of a demand than that of its competitors. In some industries, the company that is the market leader may be able to set the pattern for changes in such things as selling prices and distributors' discounts in its industry. (Also see Price Leader.)

Market Oriented

A term used to describe the way of managing a business which sets out to secure the most profitable utilisation of the company's resources by directing

GLOSSARY

ALL its activities towards winning favourable buying decisions from the prospective customers in a selected market or markets. This objective governs such things as the kind and design of products that it sells. This is distinct from the 'product oriented' company in which the whole of the business is based on producing certain products which it then sets out to sell. (See Foreword on Marketing.)

The term 'orientated' is sometimes used instead of 'oriented'. Both words are permissible and are given the same meaning in the O.E.D. The shorter word is, however, generally preferred.

Market Potential

The potential demand for a product in a particular market. (See Potential Demand.)

Market Research

Finding out who and where are the potential distributors, users or consumers, when and how they buy, and what are the conscious and subconscious motives that influence their buying decisions. (Not to be confused with Marketing Research. The two terms are sometimes misused.)

Market Segmentation

See Segmentation Analysis.

Marketing

The purpose of the marketing function in industry can be defined as follows: 'To determine and define the market or markets that will provide the most profitable utilisation of the company's physical, technical and financial resources. Then, to ensure that these resources are being used to design, produce and sell a product or range of products in such a way as to win the maximum number of favourable buying decisions from the prospective customers in the defined market at an economic cost.'

Marketing Research

A systematic study of the most suitable ways and means by which the marketing objective (see above) can be achieved most effectively in a particular company. (Not to be confused with Market Research.)

Marketing Strategy

The company's overall plan for securing favourable buying decisions from the prospective customers in its defined markets at an economic cost. It involves the co-ordination and integration of product designing, production planning, distribution planning, promotional planning and sales planning.

Mark-up

The difference between the prices at which a distributor buys and sells a product, sometimes expressed as a percentage of the price at which he buys it. (Note that a discount is usually expressed as a percentage of the price at which he *sells* it. Therefore a mark-up of $33\frac{1}{3}$ per cent is the same as a discount of 25 per cent.)

Media, Advertising

The means that are used for communicating with potential purchasers, e.g. newspapers, magazines, television, posters, direct mail, etc.

Media Selection

The study of the cost, readership and impact of various advertising media in order to select those that will secure the maximum results for a given cost.

Merchandiser

An employee whose task is to help retailers to sell his company's products—as opposed to selling to the retailers. This is done by improving the point of sale display and building special attractions or promotion in the shop to stimulate sales. (See Selling In and Selling Out.)

Merchandising

This word has a somewhat different meaning for the manufacturer as compared with the retailer. From the manufacturer's point of view, merchandising can be defined as covering all those activities which will help the merchandise to sell itself. It includes packaging, show cards and display material and the location and display in retail shops.

Merchant

A merchant, like a wholesaler, holds stocks and sells goods which are produced by others. However, he usually sells directly to industrial or trade users and consumers, e.g. a builder's merchant. (In a few trades the term is applied loosely to any distributor or retailer, e.g. a coal merchant.) In some industries, a merchant, unlike a wholesaler, fixes his own selling prices to the user.

Motivation Research

The study of the conscious and subconscious motives that influence a purchaser's decision. A better understanding of these motives is very valuable in determining the way in which the product should be designed, promoted and sold.

GLOSSARY

Moving Annual Totals (M.A.Ts.)

A periodic series of figures (usually weekly or monthly) showing the total for the twelve months up to the end of each period. Moving Annual Totals are often used for presenting sales and similar figures as the *trend* of events is very much more clearly revealed than in a series of individual totals for each week or month. Their use is even more valuable in those cases where there are seasonal variations that influence the individual totals for each period, because they remove the effect of these seasonal variations and reveal the true trend.

Multiple Shop or Store

The Board of Trade defines a multiple organisation as one that has TEN OR MORE retail branches all of which sell the same type of merchandise. A chain store (q.v.) therefore falls within this definition if there are ten or more shops in the chain.

Network Analysis

A procedure for planning and organising the various activities that have to be carried out in order to complete a project, e.g. launching a new product. It is particularly useful if there are a large number of interdependent activities to be carried out. The 'critical' activities which will govern the overall time required to complete the project are clearly revealed. (For example, an additional week spent on package design may in some circumstances delay the final completion of the project by a week whereas, in others, it may have no effect at all on the total time – the use of a network analysis would show the effect on the overall time of the week's delay in package design and whether or not it is important to take action to avoid such a delay.)

Nielsen Audits

Retail audits (q.v.) carried out by A. C. Nielsen Co. Ltd. for companies that subscribe to its service.

Non-repetitive Calling

The type of selling situation in which the salesman is selling plant, equipment or a service that is not consumed or sold by the prospective customers on whom he is calling but is retained by them for their own use, e.g. a cash register or a machine tool that is sold directly to the user. (As a result, the salesman is *not* spending most of his time making regular repetitive calls on the same customers in order to secure repeat orders.) In some industries this type of selling is referred to as 'Speciality Selling'. Quite different procedures are required for planning and controlling this type of selling operation from those that are required for Repetitive Calling (q.v.).

MARKETING AND HIGHER MANAGEMENT

Operational Research (O.R.)

Defined by the Operational Research Society in the following terms: 'Operational Research is the attack of modern science on complex problems arising in the direction and management of large systems of men, machines, materials and money in industry, business, government and defence. The distinctive approach is to develop a scientific model of the system, incorporating measurement of factors such as chance and risk, with which to predict and compare the outcomes of alternative decisions, strategies or controls. The purpose is to help management determine its policy and actions scientifically.'

Its principal application in marketing is in those situations where there are a large number of variable factors that can affect the determination of the most suitable plan, e.g. in planning a distribution network which requires the siting and setting up of a number of local warehouses and the optimum utilisation of transportation facilities. The procedure is to develop a mathematical model or formula that represents the total situation in such a way that a change in one variable will reflect the changes that will occur in some or all of the others. The solution may necessitate working out a large number of lengthy calculations, which presents no problem to a computer. The development of computers has therefore enabled this mathematical approach to be used in highly complex situations.

Optimum Selling Price

The Optimum Selling Price for a product is the selling price which will produce the maximum contribution to overhead costs and profit over a period of time, e.g. per annum. In order to determine the optimum selling price, an estimate must be made of the relationship between selling price and sales volume for the particular product. Even in those situations where it is decided for policy reasons not to sell a product at its optimum selling price, it is desirable to know this price so that the loss in profits that will result from the decision may be known.

Panel

A representative sample of users or consumers who are constituted as a continuing panel from whom information can be obtained about the purchase, usage or acceptability of a product, e.g. housewives' panels, farmers' panels, etc.

Pantry Checks

Used for obtaining information about the purchase and consumption of household consumer goods. A representative sample of households is selected and a check is made at regular frequent intervals of all the goods that are on the kitchen shelves in each household in the sample.

Psychological Selling Prices

A term that is sometimes used to describe those selling prices which are subconsciously more acceptable to the prospective purchaser than others, e.g. 4s. 11d. rather than 5s. or £498 rather than £500. (The effect is not, of course, due to the fact that £498 is £2 less than £500, as a change in price from £500 to £498 would have a very much greater effect on sales volume than would a change from £498 to £496.)

Point of Sale

The place where the final act of purchasing occurs, e.g. the counter of a retail shop. (The term is rarely used in selling industrial goods.)

Potential Demand

It is the existence of some basic need that creates the potential demand for a product or service to satisfy that need, e.g. the need to keep warm in winter or the need to occupy leisure hours. The size of the potential demand for a product is governed by:

(a) The number of people who have some basic need that could be satisfied at least as well and economically by the purchase of the product as by any other available means. (It is immaterial whether or not they are consciously aware of the existence of this need.)
(b) The proportion of these people who have the financial ability to satisfy the need by the purchase of the product.
(c) The quantity and frequency of their purchases that would be necessary in order to satisfy the need fully.

Therefore, at any given moment in time the size of the potential demand for a product depends only upon its design and selling price.

Price Plateau

There are some products, which are available in a wide range of qualities and prices, where certain narrow bands of prices at different levels within the overall range have for some reason become recognised and accepted by the buyer. Each of these narrow bands is sometimes referred to as a price plateau. Where this situation exists, many manufacturers believe that it would be unwise to attempt to sell a product at a price that was outside one of the recognised plateaux. (In its original sense, which is still sometimes used, it refers only to the final plateau which is reached and beyond which any further increase in price would cause a very sharp decline in sales.)

Price Leader

The company which is recognised in its industry as being the one that sets the level of selling prices which other companies follow. A Price Leader is usually, but not always, the Market Leader (q.v.).

Product Development

Usually refers to that part of Product Planning which is concerned with the continuing development and improvement of the company's existing range of products.

Product Diversification

The introduction of alternative or additional products which are of a different type from those previously produced and sold by the company.

Product Planning

Planning what products a company should produce; how they should be designed in order to win favourable buying decisions; what quantities of each should be produced and at what price they should be sold. Product planning is usually one of the most important aspects of the marketing function. (See Foreword on Marketing.)

Profile (Readership)

See Readership Survey.

Programmed Learning

A comparatively new method of instruction which is particularly suitable for the training of salesmen. Basically, the method involves breaking down the information to be taught into small segments. Each segment is presented in turn and tests are used to ensure that it has been thoroughly understood by the student before proceeding to the next segment. Various devices and methods have been developed for the practical application of this principle in a training course. Considerable skill is required in designing the programme (i.e. selecting and defining the segments), but once this has been done training becomes very simple and inexpensive.

Prospect

As a verb: To seek out new business
As a noun: A potential purchaser of the company's products

Quality and Reliability (Q and R)

In its marketing context, 'quality' can be defined as the degree of excellence of the product's fitness to meet the needs and requirements of the particular customers for whom it is intended, at the price which they are going to pay for it. 'Reliability' can be defined as measuring how long the product will continue to carry out its purpose effectively without the development of some fault or failure. There are many situations in which a company's reputation for quality or reliability is one of the most important factors that influence the buying decision of a prospective customer. This reputation depends both on the basic design of the products and on the *consistency* in quality and reliability of the output that leaves the factory.

Questionnaire

In the context of market research, this is a set of questions that are put to a suitably selected sample of repondents. The design of an effective questionnaire is, however, far removed from a simple listing of a number of 'obvious' questions, since a greater degree of reliability is sought. The design of the questionnaire normally requires more skill and care than any other aspect of a market research operation. Questions are usually included to check the validity of the answers that are given.

Quota (Sales)

A Sales Quota is sometimes given the same meaning as a Sales Target (q.v.). The preferred usage is its application to products for which the demand is exceeding the supply and the 'quota' is the allocation given to a salesman, an area, or a country.

Quota Sampling

A term used in market research. It is a form of sampling in which the initiative is left with the interviewer to locate a set number of respondents who have been specified by age, sex, income level or other appropriate characteristics. This is the 'quota' given to the interviewer. The quotas are designed to provide a total sample which has exactly the same constitution as the whole market being investigated. Quota Sampling and Random Sampling (q.v.) are the two most commonly used sampling methods in consumer research.

Random Sampling

A method of obtaining a representative sample in which a number of units are picked at random from the whole. In a market research operation, the units are picked at random from a complete list of the people to be sampled – rating lists and electoral registers are commonly used for this purpose. The interviewers are thus provided with the names and adresses of the respondents whom they are to interview. The procedure for the interviewer therefore differs from that used in Quota Sampling (q.v.). Either method, if used correctly, will provide a sample that is representative of the whole.

Readership Survey (or Readership Profile)
A survey of the readers of a newspaper or magazine in which the readers are analysed by sex, age, socio-economic group, buying habits, etc. Readership surveys of all the principal publications are regularly carried out for the I.P.A. for use in media selection.

Recall (Advertising)
A method of testing the impact of an advertisement by ascertaining whether it has been seen and remembered. In an 'Aided Recall' the respondent is helped with specific questions or examples. In an 'Unaided Recall' no clue is given to the type of advertisement or product being investigated.

Record of Designers
A record of over 2,000 qualified industrial designers that is maintained by The Council of Industrial Design. From this record, recommendations can be obtained for a suitable designer, either for engagement on the company's own staff or as a freelance designer.

Repetitive Calling
The type of selling activity in which the salesman is selling a product that is regularly consumed or sold by the customers on whom he is calling. Hence, he spends most of his time making regular periodic calls on existing customers to secure repeat orders and on prospective customers to secure an initial order which, it is hoped, will be followed up by regular repeat business. (See Non-repetitive Calling.)

Resale Price Maintenance (R.P.M.)
The practice in which the manufacturer fixes the minimum price at which goods are to be sold to the ultimate user or consumer and imposes sanctions on price-cutting. This practice is now illegal in the U.K. except in those cases where exemption is obtained on the grounds that the practice is beneficial to the user or consumer, e.g. where the abolition of R.P.M. would reduce the availability of the product to the consumer by reducing the number of outlets at which it could be obtained.

Retail Audits
The purpose of Retail Audits is to measure the flow of the company's and competitors' products from retail outlets to consumers. A representative

sample of retailers is selected. Receipts and stocks are checked by 'auditors' who make regular periodic visits, usually monthly or two-monthly. Such audits are continuously carried out for certain groups of products by some of the market research organisations. A continuing information service is provided to subscribers about the movement of their own and their competitors' products.

Retail Buying Group
See Buying Group.

Retail Price Index
Figures that are regularly published by the Board of Trade showing the current prices of consumer and durable goods in relation to their price at some earlier basic date (e.g. January, 1965 = 100).

Retailer Co-operatives
Retail Buying Groups (q.v.) are sometimes referred to as Retailer Co-operatives. This has nothing to do with Co-operative Societies.

Sales Coverage
The relationship between the total number of potential purchasers (e.g. retailers) in a sales area and the number that can effectively be called upon by the salesman at an optimum call frequency. The most economic Sales Coverage is likely to be less than 100 per cent if there is a large number of small outlets.

Sales Potential
See Potential Demand.

Sales Promotion
In its broadest sense, this term covers all those activities that are used to promote and stimulate the sales of a product. In a narrow sense it is used to describe those activities which lie between advertising on the one hand and personal selling on the other, e.g. display, gift offers, etc. A 'Promotion' is a particular publicity campaign.

Sales Quota
See Quota.

Sales Target
This is a term that has many different shades of meaning. It refers to some predetermined volume of sales that should be obtained from a sales territory.

This volume may, however, be anything from a sales forecast for the territory to some arbitrary higher figure which has been fixed by management in an attempt to spur on the salesman to greater effort. Sales Targets are not uncommonly developed from the past sales that have so far been achieved in the territory and are of little value as a measurement of the relative skill and effort of each salesman. (See Standard Sales Volume.)

Sales Territory

A sales territory consists of a number of existing and potential customers who have been grouped together into some suitable geographical area for convenience in calling on them. In order to obtain the most effective and economic use of the sales force, the sales territories must be designed in such a way as to provide an equal work load for each salesman. This may bear little or no relationship to the sales potential of each territory.

Salesman's Performance

A measurement of the relative skill and effort of each salesman in the sales force. (See Standard Sales Volume.)

Salesman's Incentives

See Financial Incentives.

Sampling

See Quota Sampling and Random Sampling.

Sampling Frame

See Universe.

Segmentation Analysis

Purchasing behaviour is governed by many factors which cut across the conventional sub-divisions of a market into sex, age and socio-economic groupings. Segmentation analysis consists of analysing the market for a product type into all its many and varied segments. For example, among the purchasers of a particular product type there may be those whose main interest is in getting good value for money; those who want a bargain and are looking for the cheapest; those who like quality and are prepared to pay for it; those who look for the latest in fashion design and so on – this is a simple form of segmentation. It is applicable to both industrial and consumer goods.

Selling Aids

A term that usually refers to the material with which a salesman is provided to enable him to make some visual presentation to support his selling interview, e.g. samples, brochures, etc.

GLOSSARY

Selling In and Selling Out

These terms are usually confined to products sold through retail distributors. 'Selling In' is concerned with those activities which are directed to persuading the retailer to buy and stock the product. 'Selling Out' embraces those activities such as consumer advertising and point of sale display that are designed to move the product from the retailer to the ultimate user or consumer. The same division can, however, be applied to selling materials or components to industrial users – e.g. the promotion of canned foods by a can manufacturer – this is sometimes called Back Selling (q.v.).

Shop Audits

See Retail Audits.

Socio-Economic Group

A classification used in Market Research in which social status, occupation and income of the head of the household are taken into consideration. The following groupings are those commonly used:

Group	Social Status	Typical Occupation of Head of Household
A	Upper middle class	Higher managerial or professional
B	Middle class	Intermediate management
C1	Lower middle class	Supervisory clerical and junior staff
C2	Skilled working class	Skilled manual workers
D	Working class	Semi and unskilled manual workers
E	Those at lowest levels of subsistence	Pensioners and lowest grade workers

These socio-economic groups are tending to become less significant with many consumer and durable products. Because of the increase in the number of working wives and the higher earnings of teenagers living at home, the criterion used is often the total disposable income of the family after the payment of rent, rates, etc., rather than the social status of the head of the household. The same television receiver may today be purchased by those in both the A and D groups. (See also Segmentation Analysis.)

Soft Selling

See Hard Selling.

Special Offers

A temporary inducement to purchase, often in the form of a price reduction or gift, that is used in conjunction with a particular promotional campaign. The term is usually confined to the sale of consumer and durable goods.

Speciality Selling
See Non-repetitive Calling.

Split Runs (Advertising)
A method employed in Copy Testing (q.v.). Two different advertisements are designed, half the copies of a particular publication carries one of these advertisements and the other half carries the alternative version. A keyed hidden offer (q.v.) is included to measure the relative effectiveness of each advertisement. Its use is limited to those publications which provide a split run service for advertisers.

Standard Industrial Classification
A standard grouping and classification of industries adopted by the Board of Trade. Sometimes useful in industrial market research.

Standard Sales Volume
The volume of sales that has been set as a standard for a sales territory and against which the sales obtained is compared as a measure of the skill and effort of the salesman. It is defined as: 'The volume of sales that could reasonably be expected from the territory if it was being operated by an effectively trained and motivated salesman of *average* ability.'

The standard is *not* based on the salesman who happens to be in the territory at the particular time. In a repetitive calling situation it will be governed by the relative size of the demand and the relative intensity of the sales coverage in each territory. A standard that is based on the past sales achieved in the territory is of little value as a measurement of the skill and effort of the salesman. In those cases where the sales volume can be significantly affected by factors that are outside the control of the salesmen it is preferable to define the standard as 'The *proportion* of the Company's sales that could reasonably be expected...'. The proportion that is actually achieved compared with this standard provides the measure of the salesman's performance.

Stock Turn (Rate of)
The number of times that a stock is 'turned over' in a year, e.g. if stocks are £10,000 and annual sales are £50,000, there is a stock turn of five times a year. (The rate of stock turn can have an important bearing on the ratio of profit to capital employed in the distributive trades.)

Stratified Sample
A term sometimes used in Market Research. The proportions in each stratum of the sample are identical to the proportions in each stratum of the whole.

GLOSSARY

Subliminal Advertising
   A form of advertising which is designed in such a way that the prospect will not be consciously aware of having seen or heard the advertisement. (In the U.K., the I.P.A. has voluntarily placed a ban on the use of subliminal advertising.)

Switch Selling
   The procedure in which the interest of the prospective purchaser is aroused by the offer of some product at, say, a highly attractive price. The purchaser is then persuaded not to buy this product but another more profitable product, probably at a higher price.

TAM Rating (Television Audience Measurement)
   A continuing survey of the size of the audience watching television programmes.

Territory
   See Sales Territory.

Test Marketing
   Tests of a product which are carried out, usually in a selected sample area of the total market (the test area) before launching nationally. Often embraces a test of both the product and its associated advertising campaign.

Tied Indicators
   A term used in Market Forecasting. Tied Indicators are products whose sales will directly or indirectly influence the demand for the particular product being investigated.

Trade Mark
   A brand name or symbol that is given legal protection by registration.

Trading Down
   A seller's practice of handling lower-priced products in order to secure a higher volume of sales – usually at a low rate of profit with a high stock turn.

Trading Up
   A seller's practice of handling higher-priced products – usually at a higher rate of profit with a lower stock turn.

Universe
   When used in Market Research, the Universe defines the total users or consumers from whom a sample is to be selected. The first step in sampling is,

therefore, to define the Universe. It is sometimes referred to as the Sampling Frame.

U.S.P.

A product's unique quality or appeal which is used as the basis for its promotion. Originally, the letters stood for 'unique selling proposition' but they are sometimes interpreted as 'unique selling points'. In practice, a product's U.S.P. is often an outstanding feature rather than a unique feature. The determination of the product's U.S.P. is often the starting point for preparing the Copy Theme (q.v.) for an advertising campaign.

Value Analysis

A systematic method of making an analytical examination of the materials and component parts used in a product and the precise purposes which they fulfil. Significant and unexpected improvements or economies are often revealed by subjecting a product to Value Analysis. As a simple example, even a small component such as a screw may be larger and more costly than is really necessary for its purpose, or it could perhaps be replaced by a rivet with a considerable reduction in cost if large quantities are being produced, or it may be possible to alter the design so that the fixing is unnecessary.

Van Salesman

A salesman equipped with a van containing stocks of his company's products, giving on-the-spot delivery. Van salesmen may or may not be used to obtain immediate payment without further paper-work. The use of van salesmen is often an effective way of selling economically to small outlets where only a low average value per order can be expected. The 'van' may be a suitably equipped car or estate car.

Variable Costs

Those elements of the costs which vary in direct proportion to a change in volume *that is within the limits of the situation under examination.* For example, the clerical costs in the sales office may be a fixed cost for a small change in sales volume as there would be no alteration in the size of the staff, whereas part or all of these costs would be variable costs if a large change in sales volume is being considered, e.g. twice as many orders to be processed.

Voluntary Groups and Chains

See Buying Group. The Economist Intelligence Unit defines a Voluntary Group as one that consists of one wholesaler and a number of retailers, and a Voluntary Chain as one that consists of a number of wholesalers and retailers

GLOSSARY

operating under varying degrees of central control. (These groups and chains are becoming increasingly important as buyers in the grocery trade, e.g. Wavy Line, Spar, etc.)

Wholesaler

A wholesaler holds stocks and sells goods that are produced by others. He sells to retail outlets and not directly to users or consumers. In appropriate situations, the wholesaler plays an important and economically essential part in the chain of distribution. The order obtained by the wholesaler will include a wide range of products, and he is therefore able to accept much smaller quantities of an individual product than would be economically possible for the manufacturer of that product if he was employing his own sales force to sell directly to the small retailer.

Z Chart

An annual chart of sales or other figures throughout the year. The chart contains a line for each of the following:

(a) the period total for the week or month
(b) the cumulative total to date, and
(c) the moving annual total (q.v.)

In the first period of the year the cumulative total will be the same figure as the period total. At the end of the year it will be the same figure as the moving annual total. The three lines will therefore take the shape of a Z on a completed chart and the name derives from this configuration.

Index

Account Executives, 220
Activity Sampling, 220
Advertising, 130
   advertising agencies, 200
   advertising costs, 76
   advertising objectives, 131
   copy testing, 191
   media selection, 196
After-sales Service, 33, 124
Agents, 220
Attitude Studies, 195
Audits, Retail, 167

Back Selling, 221
Banded Packs, 221
Branded Goods, 136, 221
Brand Image, 136
Brand Leader, 222
Brand Manager, 147
Break-even Chart, 52, 66
Budgetary Control, 78, 178
Buying Decisions, 26
Buying Groups, 222

Capital employed, 47
Channels of Distribution, 78, 128, 167
Check Questions, 166
Communications, Market, 127
Company Image, 136
Consumer Panels, 167
Contribution, Financial, 58, 68
Conurbations, Market, 225
Copy Testing, 191
Corporate Long Range Planning, 150
Costs and Profit, 48
Council of Industrial Design, 138, 240
Credit Facilities, 34, 124
Credit Rating, 35
Critical Path Analysis, 235

Delivery Date Promises, 33
Demography, 226
Desk Research, 157
Distribution Planning, 78, 128, 138
Distribution Research, 167
Diversification, 102
Dumping, 227

Econometrics, 227
Ego Drive, 227
Elasticity of Demand, 56
Empathy, 228
Exponential Smoothing, 228
External Marketing Services, 148

Family Income (Market Segmentation), 117
Farmers' Panels, 167
Field Research, 160
Field Sales Force, 201
Financial Aspects of Marketing, 45
Fixed Costs, 50
Forecasting, 171
Franchise, 229

Geographic Segmentation, 119

Hidden Offers (Advertising), 193
House Accounts, 230
House Style, 231
Household Audits, 168
Housewives Panels, 167

Impulse Buying, 231
Image of a Company, 136

Journey Cycle, 231

Life Cycle of a Product, 95
Long Range Planning, 150

249

Loss Leader, 232

Management Structure, 142
Managing Director, role in Marketing, 142
Market, 25
  market forecasting, 171
  market research, 155
  market testing, 177
  market segmentation, 112
  market selection, 25
Marketing, 23
  marketing management, 142
  marketing planning, 111
  marketing research, 155
  marketing strategy, 120
Measurement of Sales Performance, 206
Media, Advertising, 130
Media Selection, 196
Merchandising, 135
Motivation Research, 168
Moving Annual Totals, 175

'Needs' and 'Wants', 13
Network Analysis, 235

Obsolescence, Designing for, 100
Observational Research, 161
Operational Research, 236

Performance Measurements, 206
Personnel – Marketing, 147
        – Sales, 201
Plateau, Selling Price, 59
Postal Questionnaires, 161
Potential Demand, 17
Pricing, 55
Product Policy, 81
  product adaptation, 108
  product, definition of, 15
  product design, 121, 182
  product diversification, 102
  product planning, 181
  product mix, 68, 188
  product variety, 86
  selling prices, 55

Profitability of Products, 68
Programmed Learning, 238

Quality and Reliability, 31, 123, 184
Questionnaires, 164
Quota Sampling, 239

Random Sampling, 239
Range of Products, 86
Readership Surveys, 198
Reliability, Product, 31, 123, 184
Retail Audits, 167
Return on Capital, 47

Sales Forecasting, 171
Salesmen, 138, 201
Sampling in Market Research, 163
Screening in Product Diversification, 104
Sectoring the Market, 113
Segmentation of Market, 112
Selling Costs, 72
'Selling In' and 'Selling Out', 243
Selling Prices, 55
Socio-economic Groups, 115
Special Offers, 243
Split-run Copy Testing, 193
Subliminal Advertising, 245
Switch Selling, 245

Telephoned Questionnaires, 162
Television Advertising, 196
Tools of Marketing, 42
Test Marketing, 178, 194
Trend Projection, 174

Unit Contribution, 68
Using Sales Forecasts, 178
U.S.P., 246

Value Analysis, 246
Variable Costs, 50
Variety in Product Range, 86
Visual Aids for Salesmen, 136

'Wants' and 'Needs', 13

Z Charts, 247

GEORGE ALLEN & UNWIN LTD

Head Office
40 Museum Street, London W.C.1
Telephone: 01-405 8577

Sales, Distribution and Accounts Departments
Park Lane, Hemel Hempstead, Herts.
Telephone: 0442 3244

Athens: 7 Stadiou Street
Auckland: P.O. Box 36013, Northcote Central N.4
Barbados: P.O. Box 222, Bridgetown
Beirut: Deeb Building, Jeanne d'Arc Street
Bombay: 103/5 Fort Street, Bombay 1
Calcutta: 285J Bepin Behari Ganguli Street, Calcutta 12
Cape Town: 68 Shortmarket Street
Delhi: 1/18B Asaf-Ali Road, New Delhi 1
Hong Kong: 105 Wing On Mansion, 26 Hancow Road, Kowloon
Ibadan: P.O. Box 62
Karachi: Karachi Chambers, McLeod Road
Madras: 2/18 Mount Road, Madras
Mexico: Villalongin 32, Mexico 5, D.F.
Nairobi: P.O. Box 30583
Philippines: P.O. Box 157, Quezon City D-502
Rio de Janeiro: Caixa Postal 2537-Zc-00
Singapore: 36c Prinsep Street, Singapore 7
Sydney N.S.W.: Bradbury House, 55 York Street
Tokyo: C.P.O. Box 1728, Tokyo 100-91
Toronto: 18 Curlew Drive, Don Mills

INTERNATIONAL BUSINESS MANAGEMENT SERIES

Marketing: The Management Way
ARNOLD K. WEINSTEIN

Marketing: The Management Way, by a lecturer in Business Administration, has been written, as its title suggests, with two functions in mind. First, to present a managerial approach to the subject of marketing, and second to show how and why a marketing orientation is necessary for corporate survival.

This book should provide the practising executive with a practical approach to his very difficult job. It should also be a valuable stimulant for discussion in marketing management training courses. The chapters are short, clear, concise statements of considerations to be made in solving marketing problems. Yet they do not actually solve these problems. Rather, they present a managerial approach to them. Within each chapter there is the underlying assumption that marketing management must and can be done in a professional manner.

'Well-supported by judicious use of quotations which set out basic ideas and by adequate references. May well be considered for use on elementary courses for students specializing in Marketing or for non-specialists.'
British Journal of Marketing

Management Techniques
JOHN ARGENTI

Among the many books on management techniques this one is unique. In the first part the author describes, with absolute clarity, how a manager can select the *correct* technique to use on his particular problem, and explains the step-by-step procedure for learning, introducing and applying it. The second part is a Glossary which briefly describes over one hundred modern techniques, identifies the problems that each is designed to tackle, and indicates the standard of education which its use demands. The author gives his estimation of how much each will cost to use and the results which can be expected from it.

The techniques described range from those intended for the exclusive use of top management to those specially designed for shop-floor supervisors. This book, which is non-mathematical in form, is an essential handbook for managers at every level, in every size and type of organization.

'For the thousands of executives who are increasingly bewildered by the various management techniques being peddled these days by business schools, management training centres and journalists, Mr Argenti's book comes as a friend in need . . . deserves wide readership.'
The Financial Times

LONDON: GEORGE ALLEN AND UNWIN LTD

STUDIES IN MANAGEMENT SERIES
The Numerate Manager
F. KEAY

This is a book for the manager or potential manager concerned with strategic decision-making. Its theme is the concept of numeracy – one that is only just coming to be understood – and the role it should play. The book discusses its origins and its tools, the nature of problems, the characteristics and handling of information and the implications for the future. While it is not a textbook of techniques, it illustrates their application for the user. The text has been a valuable source for lectures at all levels given to managers attending Ashridge Management College.

'This is a book of quite exceptional importance and interest to the accountancy profession. It has the added charm and merit of being so well written that it is a pleasure to read.'
Accountancy

British Management Thought
DR JOHN CHILD

British Management Thought is an indispensable classic text for anyone with a critical interest in the development of British management philosophy. An incisive and elegantly written book, it is the most comprehensive analysis of British management thought that is available today. It is a study that will interest management teachers, informed managers, sociologists and historians.

Utilizing detailed documentary evidence, Dr Child traces and assesses the emergence and development of management thinking in Britain over the last hundred years. He considers the organizational and social problems faced by managers, and how management thinkers have attempted to provide solutions. The functions performed by management thought are analysed, and also the way in which its content was influenced by socio-industrial change and by existing ideas available to management writers. Detailed attention is given to recent development including the Glacier Project and the Human Relations school.

The book demonstrates how social science research has today brought to light many deficiencies in management thought.

'His arguments are carefully considered. The analysis of the three "continuing themes" of management theory in Britain is well balanced and illuminating.'
New Society

STUDIES IN MANAGEMENT SERIES

The Manager's Guide to Industrial Relations

L. F. NEAL   ANDREW ROBERTSON

This is a short book, by two outstanding authors. It is distinctive too in being based on British industrial experience and conditions; it is addressed to managers in England and the Commonwealth. American experience and theory are not ignored, but this is not imported wisdom.

In two brief chapters the authors trace the origins and evolution of the attitudes of managers and men from the beginning of industrialization to the Fawley Agreement. The next is an equally forthright summary of the development of personnel management and the contributions, so far, of the social scientists, leading to a similar summary of 'Trade Unions and Collective Bargaining'. Having set the historical scene, in their central chapters the authors deal squarely with the British system of industrial relations, the Shop Stewards and the survival of restrictive practices. At every point of their terse treatment they reveal their complete familiarity with both theory and practice, informed by their philosophy that 'a sympathy, in the precise meaning of the word, a fellow feeling, has to be conjured up before any constructive exchange of ideas can take place', and this is the key to permanent progress.

The problem of making changes is introduced by the statement that if management decides to introduce something new the workers know that they can only delay but not stop it. This is followed by a warning chapter on 'False Remedies', which leads to an analysis of Joint Consultation and to a penultimate survey of 'The Two Sides of Industry' – and of the very different risks they are expected to accept.

In their last chapter, 'Any Answers?' the authors emphasize that their object has been to set out in an accessible form an array of both the thinking and the events that have brought us where we are. By charting this route they enable managers and students of management, informed about other people's theories and explanations, 'to continue their own thinking in the context of reality'.

'Of the high quality one would expect from these two authors. Contains some interesting analyses of industrial relations problems.'
Personnel and Training Management

'Authoritatively written, this well-produced, concisely written book is stimulating and thought-provoking.'
Works Management